£14.70f

Library of
Davidson College

THE
HISTORY OF RELIGIONS

THE HISTORY OF RELIGIONS

BY

UGO BIANCHI

Professor of the History of Religions
in the University of Rome

LEIDEN
E. J. BRILL
1975

Translated from the Italian of the Introduction to the *Storia delle religioni* edited by G. Castellani, 6th edition, Copyright 1970 by Unione Tipografico-Editrice Torinese.

ISBN 90 04 04237 7

Copyright 1975 by E. J. Brill, Leiden, Netherlands

All rights reserved. No part of this book may be reproduced or translated in any form, by print, photoprint, microfilm, microfiche or any other means without written permission from the publisher

PRINTED IN THE NETHERLANDS

TABLE OF CONTENTS

I. OBJECT AND METHODOLOGY OF THE HISTORY OF RELIGIONS   1

    1. Questions of definition   1
    2. The history of religions as a comparative-historical science   3
    3. The meaning of historical-religious comparison. The analogous meaning of 'religion' and 'religious' . .   5
    4. The 'structures' of religion and the historical typology of religions   8
    5. Religious ethnology and the history of religions . .   12
    6. Various ways of approaching the study of religions. Other objections to the history of religions . . .   15
    7. Various sciences concerned with religions . . .   19
    8. Alternative names for the history of religions . . .   23
    9. The organization of studies concerning the history of religions   27

II. RELIGION AND THE VARIOUS RELIGIONS   30

    1. Universality and the meaning of religion . . .   30
    2. How to begin the study of religions   33
    3. Religion and religions. Forms and structures of religion   35
    4. Types of religion   36
    5. Other persons figuring in religious belief . . .   44
    6. Magic   46
    7. Power   48
    8. The 'holy'   49
    9. Religious institutions   49
   10. Sacred periods of time and history. History and 'salvation'   51
   11. Persons. Initiations. Ethnical and 'founded' religions; national, mysterio-sophic, cosmopolitic and universal religions   53
   12. Qualified 'sacred' persons. The priesthood . . .   56
   13. Sacrifice   58
   14. The knowledge of the superhuman   59

III. STUDIES AND PROBLEMS IN THE HISTORY OF RELIGIONS . . 61
   1. The sources of historical-religious thought . . . 61
   2. Max Müller and the 'mythology of nature' . . . 62
   3. The history of religions, systematically divided into periods 66
   4. Goblet d'Alviella and the 'Science of Religions' . . 67
   5. The anthropological school 71
   6. Bachofen and the 'Matriarchate' 72
   7. J. G. Frazer 74
   8. Theories on 'totemism' in the general history of religions 76
   9. The sociological school 77
   10. Lévy-Bruhl and primitive mentality 79
   11. Tylor and the theory of animism. The notion of spirits and of the soul among primitive races . . . 83
   12. The theory of 'animatism' and dynamism. 'Power' . . 86
   13. Supreme Beings and the idea of God among primitive peoples 87
   14. Myths about the origins of the world, in the most ancient civilizations 91
   15. The question of monotheism 94
   16. The Supreme Being and his *Sitz im Leben* . . . 96
   17. The primordial *dema* divinities and their mythology 98
   18. Polytheism and cosmological speculation in the more 'advanced' civilizations 102
   19. Religion in the 'higher cultures' 106
   20. Pan-Babylonianism and pan-Egyptianism 107
   21. Historical-religious and comparative aspects of the 'cuneiform' area and adjoining regions 109
   22. 'Myth and ritual' 111
   23. The 'myth-and-ritual' pattern 113
   24. Death and evil in some ancient religions of Near Asia 118
   25. Iranian-Near Eastern syncretism: Mithraism . . . 120
   26. Indo-European mythology and the ideology of the 'three functions'. Classifications and structures in myths and in society 121
   27. Cosmic and cosmogonic rituals 124
   28. From the myth to the 'logos' 127
   29. Concrete nature of the symbol. Symbology of the king 133
   30. Non-mythical religions. The God of Israel . . . 134

31.	The question of myth and the Old Testament . . .	138
32.	The meaning of the term 'myth'	140
33.	The VIth century B.C.: an 'axial epoch' . . .	142
34.	'Salvation'	144
35.	Iran and the history of religions	147
36.	The *'Religionsgeschichtliche Schule'*	150
37.	Italian Modernism and the history of religions . .	154
38.	An example of comparative investigation: Dualism .	155
39.	An Eastern example of a universalist religion: Buddhism	158

IV. MODERN PROBLEMS OF METHODOLOGY AND INTERPRETATION   163

    1. Dynamism of religions and sociology of religion . . 163
    2. The 'para-religions' 167
    3. R. Otto and the Marburg School. The 'holy'. The Religionswissenschaft 169
    4. The phenomenology of religion 178
    5. The 'history of religions' and 'comparative religion' in the U.S.A. 181
    6. Mircea Eliade and the 'Morphology of the holy'. Contrasting opinions on the 'holy' and on history . . 184
    7. Examples of 'reductionist' theories 191
       (A) Psychologism 191
       (B) Marxist sociologism 192
    8. The comparative method and the category 'religion' in R. Pettazzoni. Observations on the theme of the universality of religion 199

V. CONCLUSION 201
   The Definition of Religion. On the methodology of historical-comparative research. Comparative history or cultural anthropology? 201

Bibliography 221

Index of Modern Authors 225

CHAPTER ONE

OBJECT AND METHODOLOGY OF THE HISTORY OF RELIGIONS

1. *Questions of definition*

The history of religions, as the term suggests, is a science which has as its object the manifestations in universal time and space of that human attitude which we call 'religious': an attitude which is hard to define or describe, even before we begin to discuss its nature, origin and development. Generally speaking, the historian of religions, faithful to the positive and inductive character of his investigation, will describe as 'religious', using this adjective as a hypothetical term for purposes of research, all those phenomena which he has encountered in civilizations similar or dissimilar to those in which he has received his *Bildung* and scientific training, and which show an analogy, even if with a marked contrast of principles and forms, with what in his own cultural circle (for example, European civilization with its classical and Near East antecedents) signifies 'religion'. And in this he will not be led into an ethnocentric deviation, that is, an anti-humanist and anti-scientific deformation and diminution of perspective. On the contrary, the very fact that he is aware of the historical cultural background of the concepts of 'religion' and 'religious' with which he begins his work will enable him, once he has established the philological foundations of a research that extends beyond the above mentioned cultural boundaries, to present concretely and historically, that is, in a positive inductive manner, the scientific problems concerning cultures which he found at first to be extraneous to him. And this will be true also of the student who has another ethnical and cultural background: he also must begin the work of understanding civilizations very different from his own.

It is true that there is one initial requirement in all this effort of scientific approach [1]: the research which aims at studying civilizations and religions of all kinds, and irrespectively of the particular cultural territory to which the student belongs, must have recourse

---

[1] Or, as is usually said today, of 'mutual understanding', but the expression is a little dangerous because it does not help us to distinguish between scientific and ecumenical understanding.

to historical methodology. This means that the history of religions is based upon philological documentary research, with great attention paid to the chronological, geographical and historical-cultural localization of the phenomena, personages, texts and historical processes which form the object of its enquiry.

In other words, the 'when', 'who', 'where' and 'how' are problems which arise before and apart from any vague formulations, before any generalizations or intuitive judgments, however brilliant these may be, and in opposition to any reduction to 'today's' terms, or to merely presupposed and possibly anachronistic or undocumented 'origins'.

Genesis and development are problems and perspectives which respond to authentic research into the history of religions. This suffices to show that, in spite of any eventual inadequacy, the history of religions owes much to the scientific methodology of European historians and philologists. Today students of non-European religious history rightly protest against the great harm done to the history of religions, especially in the 19th century, by presuppositions of an ethnocentric, positivist and abstractly progressivist nature (with the consequent reduction of the primitive and exotic to the status of inferior forms, or forms less worthy of mankind). But one must also admit that certain intuitive judgments, found in many studies by Asiatic, African or, in other circumstances, American or European students, which represent certain currents of thought which are too generically 'phenomenological', are in reality quite extraneous to the history of religions. This is seen in the propensity of many of these students to reduce the history of religions to ethnology or anthropology, or, on the contrary, to interest themselves exclusively in the 'great living religions', with a particular predilection for those of India, and without paying sufficient attention to historical questions concerning their genesis, development, historical and cultural circumstances.

One may therefore say that an *a-priori* approach, typical of European ethnocentric positivism, which claimed to reduce all religion, or at least its most essential aspects, to embryonic forms which were to be sought in the religions of the 'primitive peoples', summarily interpreted, is today opposed, in certain writers on religious phenomenology, by a generalization which is itself harmful, at least from the point of view of practical research, because it is subtle and spiritually attractive. For example, a positivism which refuses to recognise religion as a living and complex element in factual history is sometimes opposed by a 'religionistic' approach which is almost purely intuitional, applied to primitive religions or to the mystiques of the living religions of the East, and which discusses at length, but generically and unhistorically, the socalled 'holy', understood as a common denominator of all religion. [2]

2. *The history of religions as a comparative-historical science*

Like all historical sciences, the history of religions approaches its subject by studying historical facts and details: what really existed and was manifest. It is not, therefore, *at least primarily*, interested in generic questions about religion, or even about this or that great religion as a whole, but in an enquiry into facts, with a view to the identification of historical processes, bound by links of space, time, objects and individual human beings. It is true, as we shall point out, that the history of religions is not to be confused with a religious historiography which deliberately confines itself to one religion, or to certain aspects of this, to the exclusion of the study of more universal historical and phenomenological problems. These problems are always essential to the purpose of the history of religions which some still define (superfluously but, if the adjective is properly understood, justifiably) as the 'comparative' history of religions. In reality the history of religions is not only a historical, but a comparative-historical study. It certainly investigates individual historical processes which are in their own way unique, although even here one cannot exclude a certain historical typology or even some of its immanent 'laws' or 'possibilities'. But it tries to see these processes as they actually developed, in their own *milieux*, and it tries to take into consideration all the problems of historical influence, of convergence or divergence in relation to other processes or *milieux*.

The comparative-historical method, then, presents the history of religions as something very different from a factual classification of particular religious histories, as they can be listed and compared in a text-book. What we must now point out is that, on the basis of what we have already said, it is clear that the history of religions has not as its primary, and still less as its only, object or as a presupposition, a too immediate and exclusive study of the characteristics of a generic

---

[2] Lehmann, in a study on *mana* (1922), protested against the too facile recourse to ethnology to support R. Otto's theory of the 'holy'. This criticism is repeated with references also to other religions, by the Leipzig followers of Lehmann, W. Baetke and K. Rudolph.

religious *quality* which might emerge too easily from the context of the facts investigated. Certainly, this also may emerge from historical-comparative research, that is, from a phenomenology firmly based on historical-positive enquiry. [3] In other words, there may result, even with all its complexities and analogies, a form, or rather an aspect (among other variants) common to all civilizations and to all men which we call 'religious'. This common 'religious' quality is of course analogically (see further on) and historically conditioned, that is, it is always open (as to its adequacy) to conceptual verification on the basis of progressive historical positive research. Nevertheless, between phenomenological generalities on the one hand and concrete individualization on the other, the philological and historical, or rather comparative-historical method will be a necessary mediator and guarantor. This method implies the investigation of cultural processes and *milieux* in which the religious facts are concrete and, as such, objects of history. And this will be true not only for all that concerns the study of those religions which are called 'ethnical', that is, religions which, like the Etruscan or the original Roman religions, or the Sumerian or Egyptian, are an integrating part of a civilization or of a culture, with which they rise and with which, or before which, they decline, but is also true in the case of 'founded' religions, that is, religions which develop through the operation of a clearly individuated Founder, although always of course, at least in their origin and early development, in the context of a culture and a history. Thus even the individual 'religious' man who is the Founder of a religion is historically localised in a context from which it is impossible to isolate him until this context has been the object of all the historical study which it deserves.

Of course the intimate and personal aspects of religion will not be sacrificed or diminished by a legitimate historical investigation which therefore will not descend to sociological over-simplifications or preconceptions. In fact, just because of his concentration on actual fact, on detail, on the individual, on what is unique, and unrepeatable, the historian of religions must be willing to appreciate the personalities of those who have in their own persons incarnated, actively and passively, the religious history of mankind. This means, among other things, that the historian of religions must beware of the 'reductionist' temptation, and of the tendency to give facile explanations; he must not consider that all the facts and personalities he comes across can

---

[3] See further on, for the concept or 'historical typology of religions'.

be 'explained' merely on the basis of an over mechanical application of a historical-cultural criterion (or, still less, of merely sociological, geographical, psychological-social or ethno-psychological criteria). He will find difficulty in studying in depth the personalities of the Founders, reformers and prophets—but this does not mean that he must have recourse too frequently to intuitive judgments or, worse still, to the exaggerated intuitionistic method of which we have already spoken, especially if by so doing he intends to isolate these personages from the whole complex historical, sociological and psychological problem. But to avoid these dangers and to build on a sound foundation the study of the personalities which are at the source of so great a part of this problem, the historian of religions will indeed have to appeal to the resources of his methodology, which is historical-positive, and avoid having recourse to generic preconceptions or to various eventual alternatives to historical research (see further on). Religion and religiosity as general concepts will certainly remain as much a problem of phenomenology and religious psychology as they are of comparative history. But one will be able to say more about this, on historical and phenomenological grounds, only at the end of an investigation, which is always undertaken from a positive-inductive angle, and never in the early stages of research and its extension.

3. *The meaning of historical-religious comparison. The analogous meaning of 'religion' and 'religious'*

The history of religions is therefore a historical science which has as its object those phenomena which, in universal time and space, we call 'religious'. Every one of these phenomena has its own peculiar individuality and character, and therefore exercises more or less a power of attraction or repulsion, or both together, with regard to other 'religious' phenomena in its vicinity. Religions present themselves for investigation as historical processes, as closely woven complexes of belief and practice, as more or less compact systems even if more or less inter-communicative. These systems correspond on the one hand to a human attitude, the 'religious' attitude (and in this they betray more or less obvious analogies) but, on the other hand, they seem to vary so much that a large section of the history and phenomenology of religions must be devoted to questions of historical-typological categorization.

Here the problem arises as to whether a given phenomenon or a given system (for example, the Buddhism of the 'Small Vehicle') deserves the term 'religion' or 'religious', not in relation to the concept of 'true' religion and the 'truly' religious in the philosophical and theological sense (as opposed to 'false' religion and 'false' religiosity) but in relation to that historical-phenomenological 'analogy' to which we have already referred, which is the special object of the history of religions.

The problem is more common than is generally thought, because it is not only the objects which are so diverse but also the spirit, intention and perspective of 'religions' and the 'religious'. In extreme cases the comparative-historical method will be put to a hard test but will show all its powers of discrimination when it discovers those characteristics which nevertheless justify from the scientific point of view the intuitions of the common man who so frequently, while remaining faithful to his creed (which sometimes renders him even more sensitive) has been able and willing to call 'religions' even those beliefs which at first (but not always and not necessarily) appeared to him strange, unacceptable or superstitious. Even here, between a genuinely fertile intuition, which must however always be verified from the historical point of view, and an improper use of ready made conceptual categories, the mediator will be the comparative-historical method proper to the history of religions. This is seen for example in the case of a Buddhist monk of the 'Small Vehicle' who might be called 'religious', but might also be denied that description because of his indifference to the essential problems of all the other religions. The comparative-historical method will draw upon all its resources in order to single out those aspects under which, concretely and positively, that form of Buddhism, or rather Buddhism as lived in that *milieu*, is 'analogous' to other more usual religious forms—an analogy which may be true when, for example, Buddhist 'atheism', or the Buddhist doctrine of the impermanence of the soul, operates concretely and historically as the radicalization of an obviously religious problem, such as that of Vedantic speculation about the illusory nature of the world of the living, in the perspective of a final liberation in the Absolute. [4]

---

[4] It is useless to observe in this connection, as H. Clavier does in *Numen*, XV, 2 (1968) p. 105, that Buddhism is a philosophy which 'wherever it becomes religious in fact [devient religieuse en fait], even in its most rigid tradition, that of the Hīnayāna, created its own divine personages'. In fact, except in the case of Amidism, it is not these personages which characterize it, or constitute its essence or final significance, and it would be strange if a non-religious doctrine and practice were to become religious merely through the accretion of elements which are to it accessory and secondary.

From what we have already said it is clear that the comparison implicit in the history of religions—a comparison which does not mean to identify things different but on the contrary to distinguish elements otherwise left in confusion, will be above all a comparison between religions, between religious systems and complexes, and not mainly a comparison of detached elements or individual phenomena. In fact these latter, separated from their context, would be misunderstood and arbitrarily identified or contrasted. Here one sees the inevitable limitations of a phenomenology which would break up history and historical processes into so many elements of belief or practice especially if the student reserved for himself the supreme privilege of putting them together again, or interpreting them on the basis of arbitrarily erected structures, in homage to religions or philosophies taken *de facto* as models. If he were to do this explicitly his method would be more legitimate but would then become a philosophy or a theology. Even then he would misunderstand the facts, or fail to render them full justice, in so far as he neglected the results of historical and positive research. Hence the danger of studies and publications, undertaken from the phenomenological point of view (on pre-established religious items: God, sacrifice, soul, salvation, religion), which do not take into account the exigencies of historical method and research.

Another danger inherent in a mistaken application of the comparative method (apart from the old claim to compare only what is linguistically comparable, a claim which however at least indicates praiseworthy scruples proper to a philological-positive approach) would be that of wishing to make comparisons in an unorganic and arbitrary manner which may even be fortuitous or capricious, and unjustifiable even from the point of view of phenomenology. This occurs in certain 'comparisons' between, say, the religion of Israel and the Chinese religions, without the necessary historical framework which would explain the contexts and, wherever possible, the geographical, chronological and historical-cultural links which might make a more positive contribution to the comparisons between one *milieu* and another. Comparative arguments have been used also in connection with the famous 'questions of rites', which would often be easier to resolve by means of some practical initiative, that is, by a concrete cultural contact, than in a mere theoretical enquiry which be abstracted from such a contact. [5]

---

[5] For example, it is incorrect or at least dangerous, to ask whether or when the traditional God of the Chinese is the true God of Christian theodicy or theology. This is not because the philosopher or theologian cannot accept a supreme concept

The historical-comparative method has still less in common with that comparative method which calls itself historical but is in reality far from being such, for it admits (as did Goblet d'Alviella) the possibility of supplying the lack of true or supposed documentary elements in the history of a cultural *milieu* or of a period by substituting elements and events taken from the history of other historical periods or *milieux*, on the basis of hypothetical evolutionary laws of universal validity (see chap. III, 4).

Our attempt to clear up this point will then be justified, if, notwithstanding, we attach a certain importance (see Chapters II and III) to a presentation of general religious phenomena which will however always imply, and sometimes explicitly contain, concrete historical-cultural references to the respective *milieux* in which they existed and still exist, and in which they have significance.

4. *The 'structures' of religion and the historical typology of religions*

Several objections have been made to the history of religions being considered as a subject in itself. Some of these objections derive from purely practical reasons. For example, its scope is said to be too vast to be explored scientifically by a single student. There is implicit in this objection the just requirement that any discussion on facts and texts must presuppose a philological (and of course linguistic) competence adequate for the purpose.

Certainly one must from the beginning concede that the historian of religions, besides having considerably enriched his own interest in comparative studies with practical experience and knowledge, must have a philological competence in some special field, a competence which can direct his enquiry and enable him to profit also by the philological achievements of others. However, it is also true that the history of religions, in coping with its own problems, cannot reduce itself to a mere summary of particular religious chronicles, each of which has to be entrusted to experts in the respective cultures and

---

of God and compare with it other concepts of Supreme Beings or Deities, etc., but because it may happen, and indeed often happens, that the Chinese concrete idea of God, in one or other period of their history, is on such occasions made the object of selection in an arbitrary way or in any case subjected to an hermeneutic which does not take account of the specific and complex character of its ideological and historical-cultural associations. As for the problem of Deity in that cultural milieu see now J. Shih, *The Notions of God in the Chinese Religions* in *Numen*, XVI (2), 1969, pp. 99-138.

philologies. In fact, whoever has any experience of inter-cultural problems, concerning the contacts and reciprocal influences between different civilizations and cultural *milieux*, must know that even in the field of religious concepts and practice, although this is often the field in which peoples are most jealous of their spiritual inheritance and most anxious to conserve it, nevertheless the phenomena of the influence of other systems, active or passive, were and still are of great importance. The cosmopolitic and universalist religions show that barriers of race, culture and language may easily and significantly be overcome in the religious field.

Moreover, even apart from the question of diffusion, which in the ethnological field is indeed much more widespread than is generally thought (forms of culture and religion studied by ethnologists sometimes show that they have migrated across cultural areas and continents, oceans and deserts formerly considered impassable) there remains the fact of the vast extension of certain well defined types of culture and religion, and of certain elements of religious belief and practice, which hold out no possibility of their lines of diffusion being traced. For example, one finds concepts like that of a Supreme Being, of an ancestor who has become the object of worship, of a fertility rite, of 'spirit' in the animist sense, and there are institutions such as the 'passage rites', initiations, oracles and other 'structures', even if this term is inadequate and dangerous because too constrictive. There is the element of sacrifice, a factor in worship which is present in most varied forms and always relative to the type of religion to which it belongs, and prayer and the priesthood, and the tendency to create formulae, symbolism and myth. But one must remember especially that very 'analogical' form or 'structure' which is 'religion' itself, whatever may be, as we have already said, the historical value of this very generic term.

One may object that these 'structures' concern religious phenomenology, with all the dangers of abstract conceptualism and arbitrary judgments involved in this, more than they concern historical research, such as is implied in the history of religions; thus—the same person could object—the comparison which verifies these structures and forms is more a question of phenomenology than of historical research. So it would be vain to hope for a truly comparative-historical method capable of studying religious phenomena throughout the whole civilised world. This is also the objection raised by Italian 'historicism' (B. Croce and others) against the history of religions, which was accused of being a typically positivist study, without any real significance for true historical research, because of its claims to be universalist and comparative. In fact, comparative research, especially on a vast scale, was accused of having at most resulted in catalogues and collections of mere heuristic interest.

Now all these objections derive from an insufficient appreciation of the comparative-historical method proper to the history of religions, and from an inadequate sense of the urgency with which, in spite of any theoretical contestation, certain problems present themselves. These demand a reply, and one which is scientifically sound. In fact, whoever studies human phenomenology will see that certain aspects of the religious element—in fact, more precisely, certain facts such as concepts, rites and institutions, are present at least 'analogously' [6] in various civilizations and function in these, because of cross-cultural influences which may still be traced, or because of circumstances (diffusion? parallel development? convergence?) which are none the less real for being indefinable in our present state of knowledge.

Hence the necessity to study these facts and processes or 'structures' [7] with first hand documentation, and with the help of a scientific hypothesis (which must be prudent and aware of its limitations) in various regions, peoples, civilizations and continents and in various types of culture. But here also is the opportunity to attempt to establish, as it were, a 'historical phenomenology' or 'historical typology' of religious facts, that is, a typology no longer merely composed of individual religious elements (specific creeds, rites, institutions, etc.) which would make it too sectional, 'horizontal' and abstract, but also a typology of historical-cultural processes, that is of 'religious histories': by this we mean an enquiry into the historical meaning of 'analogous' developments in various religions, or the development of 'analogous' religions or religious forms in different localities and periods.

A typical example of this requirement is the study of historical circumstances (which may be reproduced in various localities but are apparently almost always accompanied by influences and stimuli which can be traced historically) in which can be seen, in differing civilizations, that typical form of religious complex called 'polytheism'. This

---

[6] As we have said, the definition of the historical-phenomenological sense of this 'analogy', which is valid also as regards the concept of 'religion', is the principal aim of the history of religions.

[7] This term also presents a historical problem, unless one is prepared to accept over facile 'psychologistic' solutions, that is, to see in the 'structures' timeless 'archetypes' of the human psyche, individual or collective (see pp. 185-189, and 192 et seq.).

implies a religious concept and practice which do not arise spontaneously, and certainly not as the result of a 'naturalistic' necessity, but in relation to a clearly defined historical development, that is, in connection with the rise of the 'high civilizations' of the ancient world, characterised by the building of cities, with specific shrines and specific deities, and with the parallel development of political and religious institutions which are peculiarly apt for the organisation of a polytheistic cult. [8]

Similar problems and similar historical solutions or hypotheses arise also in the case of other types of cultures and religious forms which may be reconstructed by students of cultural history. Such are, for example, the very ancient civilizations of the primitive hunters, with certain fairly constant forms of religious belief and practice (hunting rites, tribal initiation rites, etc.).

Apart from the 'ethnological' civilizations it will be even more useful for the historian of religions who is alive to comparative-historical problems to make use of written sources or of those other elements for investigation in which the 'literary' civilizations abound. The enquiry will be all the more meticulous, the more specific the type of historical problem to which it leads, revealing eventual links much more closely circumscribed in space and time. But here also appear historical problems of an amplitude which it would be difficult for a historian to perceive if he were insensitive to questions of comparison. One must try to imagine what the investigation into a phenomenon like gnosticism or, even more, dualism (in the sense in which this term is used in the history of religions) or into other problems, to be dealt with in the third chapter would be like if the comparative-historical problem were neglected, even in its concretely typological aspects. This is all the more obvious if one reflects that other branches of study would immediately invade the field destined for historical-phenomenological comparison, and we should see philologists and historians interested in a given civilization or historical period basing

---

[8] As we see, this is very different from research founded on the positivist dogma of the 'laws' of historical evolution, and is also a very different concept from that of the 'analogous developments in different religions, under the influence of similar factors', of which M. Clavier speaks, *op. cit.*, p. 108.

Even if this may sometimes be true in other cases, this type of analogy is too extraneous to the interior dynamism of history, common, by hypothesis, to religious processes which historical typology finds similar. This is proved by the type of example which Clavier adduces (evil influence of prosperity or privilege over the religious life of a community), examples which clearly imply the application of criteria not necessarily valid for every type of religion cf. p. 166 n. 8.

their enquiries, with regard to the more general localization and comparative interpretation of the facts and structures they are studying, on theses borrowed from phenomenologists, philosophers, sociologists and theologians, all of which theses are legitimate in their own field but not the product of that comparative-historical method which is typical for religious-historical research.

Finally, the judges of these conflicting claims will be, in this case, the facts themselves. If the historians of religions, with their comparative-historical studies, have encouraged philologists to pursue new knowledge, or if they have revealed the existence of relationships, not previously noted, between various phenomena, or even if they have merely raised new problems, they will have given proof of the scientific legitimacy of their field of studies, and certainly they have done this many times already even if—on other occasions—they have strayed from the right path. And it would be wrong to object that they have achieved these ends merely through their individual philological competence or their skill in related fields—for those problems and those results often have a much wider range than that of any system of enquiry relating to a single ethnical group or a single cultural *milieu*.

5. *Religious ethnology and the history of religions*

It happens sometimes that in common parlance the 'history of religions' is said to be almost, if not quite, the same as 'religious ethnology'.

This identification is of course mistaken, since the object of the history of religions is not only more extended, including also the religions of the more advanced civilizations and the great universalist religions, but is from other points of view also different from religious ethnology, which is primarily a part of general ethnology, whose special object being the history and typology of civilizations without written records.

Nevertheless we cannot deny that religious ethnology has had and continues to enjoy great prominence in studies connected with our own subject, and this is for reasons both historical and methodological. As we shall point out in Chapter III, studies in the history of religions, or at least studies connected with this, were, not only in the first investigations of the eighteenth century but also in their hey-day in the nineteenth century, largely confused with the studies of an Illuminist and evolutionist anthropology, which sought the essence of religion in its origins and identified these with embryonic and shadowy manifestations of a primitive or 'savage' conception.

This method of procedure gave rise in time to a twofold reaction. On the one hand, ethnologists, particularly those of the historical-cultural school, contested the validity of the reasoning of the evolutionist school. On the other hand, many students of the phenomena of religion challenged the wisdom of seeking its essence and significance in primitive religious phenomena (or indeed in folklore or even, as occurred in certain psychologistic circles, in infantile and para-normal manifestations). In any case, it was and still is objected that studies based mainly or exclusively on these materials cannot say much about the power and importance of religion in the history of the spirit and the history of culture. It is as if the achievements of Christian history, or of religious India, or of Greek religious thought, were less meaningful, from this point of view, than the 'stammerings' of a savage, and not something new and infinitely greater than these. The objection is certainly valid and significant from the point of view of historical research and the comparative-historical method. In fact, it seeks to give due importance to the true concept of history which is that of the original, unique and progressive creation of human and cultural values which, if on the one hand potentially implicit in common human nature, are on the other hand historically localized and real in a history which leaps, or at least marches, forward at its own pace.

However, if must be added that the history of religions not only cannot fail to consider as its object and within the ambit of its scope, universal in time, space and culture, the religions of primitive cultures: it must also give these a very special attention, because of the contribution they may make to the theme of genesis and development, which is of supreme interest in comparative-historical studies connected with the history of religions. It is however true, and the evolutionists, like certain phenomenologists today, were wrong to forget this, that history knows many geneses, as many as the processes of which it consists.

In this connection another very delicate point deserves our attention. It has been observed that the civilizations and religions studied by ethnologists should not be described as 'primitive', since this adjective is much more legitimately applied to pre-historic civilizations. In fact, the civilizations studied by ethnologists, that is, the cultures of peoples without written records, whose customs and brief history (brief, as known to us!) have become known to us for the most part only in recent years, have behind them a long road as time-laden as our own, and so are anything but primitive: in fact the 'savages' of today are our 'contemporary primitives'.

This objection too has a certain, but very partial validity. In fact, 'quantitative' time is one thing, and is certainly the same for a New Yorker as for a Melanesian of the virgin lands of New Guinea and as it was for their respective ancestors; but 'qualitative' time is quite another thing. It is 'cultural' time, the time needed for the dynamic impulse of cultural evolution and revolution in New York and in Melanesia, as in their respective cultural *milieux* and histories. Therefore, as has been rightly pointed out, it is we (the advanced civilizations, or high cultures) who are the 'real ancient' ones.

We find a concrete proof of this observation in a concept acquired by modern ethnology: the so-called 'more advanced' cultures or 'literary' civilizations, from those of ancient Mesopotamia, Egypt, etc. to modern civilizations in various continents, are not 'more advanced', that is, more complex and culturally rich and productive, by virtue of a purely conventional comparison with the so-called 'inferior' (or illiterate) cultures, but effectively represent, in terms of historical-cultural dynamics, a 'further' and therefore more advanced product than these. And this is true whether the 'more advanced' civilizations are to be traced, by a historically proved diffusion, to the ancient Mediterranean and Near East civilizations, or whether their affinities with these are merely due to a historical typology of the kind we have already mentioned. The so-called primitive cultures, which naturally include, in a special category, the pre-historic cultures, do not belong to that historical process which, beginning in Mesopotamia or possibly elsewhere, many thousands of years before Christ, has produced the 'more advanced' civilizations by a sort of complex cultural accumulation. Thus those cultures which have remained extraneous to this process may legitimately be defined by a unitary term which characterizes them all, and this term way well be, in contrast with that of 'higher' or more advanced civilizations, that of 'primitive' cultures.

Naturally it may be objected that few—or possibly even none—of the civilizations studied by ethnologists are now at the beginning of a process of development similar to that which produced the 'higher' civilizations, and that therefore the cultures of present day illiterate peoples are not involved in this dialectic of 'earlier' and 'later'. This is all the more true since various so-called primitive cultures may quite fortuitously be very youthful, possibly because of some event in their past history. For example, if some populations took refuge in thickly forested regions, this was followed by a consequent withdrawal from their cultural system and a relative adaptation, impoverishment and 'specialization'. But it is nevertheless true that, on the whole, the line of development of the 'higher' cultures, that is, the historical process which has produced them, is the only yardstick and main point of reference which permit us to form a criterion in questions of the 'primitiveness' or 'modernity' of cultures as a whole, naturally apart from those ulterior internal specifications which are valid not only for cultures extraneous to the process of 'higher' civilization, but also for those already involved in it.

Moreover, it is undeniable (even if each case has to be verified separately, in order to avoid falling into the snare of the too obvious) that illiterate civilizations may in some way be classified together, not only by contrast with the higher cultures, but also because of characteristics which make them specifically comparable from certain points of view, even if they do not really resemble each other, and many of these shared features are obviously archaic (which permits us, within certain limits, to set aside, in this very generic question, the case of 'regressive' civilizations). Finally, one must remember that several of these same factors could be common to prehistoric civilizations as well as to those studied by ethnologists. Here too one must avoid the snare of considering as identical or analogous anything which, in a pre-historic or an ethnical culture, may be only apparently analogous but in reality historically dissimilar. We shall nevertheless trust to genuine similarities, which no one in fact will contest. To confine ourselves to one example, who would have recognised the historical-religious significance of a rhomb in Sicilian folklore if rhombs had not figured as typical initiatory ritualistic instruments, testified by various ethnologists, and if rhombs of an undoubted ritualistic significance had not been known even to students of prehistory as well as of classical antiquity? Many more examples might be cited, hunting rites, sacrificial customs, the general aspect of certain cultures, etc.

6. Various ways of approaching the study of religions. Other objections to the history of religions

Other questions may be raised concerning the method and object of the history of religions, especially by students of the 'great living religions'. As a general rule one must point out that the history of religions is just as much interested in those which have disappeared

—although it is very hard to find a religion that has disappeared completely, with all its elements and aspirations—as in religions alive today. This is because both types are included in those vast historical panoramas with which the history of religions is concerned, and also because whether a religion is practised or not does not affect the principles of methodology but only—and this is in itself quite considerable—the nature of the respective documentation to be utilized. Moreover, an analogous difference may be seen, in this connection, between the religions of pre-history, philologically mute and articulate only through archeological remains, and the religions of the 'literary' civilizations that are now spent and are articulate only through texts which are often of unsurpassed splendour and cultural and documentary value. It may indeed be said that some scholars who have been trained in humanistic studies may find it easier to understand—at least apparently, for one must never underestimate the differences dividing centuries and cultures—the texts of Seneca or Virgil or even the spells of the Arval Brothers, than some popular beliefs and practices of today. Tylor and Frazer were justly reproached for their very theoretical reconstructions of the dawn of religion among men. Analogously, the living non-European cultures, civilizations and religions may be more alien to the student of the history of religions, not to speak of the common man of our own lands (especially if he has only a minimum of culture) than the religions of classical antiquity or of German mythology, which he studied when at school. And this is true even today when there is so much talk about cultural 'pluralism'.

The history of religions thus studies with equal right, and substantially with the same method, all religions, setting up a hierarchy of importance only in the case of those problems which are most crucial in a historic survey of religions and of religious civilizations. So it emerges that there really exist, in the history of religions, certain important problems highly significant for this branch of study (See Chapter III). There is for example the question of archaic forms of religion, in connection with which the history of religions made many of its initial enquiries, or the problem of the Indo-Iranian religions, or the question of the mutual relations between religious *milieux* of the ancient Near East (Mesopotamia, Syria and Palestine) or questions relative to Christianity and the ancient religions of 'salvation', or Islam and its relations with pre-Islamic Arabia and with the Biblical religions; or even, although these are much less frequently considered, questions relating to the mediaeval 'heresies', a field of enquiry too often left to mediaevalists, with the danger of a diminished awareness of the indispensable comparative historical method. Finally, there are the questions about the diffusion of Buddhism and its multiple forms, in relation to the various regions to which it spread and their respective cultures, etc., an enquiry often left to the Orientalists alone, or to the sociologists, who have indeed made a good and useful contribution to this problem.

One may add that the objectoins to this 'equalitarian' attitude of the history of religions proceed from various quarters. They may be raised by experts (or other scholars) who are particularly interested in the international, social, political, ecumenical and religious problems of today, naturally inspired by motives corresponding to their respective points of view.

Therefore, those who today, actuated by motives that may be very varied or even contrasting, interest themselves in the fate and function of religion and religions in the modern world or in certain types of modern civilization (for example, in 'industrial' as opposed to 'peasant' civilizations), may be surprised to learn that the history of religions is still much concerned with questions that now seem to them ephemeral, or of interest merely to scholars, and will include this branch of study in their general criticism of the 'abstract' nature of traditional humanistic studies.

Now no one denies the historical interest of religious forms and tendencies in the modern world, and no one denies that this is material for the history of religions (which is therefore mistaken when it frequently leaves similar subjects to sociologists and students of cultural anthropology, or even to politicians and to journalists). Nevertheless, the criticism against a history of religions which is said to be too much concerned with remote times and problems shows an inveterate incomprehension of the historical problem involved. This is not only because the historian is not—as may be commonly thought—for ever brooding over remote, lost things but because to reconstruct a historical process is a work, if not of contemporary interest in the sense desired by an exaggerated historicism, certainly of immediate interest for the understanding of today's world. We often find this easier to understand when we know the origin of some of its structures (or even of some of its contestations) than when we merely study the most recent developments of a present situation. Now there are some problems, among the typical problems already referred to, which the history of religions cannot afford to neglect, for fear of destroying itself;

this explains why in recent Congresses of the history of religions many scholars have been dismayed to see certain important fields given too little attention, or abandoned to the respective specialists (in the field of Orientalism for example), or certain historical or cultural areas or periods considered more significant than others which are certainly no less essential.

Another objection may be raised by scholars who are interested in the history and phenomenology of religions for reasons that are not purely scientific but derived also and above all from too indiscriminate a phenomenological outlook, which is marked by a certain religionistic intuitionism of which we have already spoken, or from a generic ecumenicalism. These scholars, interested mainly in the great living religions, although admirable and praiseworthy in other fields, seek to promote a 'mutual understanding' between religions and religious peoples which is not based solely on a religio-historical foundation and does not use a religio-historical methodology.

In this group there are many who favour a sort of transcendental theosophical unity of religions, or even syncretistic forms—and these finalities too are in any case different from the aims of the history of religions. Naturally this science does not presuppose agnostic or reductionist philosophies, or confessional (or anti-religious) positions, but only insists on the correct application of the positive-historical methodology which determines its object and its purpose, as will be better explained later on.

Others, without going so far as this, nevertheless assert a principle which is not easily acceptable in our studies: they maintain that a statement on a living religion, different from one's own—or different from the religion in which one was born—is valid only if the adherents of this religion will agree to it, that is, if they consider that they are faithfully portrayed in the book in question [8a]. But this principle too is not in accordance with the methodological principles of religio-historical research. In fact, apart from the fact that it would render futile all historical studies on ancient religions, the fact remains that the followers of a religion, although they may be representative of the average feeling of its adherents today, are not always good interpreters of their religion as it was in the past, or of the historical interpretative problems closely allied with it. Or better, if they are,

---

[8a] This in the context of the question of 'mutual understanding' (see above, n. 1): cf. W. Cantwell Smith, in Eliade-Kitagawa, *The History of Religions*, Chicago, 1959, pp. 42-54. See also below, pp. 23-23 n. 9.

from various points of view, competent interpreters of their religion as it is today, or even of one of its living traditions (and they are often more intelligent, better informed and more sensitive than many pretentious experts without sensibility or acumen) on the other hand it is no less true that their interpretations can never *simpliciter* be translated into religio-historical motivations, for this would be legitimate only on the basis of the methodology proper to this science, which does not claim to say or to know all there is to be known about religion, but must say what it has to say on the basis of its own pertinent methodology.

Moreover, they are not bound to study or to adopt the historical and comparative-historical, or even merely generically phenomenological presentation of the problem presented by their own religion. Yet it is true that their testimony and, within certain precise limits, their co-operation, may be useful for the study not only of the tradition and present-day situation of the religion in question, but also of the evolutions and deviations at present active in it, evolutions and tendencies which for present and future purposes are no less pertinent to the history of religions than are questions of pre-history or antiquity.

Equally obvious is the reply to those who object that the history of religions places all religions on the same footing, whether this objection is raised from a 'confessional' standpoint, or from the standpoint of 'historicism'. On the contrary, if the history of religions applies the philological and comparative-historical method to all religious phenomena, it does so in order to identify every one of these facts and processes and their respective positions in the framework of history, and to do this it needs to use means provided by the historical method. Moreover, this does not imply any 'superior' attitude on the part of the history of religions in the study of religious phenomena, but only a definition of its own competence, as we shall show later on.

7. *Various sciences concerned with religions*

It is also important to distinguish the history of religions from the other sciences which in one way or another are concerned with religion and religions. This is necessary, particularly but not exclusively, as the properly philosophical and theological problem of the 'question of value' or 'question of truth' (*Wahrheitsfrage*) is concerned, or of the question of the absolute value of religion or of a religion (*Absolutheitsanspruch*; see also below, on pp. 34 n. 3 and 177 n. 28).

But already in questions which do not imply the 'question of value' or the 'question of truth' certain discussions of relative competence may arise between the history of religions and other fields of learning. We have already referred to a certain 'phenomenology' which claims to be independent of clearly defined philosophical systems, although it is obviously much influenced by them, but we could speak also of phenomenology in the technical sense of the term, as used by Husserl, or of phenomenologies of religion defined in more traditional philosophies, including those of Kantian origin. This philosophical phenomenology often sets out to establish the typical concept of religion without sufficiently taking into account the methodological requirements of the history of religions.

We have also spoken of that phenomenology of an irrationalistic intuitionistic type which relies too much on intuitions, however efficacious these may be, like that of the 'holy', or of an 'ultimate' which is said to underly all religious manifestations and, in the final analysis, is their meaning. In certain forms more interested in religious typology the manifestations of this 'holy' element or this 'ultimate' are classified in various hierophanies, substantially homologous, while religion is considered to be a 'transcendence' or a 'breakthrough' from 'this' world and 'this' universe—a view which, although in one sense capable of fertile development, in other senses, and in certain of its corollaries, remains arbitrary because it is over-simplified and generalized. This is seen, for example, when religious value is identified with the primordial and the a-historical, continually compromised and diminished by the passing of time and ritually restored in religious ceremonies.

Other observations, with very different cultural references, must be made about philosophies with a sociological-dialectic basis, like those which are attached in some way to Marxism as a philosophy. The studies pursued with this preconception about religion and religions, even when they are not merely the application of theoretical schemes, reveal an obvious introduction of extraneous arguments which distort the result, altering and restricting the sphere of enquiry, as well as the whole of the heuristic patrimony of evidence. This, as we shall point out, does not mean a prejudicial assumption of the notion of the 'religious' as an *a priori* element in the history and nature of man, for such a supposition has no place in history as part of an inductive-positive methodology. Similarly, the history of religions must not be confused with certain 'explanations' of religious phenomena based essentially on sociological and psychological studies, or 'reductionist' theories, since these systematically reduce the 'religious' to the 'social', and this is particularly true of the French sociological school of Durkheim and Mauss, or to the 'psychical'. Here also it is not a case of admitting, for the history of religions, the religious element as an *a priori* category of the spirit, but rather of recognising that the sociology and psychology of religion, although these are precious auxiliary sciences for its history, nevertheless belong, as Pettazzoni observes, respectively to sociology and psychology, and so have for their specific object not religion but, respectively, society and the psyche. From this it clearly results that the presentation of their problems, the documentary materials they examine and the aims of their research do not cover the vast extent and complexity of the religio-historical problem of religion and religions. Here also nothing can *a priori* prevent religio-historical research from suggesting or putting forward reductionist conclusions, or even conclusions contrary to these; what one *cannot* accept is that research should be confined to a sociological or psychological enquiry, and that this should be an *a priori* of the inductive argument and of the historical interpretation (as it would be in the case of the Marxian preliminary division into 'structures' and 'superstructures' of the historical process *in toto*).

From what we have already said one clearly sees—on the other hand—the impropriety of an assertion frequently made that the historical study of religious phenomena is substantially possible only for one who has a personal religious faith or, as some followers of R. Otto maintain, has a 'gift' for perceiving the 'holy'. The example most frequently quoted in this connection is that of a man born blind who will never be able to perceive colours. But an admission of this kind conflicts with the characteristics of every historical science, for which the arguments must be valid *erga omnes*, and particularly with regard to all those who fulfil its methodological requirements. Other qualities and pre-conditions are not insisted upon, for fear of making the student of religious history too sectorial in his attitude to scientific problems and human research. Apart from the absence of any presupposition of *a priori* systems, such as those already mentioned,—sociological and psychological, and even phenomenological or philosophical (at least in so far as these philosophies define religion and its exemplary forms), theological and 'confessional'—apart from all these, it is legitimate to require that the students even of specialised subjects should be gifted with some 'sensibility', that is, a profound and genuine interest in the whole range of the investigation of religio-historical problems as such, coupled with an awareness of and an interest in all the problems of history and civilization in general.

The history of religions has then no confessional or anti-confessional bias and its valid motivations and arguments are those which result from the strict application of the inductive-historical method. Nor has it any grounds for incompatibility with, or dependance on, the philosophy of religion (see the following chapter) or theology as such.

If a science declares itself in relation to its object and bases its enquiry on its own method, which gives it its autonomy, then these conclusions are clear. In fact, one must point out that the object of a science is so strictly connected with its method, that is, with its means of research, that it is in some way identified with it. This means, moreover, that the history of religions is not generically the study of religion but the study of religion as a phenomenon and fact of history and, as such, capable of investigation by a historian.

This does not signify agnosticism, which instead implies a precise philosophical position not pertinent to history as a science; nor does it properly mean 'neutrality', another concept implying anyhow a reference to philosophical controversy, and so extraneous to religio-historical methodology and scope.

Finally, the double-edged objection that the historian of religions is always (or should always be) a man involved in a vast system of problems and involvements falls to the ground. Naturally, if one wishes to avoid being ingenuous or easily deluded, one must admit that the historian in general, and the historian of religions in particular, may be influenced, in setting up his working hypotheses, by his own way of viewing the world and religion, and this may add a more lively interest to his enquiry. Nevertheless, the fact remains that his research and his conclusions in the sphere of the history of religions, that is, not only his descriptions of religious phenomena but also his well documented accounts of particular historical processes and of general historical typology, will be valid and defensible, in so far as he is able to rely on a pertinent use of positive-historical methodology, which must be both strict and open to verification by anyone whose competence is based on the principles of this methodology. [9] An inconfutable

---

[9] So we may reply to an objection like that raised by B. Schwartz (Kitagawa, *op. infra cit.*,): 'The illusion of complete non-involvement, with all the self-deceptions it nourishes, is more detrimental to objectivity than a lively sense of involvement controlled by the desire to understand': a remark which, in order to be proved objectively, would need further distinctions, and which we quote merely as a useful description of the psychological state of the student of the history of religions.

proof of the correct application of this will be seen when the historian of religions succeeds in bringing to light concretely new aspects of the problem in question, some of which had been previously ignored—that is when, even before suggesting new solutions, he has indicated new problems which his investigations have shown to be really present.

For these same reasons, there is nothing to prevent the history of religions, when not 'instrumentalized', from making useful and sometimes necessary contributions to other studies on religion, religious sociology and psychology, etc., and may also facilitate mutual understanding among religious people or people *simpliciter*—and this cannot be an object of indifference to any educated person. It does not however constitute in itself either an object or an end of religio-historical research, since it signifies something different from the 'understanding' of the historical dimension of religious phenomena.

8. *Alternative names for the history of religions*

The most obvious name for the positive and comparative study of religions is 'history of religions' because this exactly describes the historical nature of this study and because it has in fact been adopted

---

One must reject a distinction between the religious involvement and the cultural (and political) involvement of the student of the history of religions, which suggests that the former, unlike the latter, would impede a historical—religious research. In fact both, if for different reasons, may (with their working hypotheses and desire to understand) disturb as well as promote historical research and judgment. These all have differences of outlook which would require long and pedantic study to analyse and distinguish there. What is essential is a prudent and above all verifiable application of historical methodology, without recourse to prejudicial extraneous elements which prevent the student from seeing and taking into consideration all aspects of the question. This would happen in the case of the application of 'religionistic' ('phenomenological') preconceptions (in the sense explained on p. 20) or confessional or 'reductionist' presuppositions (sociologistic and psychologistic hypotheses transformed into theses, under pretence of a dialectic cooperation between theoretical thesis and concrete research); the same in the case of philosophic-systematic presuppositions, including the philosophy of B. Croce's absolute historicism (*storicismo assoluto*) and of Marxism. Even more negative would be a postulatory disinterest in religious phenomena shown by anyone who wished to study them for sociological and psychological purposes. We have already spoken about the significance of the 'sensibility' required of a student of the history of religions. W. Cantwell Smith's alternative between 'secular', 'detached' studies and studies [of Comparative Religion] 'carried out by religious people for religious people' (*Comparative Religion: Whither-and Why?*, in Eliade-Kitagawa, *The History of Religions*, Chicago 1959, p. 45 et seq.) is moreover inacceptable as far as Theology (or Comparative Theology) are not concerned. In our opinion that alternative secular-religious fails to reach the core of the question, which is the *methodological* autonomy of the history of religions, with the above mentioned pre-requisites indicated as pertaining to this (and this does not mean 'studying religion from above').

by those scholars who, even if their methods are sometimes gravely defective, have set themselves the aim of an inductive-positive study of religions as facts and processes, open to investigation and identification by historical research and embodying the religious experience of mankind. [10]

Other terms sometimes used are: the 'science of religions', 'the phenomenology of religions' (or 'of religion'), and comparative religions'. (The term 'comparative history of religions', although once used in the Latin countries or in Germany, is really restricted to the concept of the history of religions *tout court*, once this is conceded to be a comparative science or, more precisely, a comparative historical science).

These alternative terms for the history of religions are in reality only partly satisfactory; one may say they are valid only in so far as they do not compromise the competence of the historical method.

We have already spoken of a 'phenomenology of religion' which be not based on a true comparative historical enquiry and indeed rejects the constant control of such an investigation. Without this it can lead to an equivocal 'philosophy of religion' which, while claiming to describe religious phenomena in its own way and to identify essential characteristics, is in reality falsely positive and even falsely objective, and this is also true of a certain 'philosophy of religion' which asserts that, without a 'criterion of value', it wishes to define religion itself. In reality it is inspired by an exemplary concept of the same, based on its own assumptions. If these assumptions are declared and justified, then the notion of an exemplary phenomenology of religion elaborated by a philosophy of religion becomes more legitimate, but it already belongs to the field of the philosophical elaboration of a system of religious concepts, that is to philosophy itself. [11]

'Comparative religion', even when it does not assume, as it does sometimes, any of the 'religionistic' attitudes of the phenomenology of religion, cannot properly be identified with the 'history of religions'

---

[10] Therefore we consider the term 'history or religions' (as used in French, Italian or English-American studies) to be preferable to the corresponding German *Religionsgeschichte* which considers 'religion' in the singular. The fact that the history of religions considers them primarily in the plural, as historical facts to be individually studied, naturally does not prevent its research extending also to the sense of 'religion' and 'religious', a sense which, as we have said, is merely analogous, not univocal for the historian and the phenomenologist mindful of history.

[11] By the term 'philosophy of religion' will be better understood a reflection on the reciprocal conceptual implications of one or more systems of religious representations.

because of its 'modus comparandi', that is more formal and abstract than truly historical. And if 'comparative religion' aims rather at rendering the various religions mutually 'comprehensible' across the barriers of the various confessions but studied from their respective points of view, then it is more similar to a 'comparative theology' of the type known in America last century. [12] If it tends to promote the understanding of the religious motivation of the faithful of various creeds, then this is also an aim of the history of religions, which tries to fulfil it by its own methodical instruments (see the preceding paragraph). [13]

The 'science of religions', finally, should as its name suggests include all those studies which seek to treat religion methodologically by the scientific ascertainment of facts and of the various systems of relations to which they belong; it therefore includes history, sociology and psychology of religion. One may however doubt whether these three spheres of study may constitute a unitary science of religions, or of religion (the German *Religionswissenschaft*); [14] in fact, as we have already noted, the second and third belong primarily to the realms of sociology and psychology, their proper object being not religion but, respectively, society and the psyche. In so far as they relate to religion they must be considered as auxiliary studies for the history of religions, also because the data on which they work, although

---

[12] Cf. below, p. 181-183.

[13] Cf. above p. 18. In our opinion, there are grave limitations, from the point of view of the history of religions, in the views of Wilfred Cantwell Smith, *Comparative Religion: Whither and Why?* in Eliade and Kitagawa's *History of Religions. Essays in Methodology*, Chicago, 1959, p. 31 et sqq. and in his desire to effect a 'personalization of comparative religious studies' (*op. cit.*, p. 33 et sqq.). He gives a typical definition (*op. cit.*, p. 52) of the scope of *'Comparative Religion'*, which is 'to construct statements about religion that are intelligible within at least two traditions simultaneously'. What means here epistemologically, 'intelligible'? Moreover, the author recognises that the historical interest which inspires him is more in religiosity itself than in the various religions (*op. cit.*, p. 55); cf. also below, p. 165.

Elsewhere, especially in England (with S. G. F. Brandon and others) *'Comparative Religion'* indicates a type of research not dissimilar to that implied in the history of religions, but on the basis of a comparative method understood in a wider sense. Also the scope of the recently issued English review *Religion* is rather wide. The periodical *Studies in Comparative Religion* edited in England an dcontaining articles on the line of Guénon is not in the ambit of the history of religions. Among its collaborators is Frithjof Schuon, the author of various volumes showing this orientation, in the wake of Guénon (cf. also E. Zolla and others).

[14] One must remember that this term goes back to a time when scientism was proposed as a substitute and rival for metaphysics and theology; meanwhile it expressed itself in sociology of a naturalistic type, ignoring historical methodology and monopolizing the study of religious phenomena.

acquired independently as a result of investigations or collections of facts, statistics, the identification of affinities, determining factors, etc., must be framed in a concrete historical context which cannot be generalized. Certainly, laws of a natural or naturalistic character can also be elaborated by the religious sociologists and psychologists (in so far as the determining factors, dependent on the nature of the psychical and social structures, can be identified) and as such can be assigned their proper value, which however can never be absolute, in the history of religions. But these determining factors must always be verified in actual history, just as, in quite another field, the 'law of demand and supply' is natural and deterministic but always verified in the *milieu* of a particular society and of presupposed forms and goods, by means of which this society carries on its exchanges. [15]

Problems of the following type will not therefore be the concern of the sociology and the science of religions. They will not be interested, for example, in whether wealth and the support of authority is *in absoluto* useful or not to religion, unless it is made clear, with references to historical research and historical typology, what sort of religion is in question: whether it is a religion of the Messianic-prophetic type, with an eschatological aim, or a religion of the cosmic-political type such as that of the ancient Egyptians, in which the Pharaoh is both son and representative of the Deity, and Lord and Owner of the land. If sociologists were to identify diverse types of religious societies or even, with the aid of cultural anthropology and ethno-psychology, diverse types of religious civilizations, they could do this only by constant reference to historical research concerning these civilizations and religions; otherwise they would run the risk of building on a hypothetical basis. [16]

---

[15] Naturally, in some cases, philosophical reflection and religious faith, or even, sometimes, common human experience, may affirm the character and the generically human (which means 'natural') foundation of feeling, behaviour, etc. But the historian must always verify these affirmations, in order not to deduce from them methodological or interpretative errors in the course of his work, or make incorrect generalizations in descriptions of factual circumstances.

[16] These are the objections that may be raised, against a methodology like that of Toynbee, concerning cultures and religions. Cf. chap. IV, p. 177 n. 28.

As regards the science of religions, M. P. Nilsson's reflections *Letter to Prof. A. D. Nock on some fundamental concepts in the science of religion*, in *Harvard Theol. Review*, 42, 2 (1949) relating to what he calls the 'science of primitive religions as such', must be taken with reservations for reasons already given. He writes (p. 74; the original in German, as a quotation from his *Geschichte d. gr. Rel.* I, p. 34 et seq.): 'This branch of learning is called a 'science', not a 'history' of primitive religions, because it represents the structural affinity of religions, not their

9. *The organization of studies concerning the history of religions*

The history of religions first began to flourish in university circles in the last few decades of the nineteenth century. It was then taught at Leyden, (Holland, with Tiele and Chantepie de la Saussaye, has a place of primary importance in these studies), in Oxford (with Max Müller), in Copenhagen and Geneva (from 1873 onwards). In 1880 De Broglie began a course of History of non-Christian cults at the Catholic Institute of Paris, [17] a course which some years later was to change its name, and to some extent also its subject. Soon afterwards there began to the *Collège de France* the courses of the History of Religions given by Albert Réville, the content of these lectures was published in the *Prolégomènes de l'histoire des religions* which appeared in a third edition in 1881 (the inaugural lecture was also edited). Meanwhile, in 1880, there appeared the *Revue de l'histoire des religions*, the first [18] specialized review (still flourishing). Among its first collaboraters were A. Bouché Leclercq, P. Decharme, G. Maspéro and C. P. Tiele, while M. Vernes was its first Director. Equally important was the institution, in 1886 in Paris, of the Vth Section, called 'of religious sciences', of the *Ecole pratique des hautes études*, at the

historical connection or their actual evolution, for which we have not even enough material to work on. When it presents a series of concepts, for example: power, the powers, spirits or gods, or faith in the dead's return or in the soul, this is always a logical sequence; and yet it is often confused with a historical sequence, and faith in power is often represented as if it were anterior to faith in beings endowed with power...'. Nilsson makes these observations (the last of which is certainly just) in the context of a rehabilitation of the concept of evolution, but one does not see what sense there may be in a study of concrete facts, in 'logical' sequences, since logic, in scientific studies, is what emerges from the facts and from the actual relations between facts, and not from theoretical extrapolations, like those of evolutionistic ethnology. It matters little, to return to Nilsson's example, that the primitive calendars were always constructed with the same 'simple' elements, such as references to the position of the sun or moon, or the movement of the seasons and stars (on what else could they more obviously be based?); what matters is the method and context of these references, which is never a simple matter but a compound of ideological elements of every kind, and this is the object of historical research, and not the result of 'logical sequences'. And if, as Nilsson says 'evolution varies and is different in certain parts of the world' (p. 74) it follows that *this* evolution is history itself. But history is not necessarily a reconstruction of processes and developments, but, when the material at its disposal permits nothing more, fulfills its function by describing its object, distinguishing and individualizing it and wherever possible noting its course in time and space (as in the 'historie' of Herodotus).

[17] De Broglie wrote one of the first treatises expounding the general subject, controversial like all the generic treatises of that time, especially in France, which were apologetic or, on the contrary, anti-clerical in their orientation.

[18] In 1898 appeared the *Archiv für Religionswissenschaft* (Leipzig) which ceased publication in 1942.

Sorbonne, in connection with the suppression of the famous Faculty of Theology of this university.[19]

Certainly, although the history of religions was instituted (as the *Revue de l'histoire des religions* explained) with the aim of treating religion and religions from the historical angle, the spirit of the age was such that whoever dedicated himself to these studies, 'lay' or Catholic, especially when he was dealing with the great problems that were (or were considered to be) his concern as a scholar of the history of religions, found himself immersed in a dense series of problems and arguments that was not very conducive to a clear and methodological distinction between historical research, philosophy, exegesis and theology. This difficulty is clearly seen in the writings of De Broglie,[20] as also in the polemical speech of Goblet d'Alviella, introducing the first Course of the History of Religions in the University of Brussels (1884) entitled 'Prejudices in the scientific study of religions'. There was a similar situation when in 1886 there was established in Italy a chair for the History of Religions, occupied by B. Labanca, which however was transformed two years later into a chair for the History of Christianity.[21] In the German Universities the

---

[19] *Problèmes et méthodes d'histoire des religions, Mélanges publiés par la Section des Sciences religieuses à l'occasion du centenaire de l'Ecole pratique des Hautes Etudes*, Paris 1968. At first the subjects treated were the following: the religions of India, the Far East, Egypt, the Semitic peoples, Greece and Rome, the history of the origins of Christianity, the history of Canon Law, of dogma, of the Christian Church and Christian literature. In 1888 were added the 'religions of uncivilized peoples'. There is still a large number of articulations but, among the *directions d'études* there is none relating to the history of religions as such (we mean object, method and comparative problem of the same). This is only partly justified by the 'practical', highly philological, specialized research of the *Ecole* (see n. 21).

[20] See p. 27, n. 17.

[21] The first permanent Chair of the History of Religions in Italy was held at the University of Rome, 1924-1953, by R. Pettazzoni, who also founded there, in 1925, the periodical '*Studi e materiali di storia delle religioni*'. In those years and in the years immediately preceding, other Reviews flourished, including '*Studi religiosi*', '*Bilychnis*' etc., especially relating to theological matters. They were more or less dissident in their views and showed a great interest in the history of religions without, however, identifying themselves with its aims. Pettazzoni treated the methodological aspects of historical comparative study and aroused the criticism of Crocian historicism. Cf. above, p. 9 et seq. In 1935 was established in Milan a Chair of the History of Religions, held by U. Pestalozza. There are at present in Italy four established Chairs for this subject and study. In international circles the richest centre of special historical-religious studies is the *Section des Sciences religieuses* of the *Ecole pratique des hautes études*, at the Sorbonne. As we have said, there is no special teaching of the 'history of religions' because of the nature of the research conducted by the Ecole itself. Moreover—it would seem—the history of religions, as such, is treated in Paris with some reserve (true, there was until recently a Chair of the History of Religions at the *Collège de France*, held by H.-Ch. Puech). Even in the School of the Science

atmosphere was less agitated, because of the long pluralistic tradition of the relative cultural and religious *milieu*. [22]

Naturally, we cannot here trace the entire course of the organisation of studies in the history of religions in the following years. [23] To form an idea of this it is enough to refer to the Acts of the International Congresses of the History of Religions held in Paris (1900), Basle (1904), Oxford (1908), Leyden (1912), Lund (1929) and Brussels (1935). The first Congress after the second world war was held in Amsterdam (1950) under the presidency of G. Van der Leeuw; on that occasion was founded the International Association for the History of Religions, of which the Presidents have been the Dutch scholar G. Van der Leeuw, the Italian R. Pettazzoni, the Swede G. Widengren and the present day President, the French M. Simon. In 1954 the I.A.H.R. launched a new periodical devoted to the history of religions, *Numen*, accompanied by a series of international bibliographical bulletins concerning this subject and two series of 'supplements' in the form of monographs (resp. dissertations) written by various authors. The following Congresses, organised under the auspices of I.A.H.R., were held in Rome (1955), Tokyo (1958), Marburg (1960), Claremont in California (1965), Stockholm (1970), with meetings for auxiliary studies in Strasburg (1964), Messina (1966), Jerusalem (1968), Turku (1973). (The 1975 Congress is to be held at Lancaster). Since the Tokyo Congress the I.A.H.R. has extended its activities to Asiatic nations. At the same time, as we have already observed, it has re-examined some questions of the exact interpretation of the nature of studies in the history of religions. Naturally, some other spheres of study, which also base their work on the historical-inductive method, come more or less within the ambit of the interests of the history of religions. As regards regular meetings for the purposes of study, particular interest is attached to Congresses of anthropological and ethnological sciences, for their studies connected with religious ethnology, which has always played a prominent part in studies for the history of religions. But Congresses of oriental studies, archeology, Biblical sciences and patrology also frequently produce historical-religious treatises or primary importance.

and Theology of Religions opened recently in Paris at the Theological Faculty of the *Institut Catholique*, there is no History of Religions. But this does not mean that this branch of learning is not taught, and its typical problems not studied, in the various cultural *milieux* of France today.

[22] For the history of religions in Germany see the volume by K. Rudolph, quoted on p. 174. For 'Comparative Religion' in England and the U.S.A. (where the term 'history of religions' is also used) see pp. 25 et seq., 181-183.

[23] For this see chap. IV.

CHAPTER TWO

RELIGION AND THE VARIOUS RELIGIONS

1. *Universality and the meaning of religion*

The reason for the student's interest in the historical study of religions is at once obvious when we consider the universality of the religious element in all civilizations, from the most ancient to the most modern, from those most remote in space to our own. It is clear also when we consider the determining influence religions had and still have in these civilizations which, as R. Pettazzoni observes, can only be understood when their religions are understood. Finally, it is obvious when we consider the profundity of the existential and spiritual interests involved in religions, not only in the context of their external institutions but also in that of the inner life of individuals—an inner life to which, no less than to social and historical-cultural structures, however important these may be, is entrusted the essential dynamism of the religious phenomenon in history, in spite of the theories of sociologists who follow Durkheim.

The universality of the religious element in the history of human civilizations, although not considered as an *a priori* factor in the history of religions, an inductive science which therefore may not assert anything which is beyond the reach of its investigations, is well attested objectively if we bear in mind what we have already said about the 'analogous' meaning of terms such as 'religion' and 'religious' (see above, p. 5 ff). Every attempt to discern or, even more, to presuppose in an evolutionary and historical system the existence of peoples entirely without 'religious' notions is regularly frustrated by the progress of ethnological studies. This hypothesis of an a-religious phase of primitive mankind, put forward by Lubbock in the last century, cannot be proved. What is more, the undoubtedly archaic nature of beliefs of a theistic type which, according to these evolutionists, must have been the most recent to appear (because most similar to our present day beliefs) has been made quite clear. Ethnologists also refute the suggestion that ethical notions come at a later date, or that in archaic civilizations they had no connection with religious ideas.

Apart from the question of individual atheism—which in various forms, commensurate with the respective concepts of religion, was present long before the modern age and, as we know, is possibly not always true atheism but is sometimes caused by particular reactions, variously motivated, expressing itself in arbitrary and generalizing formulae—one must consider, especially today, the question of mass atheism, which seems to prevail in certain highly politicized societies, as for example in the 'aristocracies' of Nazism or, more explicitly, in those societies which are more intent on the 'scientific' diffusion of Communist materialism. In both cases, moreover, we are faced with a political-cultural phenomenon (in some cases similar, though more radical and more widely diffused, to certain illuminist-deist, positivist-materialist and historical-idealist episodes in the history of liberalism) that cannot abolish the 'religious' connotation of the relative civilizations and peoples. These therefore cannot be described—at least for the present—as a-religious civilizations or peoples, whether with regard to their commonly shared convictions or to the more or less conscious motivations of their behaviour and civil institutions. This is shown by the introduction, in these latter, of 'ritual' forms which, although purely secular, seem to retain something of the religious forms they have superseded, as for example in the solemnization of weddings in the U.S.S.R.

But the universal presence of the religious element is interesting not only as an expression of historical-geographical diffusion but also as an expression of the variety of spiritual manifestations. The study of the fundamental elements of religion excludes the possibility of this latter being a product of one or other spiritual faculty with exclusion of the others, or of this or that psychical or social structure. No religious form is reducible to the mere expression of a feeling, un-anchored to conceptual determinants. Nor can it be reduced to mere agnostic voluntarism, or to a frigid philosophizing rationalism. In no historical religious forms do we find an absence of the elements of personal religiosity, able to animate and actively embody traditional norms and beliefs. No religious doctrine or institution denies the existence of mysterious and transcendent truths, or of a destiny incompatible with mere worldly interests. In fact, the irrefutable presence of existential interests and needs in religious manifestations is itself, in religions, elevated to a typical hierophany, that is, a manifestation of the presence and fundamentality of the divine, understood as the source of life, of daily life, but also as a sure indication of a loftier purpose, without which man is something less than man.

The 'holy' is thus understood as the source, the foundation, the purpose of existence, but not necessarily in the sense, implicit in M. Eliade's research and developed by him in many ways, that religious civilization finds its essence in a 'return to the origins', fearing and denying the course of history or the visible world or even, as E. De Martino asserts, that religion has a de-historicizing function, intended to save man from the terror he would feel when faced with the 'risk' of existence and of historical creation. On the contrary, the existence of religions which include the concept of the 'history of salvation' throughout the course of human history implies, as even these authors at least partially admit, a different outlook, although still orientated towards transcendence. The autonomy of the temporal and the secular, and even certain aspects of secularization [1] itself, have shown themselves to be not incompatible with Christian experience and even to be, to some extent, postulated or encouraged by this. It is nevertheless true that religion, in the great universalist as well as in primitive religions, in which the religious-social texture—at least as far 'externals' are concerned—is undoubtedly more difficult to disentangle, presents itself as the total meaning of life, even in man's most intimate self, his conscience. And the great landmark of death (like that of birth or of any very significant existential event) is always present to urge every man, and every human society, to extend the panorama of life beyond what is merely visible. This is the 'dialogue' with the transcendent, and this is what we call 'religion'.

Moreover, to define this it is insufficient to draw up preconceived schemes which do not take facts into account—not only external, institutional facts but also the phenomena of the inner life which are not only the effect but also the main cause of these. Nor will any definitions of religion suffice which, in order to ensure their general applicability, are based on preconceived lowest common denominators, as for example in the case of the theory of 'primitive animism' elaborated by Tylor in the nineteenth century. Animism, understood as a belief in 'separate' souls, revealed in dreams or other similar experiences, and expressing itself frequently in concepts like the worship of the dead, or of supernatural 'presences' in this or that natural entity, is by no means the lowest common denominator or even, as Tylor asserted, the most ancient and embryonic form of religion.

It is certainly not easy to formulate a positive-historical definition

---

[1] See e.g. the monograph, *Problemi universalistici del cristianesimo*, in G. Castellani (ed.), *Storia delle religioni*, 6th edit., Turin 1971, vol. IV.

of religion. It must be sufficiently elastic for a historical approximation and, at the same time, it must bear in mind the documentary possibilities, often diverse, offered by the various special sciences (ethnology with its studies of the living world of primitive peoples, prehistory, which works on fragments only, and can, therefore, lead to inductions which are not always trustworthy, and philology with its analysis of texts, etc.). In any case, *at the very basis of religion, we usually find belief in one or more powers, conceived as superior persons older than human beings and independent of them. Man, and the human collectivities, adopt an attitude of dependence on these beings, and this is reflected in their conduct, ethical or ritual, and in a belief in the possibility of communicating with these higher powers.* Nevertheless, every interpretation of life which admits of an otherworldly life has an essential connection with religious thought. *In other words, religion implies a 'breakthrough',* [2] *in the sense that one of the first characteristics of the religious element may be discerned in the establishment of a relationship with a super-human power which is understood to condition the life of the world and life in the world.*

2. *How to begin the study of religions*

As we have already said, in approaching the historical study of religions the student must adopt the most methodologically comprehensive attitude, in the sense that he must take into consideration not only those elements which seem most appropriate for any exemplary definition of religion, but also those elements which, though more or less similar to the preceding, may nevertheless, according to the religious standards of his own time and *milieu*, appear less adequate to the needs of an awakened religious conscience. The history of religions, as a historical science, must start with the facts, classifying them according to their apparent homogeneity or resemblance and also, contextually, differentiating between them, since the task of comparison is to point out not only similarities, but also differences, analyzing and interpreting them in their development, their historical associations and, within certain limits, their nature.

In other words, two dangers, already referred to, must be avoided. The first is that of using a method which, like the positivist-evolutionist

---

[2] For closer study see U. Bianchi, *Problemi di Storia delle religioni* (Series *Universale Studium*, No. 56) Rome 1958, pp. 116-119 and 132 et seqq. (= *Probleme der Religionsgeschichte*, Göttingen, Vandenhoeck & Ruprecht, 1964, pp. 79-81 and 88 et seqq.). For the concept of the 'breakthrough' see also above, p. 20 and below, p. 191.

method adopted by Tylor, the founder of the theory of 'animism', claims to start from a religious *minimum* found in all religions, and identical *in nuce* with the beliefs of primitive societies ('primitive' understood evolutionistically) in which the most embryonic, shadowy and 'savage' forms are considered the most ancient and so influence the interpretation of all religious evolution. This would lead to the error, for which the French sociological school and other interpretative trends have been reproached, of studying religion merely on the basis of 'primitive' documents or rather or certain primitive elements chosen from among those which seem most elementary (e.g. 'animism', 'totemism'), thus precluding any serious interest and research in the whole field of the study of religions, whether of the primitive or, more particularly, of the most advanced cults.

One might also fall into the error, rightly condemned when found in irrationalistic, modernist schools, etc. of studying only a certain *animus* or religious inspiration, the so-called 'feeling for the holy', which is found even among primitive peoples, and neglecting the study of the content of the various religions in question. But it is this content which is essential for an understanding of the religions themselves and of the history of the religious phenomenon in its concrete and historical reality as well as in its true significance.

The second danger, instead, is that of proceeding, in historical questions, with a certain intellectualist rigidity of principles which, because it presumes to define or to presuppose too much on a theoretical basis, runs the risk of misunderstanding the phenomena in question, comparing them too arbitrarily with 'patterns' or systematic formulae which are not always appropriate. This danger is found, for example, in certain studies of the Viennese cultural-historical school which have tried too glibly to reconstruct perfect monotheistic forms among primitive peoples studied by ethnologists, and also in a certain philosophical phenomenology of religion. This science, while it claims to determine the characteristics of religion on a positive-historical basis, without, however, subjecting them to a judgment based on criteria of value and truth (this being reserved for a later stage) seems at times to postulate, in the choice and description of an 'exemplary' phenomenology and of a pattern of interpretation, that very judgment, however correct and legitimate it may be in its own sphere, which it claims to have excluded (cf. chap. 1). [3]

---

[3] Particularly pp. 15-19. Concerning the 'judgement of value' see also our observations in *Problemi di Storia delle Religioni*, Rome, 1958 (Series *Universale*

For these reasons also the historical-comparative method, which we have dealt with at length in the preceding chapter, is most valuable. The first advantage to be gained from this method is that the student does not examine merely the details, which may sometimes appear analogous and yet are in reality of a very different portent, but must approach the whole complex of phenomena, that is, consider not only themes, motives, details of creeds and cults, but the whole system of which these form an integral part, and judge the details in the light of this whole. He must, that is, consider religious systems or (as phenomenologists of religion say) 'structures' (i.e. religions) and not merely ideological and ritual fragments. This approach would free the comparative method of much of that arbitrariness from which it would inevitably suffer if it concentrated only on the fragmentary and the particular, and would at the same time create the most solid basis for research, the philological-historical basis; this so more, when those systems to which we referred were once in contact with each other, spatially and chronologically. Tradition or revolution, slow evolution or sudden forward leap, syncretism or originality: historical research, applied to detail but attentive also to holistic and comparative study, may pronounce judgment on all these cases, without assuming preconceived attitudes of an individualistic type (such as seeing new and original elements on every hand) or of an evolutionistic type (claiming to indicate a pre-existent and determining cause for everything) or even of a dialectic type because this dialectic would adopt the conclusions of this or that 'philosophy of history' or 'theology of history'—conclusions which must be judged in their own sphere of study, which is not that of the history of religions. [4]

3. *Religion and religions. Forms and structures of religion*

When he comes to the question of the variety of religious forms, the first thing the historian has to do, therefore, is to study them objectively and examine the problem of their first manifestations and their development. In doing so he must make use of terms and concepts appropriate to the religions in question. For example, he must be particularly chary in his use of the terms 'god' and 'deity'. The content of these terms differs notably (even when it is to some extent analo-

---

Studium, No. 56) pp. 20-24 (= *Probleme der Religionsgeschichte*, Göttingen, Vandenhoeck & Ruprecht, 1964, pp. 15 et seqq.) and in this book *infra*, on p. 177 n. 28.

[4] This does not mean that the history of religions is reduced to a descriptive study: the historical enquiry always includes interpretation, but this is always based on a specific method, the comparative-historical method on a positive inductive basis.

gous), as does the content of other terms which more or less correspond to these in the various religions, for example, in the classical Greek religion and in the monotheistic religions of the Old Testament and of Christianity. The terms 'god' or 'deity' are not always appropriate for superhuman beings, either in the polytheistic or the monotheistic sense of those terms. There are beings, like the angels and devils of the monotheistic religions, which are in no sense divine and can, therefore, be included in a monotheistic system. And in certain religions there are also primordial entities, of a more or less pantheistic nature, that are quite different from a polytheistic god like Apollo, or a Creator like the God of the Bible: for example, the Indian Brahman or the Chinese Tao. Moreover, primordial beings of an animist and naturist type (the sun as a primordial 'spirit', the sky as the progenitor, the *dema* deities which, slain at the beginning of the world, were transformed into vegetable foods etc.) cannot be described as 'deities' in the same sense as the others we have mentioned.

We will now give a short summary of the typology of religion and of religions, leaving the historical account of religion(s) (the only one that really counts in these studies) for the following chapter.

4. *Types of religion*

A classification of religions based on their respective beliefs will probably discard schemes like those which were fashionable in more or less recent scientific literature and are still popular with many. It will therefore not be necessary, in the case of every religion, to present the dilemma 'monotheism or polytheism'. This is partly because there may be religions that seem to embody forms which in relation to those two types, rather than intermediary, are partial or embryonic, or un-systematic (referred to by some scholars in theoretical terms of doubtful validity such as *henotheism* or *monolatry*). But it is more due to the fact that there exist religions which avoid such a classification because they include divine beings or entities which express neither the monotheistic nor the polytheistic concept of divinity. Among these beings are many of the spirits of animism and manism which are frequently, but not always, considered to be subordinate to a Supreme Being of a theistic or monotheistist type, but which are nevertheless often systematically made the object of a popular worship, awe and veneration which are clearly orientated, spiritually and ethically (or unethically) in another direction. And this practice is not a tolerated or occasional phenomenon, as is the case with the 'superstitions' of a monotheistic *milieu*, but is codified and institutionalised. The religions of a more or less explicitly 'pantheistic' type are in quite another category. [5]

Those concepts of animistic, manistic and fetishistic religions which have been and still are fashionable must nevertheless be the object of more severe criticism. [6] It is difficult to find a religion that is *only* animist, that is to say, does not recognise other superhuman or divine figures such as that of a *Kulturheros*, or of a Lord of animals, or that of a Supreme Being, understood as a Creator or at least as having been particularly active at the time of creation and interested in the observance of the tribal laws he instituted.

Special difficulties arise, with regard to definitions of this kind, in the case of the religions of primitive peoples; here one must be very careful about using systematic terminologies more appropriate for the great historical religions. Even the use of the term 'monotheism', for those primitive religions which attribute special importance to the figure of the Supreme Being, cannot easily be justified. This is not because monotheism must necessarily be extraneous to primitive civilizations, or because it must necessarily presuppose an anti-polytheistic revolution, according to the theory of R. Pettazzoni (see pp. 87 et sqq.) but because, for one reason or another, a precise and discriminatory definition of the relationship between the Supreme Being and other superhuman beings is not always found. Notwithstanding, it remains true that Lang discovered the existence of the notion of Supreme Beings among primitive peoples and in their most ancient cultures [7] (a conclusion which was still further elaborated, though with some exaggerations and oversimplifications, by W. Schmidt and his school) and his discovery is still considered to be definitive and

---

[5] Concerning this concept see further on.

[6] Still more decisively (p. 71 et seq. and p. 83 et seqq.) must we exclude the theories, sustained respectively by Tylor, Spencer and Comte (and in another form by Lubbock) of the primordial nature of these forms. Furthermore, one must reject the concept of a *totemistic* religion (see further on) and even more, the idea of a totemistic origin of religion. For Shamanism see p. 57. For the concept of Animism see p. 83 et seqq. Manism implies a particular form of the worship of ancestors as givers of life, fecundity and fertility. They must be propitiated and, as it were, integrated in a world beyond which does not preclude them from participating in certain festive rituals, and generally preserves the unity and solidarity of the members of a clan. Fetishism means a belief and a cult which imply the intensive manipulation of objects inhabited or rendered efficacious in a not definitive way, by spirits of the dead, natural spirits or 'forces' of a magical nature. It is a relatively rare phenomenon (typical of Guinean Africa).

[7] For the use of the term 'primitive' see above p. 13 et seqq.

revolutionary with regard to evolutionistic trends, while the absence of an absolutely primordial character in ethnological animism and manism, understood as systems of generalized belief and practice, is also confirmed.

Historical religious studies make even clearer the fact not only of the comparatively late appearance of polytheism but, still more, of its rarity in the primitive world (Pettazzoni, James, Jensen, Brelich) and of its appearance in those peoples who are now emerging from their primitive conditions or have already entered that 'barbarian' state which resembles, or even sometimes identifies itself with, the rise of more advanced civilizations (Polynesian, Mexican and Peruvian, the cultures North of the Gulf of Guinea, etc.). The classical polytheistic regions are those of the most advanced ancient civilizations, such as the Mesopotamian, Canaanite-Phoenician, Egyptian, Greek and Roman-Hellenistic, on which the most typical polytheistic forms are to be observed. However, polytheism is far from constituting that obligatory phase in the religious history of mankind that some theorists have supposed. In fact, it did not evolve in the direction of monotheism in those very cultures which developed polytheism most clearly and completely, for example, in the Mesopotamian or Greek religions. There were indeed in these religions and mythologies some instances of the belief of One-ness of God (as in the Greek-Orphic speculations about Zeus-*arché*) which are, however, not at all the same thing as monotheism in the religious-historical sense of the term—in fact sometimes they have more affinity with a monism of the pantheistic type—and which in some instances have a merely episodic and personal significance, like the Egyptian monotheistic reform of Amenhotep IV., or have, alternatively, the character of monolatry.

The characteristic figures of the polytheistic pantheons all have this typical feature, that they are of the 'departmental' type, that is, associated with certain cosmological or natural entities. They are not, however, exclusively bound to these for they have also an anthropomorphic character and a dominant role with 'political' functions in this or that city, region or sanctuary. For example, we find the sky god, the sea god, the god of the Underworld in the famous Homeric tripartite division (Il. XV 191 et sqq.). One of these gods, generally the sky god, sometimes more or less identified with the sky, exercises a universal dominion and has an ethical validity, thus resembling those Supreme Beings of primitive peoples to whom we have already referred. Polytheism in fact emphasizes that these Supreme Beings are frequently associated with the sky, in a naturistic sense. Hence the tendency to develop a new and licentious mythology (cf. the Greek Zeus). As a heavenly god and ruler of the entire pantheon, the Supreme God of these polytheistic religions is sometimes contrasted with a god of lower rank, who is atmospheric, youthful and impulsive. In the Canaanite-Phoenician mythology Baal is contrasted with El, and in the Mesopotamian religion Enlil is contrasted with Anu, the sky god, who, unlike the Canaanite-Phoenician El, accentuates the naturistic references because of his different (Sumerian) origin.

On the other hand, the polytheistic pantheons, by their very nature, are open to the most varied divine beings, and permit ever new accessions to Olympus (the case of Dionysos, etc.).

The same pantheons, if from one point of view are hierarchical in structure, from another point of view they may easily fall into anarchy, syncretism, or even into pantheism in the original sense of the term, meaning that a complex ('pantheos') deity contains within himself the attributes, names and essences of all the others. As we have said, only the tendency towards an ill-defined theosophical unity of the divine permits these complexes to subsist, but they undergo transformations, as they did in classical or oriental paganism, when exposed to the onslaughts of a rigorous Christian monotheism.

As for pantheism, or rather *pan-entheistic* or *theo-pantistic* monism, [8] this is the doctrine of a Deity that is primordial in a very particular sense, transcendent, identified with the One but incarnate in a multiple world which is, as it were, his body. This is the divine substance which underlies, and in a certain way identifies itself with, the visible universe and its parts, which sometimes (as in the concept of the universe as a macrocosm corresponding to the microcosm which is man) correspond to the limbs of the God (in India, in the famous vision of Markandeya, in the Mahabharata, and in the *Veda*, (in the hymn to Purusha), or in Greece (in the Orphic hymn to Zeus, quoted by Plato, or in Stoic theology). This religious concept, which often implies a hostile attitude towards the visible world considered to be illusory (Indian concept of the *Maya*) or tyrannical (Gnostic concepts) represents a phenomenon which is far from being primordial in the history of religions. This is contrary to a theory which tends

---

[8] Panentheism means the Deity is *in* all things, theopantism means the Deity *is* all. Scharbau considers this to be more comprehensive and more open to 'transcendence' than an other (pantheistic), omre 'material' assertion which says: all, or 'the whole' is Deity. In fact, in the case of theopantism the Deity exceeds the whole, in fullness and quality—the world being, as it were, his body.

to see in it a very ancient religious form. The formulation of this theory was encouraged by a certain inadequacy in the typological analysis of the characteristic entities of the monist-pantheist doctrines (the *Brahman* in India and the *Tao* in Chinese speculation and, within certain limits, *Zurvan*, a personification of time which then becomes 'destiny', with astral connections, in some Iranian speculations). These entities have been arbitrarily assimilated to, and taken into comparison with, the figures of the 'great gods' or highly personalised Supreme Beings, like those primitive beings we have already mentioned or those, more or less typologically and historically connected, of the great historical monotheistic religions (Old Testament, Judaism, Christianity, Islamism and, within certain limitations of a dualistic nature, Iranian Mazdaeism) and of polytheism (Zeus, Jupiter, etc.). It is true that in certain cases the Absolute, monistically and theo-pantistically understood, is more or less implicitly and unconsciously given the characteristics of a personality, which is in one way very remote and formless and in another way living and experienced. A relationship is thus established with this Absolute, a relationship which seeks by all possible means to exalt its remoteness and inaccessibility and also its transcendence. At the same time this Absolute is believed to be accessible in an inner life which, although understood philosophically in the immanentist sense, also seeks to express the transcendentalist concept and the aspiration towards a relation with the 'altogether other', and to find the deity not in the external aspects of nature but in the spiritual depths of the soul. A confirmation of the frequent recourse of monism to religious expressions, in the theistic and personalistic sense of the term, is offered by the fact that Indian mystical thought frequently wavers between these two poles (inaccessibility of the Supreme Being and accessibility in the inner life), a wavering which however only with difficulty reaches the idea of a unequivocal transcendence with regard to the world. This, in the monotheistic religions, is expressed in a concept of creation, which, even when it differs from the philosophical notion of the *creatio ex nihilo*, is typologically and historically different from what, not only in religions of a monist trend, but also in those which tend towards polytheism, implies a mutual participation in essence between the deity and the universe. In these latter religions even the greatest gods are derived from cosmogonical origins, or at least in turn reveal and incorporate these origins, like the Zeus of Homer and Hesiod or, respectively, the Zeus or the Phanes or even Dionysos of Orphic doctrines, tending towards monism.

The Greek Orphic doctrines are interesting in this connection because, no less than well known Indians conceptions (*Vedanta*), they show a convergence of monism and dualism, and thus imply the concept of a hypostasis of the divine involved in a story of death (myth of Zagreus) or of a cycle of the One and the Many, or of Love and Discord, cosmic factors of union and separation, with the concept of the decadence of divine beings who have fallen into the world of division, of contest, of birth and death (Empedocles). Many of these notions are found in Platonic dialectic dualism, although here they are framed in a more harmonistic vision of the cosmos. They reappear however in all their harshness in Gnosticism, which attributes the creation of this world not to God but to an inferior Demiurge who imprisons therein the substance of the spiritual beings which he cannot appropriate to himself because he is congenitally alien to them. Such a Demiurge is often described as a malign being [9] and is found in Manichaean Gnosticism, as part of a dualism even more radical and symmetrical (God and Anti-God, both primordial beings) [10]—and in the dualism of the mediaeval Bogomiles and Catharists. All these are movements which are not properly Christian heresies but rather a renewal of dualistic doctrines already present, as we have said, in ancient Orphism and Pythagoraeanism, as well as, in a more articulate form and therefore susceptible to a Judaic or Christian interpretation (see Philo and the Platonic Fathers) in Platonic thought. This idea of an inferior Demiurge was not of a later origin, as we shall show when we speak of the inferior Demiurge in certain mythologies of primitive peoples.

With regard to dualism, we add that, in a different form, dualism of the Zoroastrian type, two spirits (*manyu*, one beneficent and the other destructive) are radically and symmetrically opposed. Later on we find simply a God and an Anti-God, Ohrmazd and Ahriman, and

---

[9] He is sometimes identified with Destiny, in the astral sense, from which the soul sought to free itself by ascending in flight beyond the planetary spheres (Mithraism, Gnosticism), but which often produced an amoral acquiescence in these cosmic forces (astral bodies, archons, etc.).

[10] The gnostic dualism, like the late form found among the Cathars (divided by this into two sects), may be 'radical' (or 'symmetrical') or 'mitigated', which means respectively denying or admitting that the Demiurge was derived or 'created' by God. This latter belief was held in systems of religious thought influenced by Christianity, like those of the Bogomiles and of some of the Cathars. But these two variants are in the last resort irrelevant, because both express, no less in their psychology than in their religious and metaphysical presuppositions, real dualism, as we shall define it further on.

although this Zoroastrian form of dualism may be similar to the others in some respects, in other respects it is different. In fact, it attributes to the destructive spirit or Anti-God not the creation of this material world (which therefore is not to be condemned *per se* as it is by the Manichaean Gnostics: instead it is to be highly esteemed) but a destructive intervention in God's creation (Ahriman does not belong to God) or, as in the later texts, a counter-creation, that is, the creation by Anti-Gods of a world of evil, of beings *substantially* and *cosmologically* evil. Christian theologians, from Clement of Alexandria to Methodius of Olympus and St. Augustine, have always rejected this doctrine; they see the origin of evil in this world not in a presupposition of natural causes or in a substance, but in creature's lack of a due good that is forfeited because of the creature's misguided use of his freedom.

In conclusion, dualism, as a phenomenon in the history of religions, [11] answers to the following definition: dualism means all those doctrines and myths which, even among primitive peoples, admit of a dichotomy, that is, of a sharp division, or even an opposition, between the principles which, whether co-eternal or not, are at the basis of the existence of whatever is found in the world, whether created by God, or by a Demiurge, his rival, or by an Anti-God, or even by such principles as, in India, Māyā (Illusion) or prakṛti (Matter). Forms of dualism have been found among peoples studied by ethnologists, like those religions already mentioned in which a 'trickster' Demiurge, often foiled but at other times invincible, successfully opposes the Creator, in the context of the events of creation, which therefore swerves in a wrong direction no longer in accordance with the Creator's plan. In the great religions or in the great metaphysical systems, different dualistic forms may be reduced to three: a) Zoroastrian dualism which takes a more positive evaluation of the world, in which the corruption of evil breaks in from outside, and from which it will finally be expelled; b) the anti-cosmic dualism of Gnosticism (including Marcionism, Manichaeism, Mandaeism, Bogomilism, Catharism, etc.), for which evil is the world itself, because

---

[11] Philosophers, instead, generally employ the same term to indicate non-Monist doctrines, that is, doctrines which admit transcendence, in the sense of the complete distinction between God as a creator, and the created world. A confusion between the two interpretations of 'dualism' runs the risk of not giving a sufficiently specific account of the characteristics of the dualist doctrines (in the historical-religious sense). (See below, on the Monist tendencies typical of dualistic religions). Concerning the whole question see *Le origini della gnosticismo, Colloquio di Messina*, 13-18 April, 1966, Leiden 1967, and particularly pp. XX-XXIII.

it was made of a shadowy substance not created by God, and shaped and directed by a Demiurge who also created man's body, in which the spirit is imprisoned and awaits liberation—generally as the result of a message from on high—from the power of the Demiurge and of destiny; c) a third form, metaphysical-dialectical dualism, found in Plato and in all Platonic thought but present also in Orphic doctrines, as for example in Empedocles and in various aspects of pre-Socratic thought. The constitution of the world results here from the opposition of two irreducible principles which, although complementary, are generally differentiated by an inequality of value. For example, there is the Platonic doctrine of the idea (eternal model) and of the *chōra* and the *anankē* ('receptive extension' or 'matter' and 'necessity'), or that of Empedocles concerning the two principles, Love and Discord, who unite and, respectively, destroy the unity of the Sphairos, the One, or the Pythagoraean notion of the *monad* (Oneness) and *dyad* (Duality): conceptions which seem to have exerted a great influence over the history of Greek mystical, cosmogonical and soteriological thought and which are more or less akin to others of a Heraclitean, Eleatic or Anaxagoraean origin, some of which through Plato, Aristoteles and the Stoicians, have furnished even non-dualistic doctrines with important ideological elements (for example, Christian philosophy with the definition of the metaphysical concept of the Absolute Being and of transcendence). [12]

On the other hand, as we have already pointed out, dualistic doctrines (in the strict historical religious sense, that is the doctrines we have already mentioned) tend to express also monistic attitudes, in the sense that they emphazise the consubstantiality of the beings (divine and demonic) that surround respectively the two opposite principles with these principles themselves—a consubstantiality which impels Zoroastrian theology to conceive the beings created by Ohrmazd as made of his own substance, 'light', or which impels neo-Platonism towards the conception of an 'emanation' from the One, and Gnosticism to admit the consubstantiality and to a certain extent even the transpersonal identity of the Saviour (and in general of the whole

---

[12] The absolute dialectical principle and its implicit dualism, in the sense used here of this term, has instead operated in various forms of modern thought, from Hegelianism of the right and left wings to psycho-analysis and radical existentialism. Cf. by U. Bianchi, *Le dualisme en histoire des religions*, in *Revue de l'histoire des religions*, vol. 159 (1961) pp. 18-46 and *Péché originel et péché antécédent*, ibid. vol. 170 (1966) pp. 117-126. (See also, as for existentialism, the last chapter in H. Jonas' *Gnostic Religion*).

divine world) with the Saved—the Saved being an emanation of the divine world which has fallen into the lower world. In this way the Western dualistic doctrines, here discussed, seem in their use of monistic forms [13] to have resembled those systems of Indian monism, in their turn influenced—as we have seen in the case of Māyā, cosmogonic Illusion—by dualistic and anti-cosmic views, at least in so far as they opposed a visible illusory world, with its circumscribed gods, to the transcendent and divine substance or the *Brahman* and *Atman*.

Still with regard to Gnosticism, we must point out that, besides being a historical phenomenon found in the well known systems of the IInd and IIIrd centuries A.D. (and in the late-antique and mediaeval forms already mentioned) it is also a type of interpretation of the divine and of its presence or absence in a world in which it is alien and incompatible. This type, and it is hard to say whether its diffusion implies in every case a specific historical derivation, is found again, as we have said, in forms of Greek mysticism (Orphism, Pythagoraeanism) which, when applied to traditional mythology, lend it new meanings, adopting the theme of the fallen god in an anti-cosmic sense (as we shall explain later, with reference to the various concepts of salvation). As for Gnosticism proper, it is also found in forms which have, as it were, clustered parasitically around different religious conceptions, such as Christianity (e.g. the Gnostic heresies in the bosom of the Great Church, and rejected by her as alienations), Judaism (the Cabbala, not always rejected in the same way), Islamism (especially in certain Shiite trends or in some sects with markedly specific gnostic features). This suggests the problem of a *Weltgeschichte* of Gnosticism.

5. *Other persons figuring in religious belief*

Having drawn up a summary typology of the content of religions, mainly of those most systematically expressed, we must now refer to other figures which play a very important religious role in primitive religions. Particularly significant is the figure of the 'lord of animals' who, in certain primitive societies, seems to be more or less analogous

---

[13] Strengthened, for example, in gnosticism by concepts concerning the spiritual, understood not only as a divine emanation fallen into this world, but also as the principle animating this material world itself, which has form and life (as in the Ophitic doctrines) as long as it bears the imprint of the divine-spiritual element, which is however destined to free itself from it.

to a Supreme Being, a Giver of life and food. Some scholars have chosen to see in the lord of the animals a religious figure typical of a primitive civilization of hunters. In fact, the lord of the animals is very much at home in an ideological and existential system like that typical of certain civilizations of 'hunters of the steppes' (Bushmen) and of hunters of the equatorial Forest (African and Asiatic Pygmies) or of the Arctic and Sub-Arctic regions. The Supreme Being, among these hunting tribes, is frequently associated with the origins of the world and of civilization, of the institutions and weapons of the chase, ethical and tribal norms, etc. And he is frequently endowed with heavenly and 'fatherly' or providential attitudes, and associated with the destiny of man in the world beyond, which is often a 'heavenly beyond'. It is moreover impossible to distinguish some of these elements of his personality as later accretions, belonging to a 'more advanced' hunting age.

If the lord of the animals is frequently a typical figure of the Supreme Being, he is to be mainly distinguished from a figure substantially different from this, that of the 'trickster' Demiurge, an ambivalent type, selfish, cunning and yet sometimes foolish, who intervened, with or without success, sometimes beneficently and sometimes destructively, in the initial epoch of the world's history. He often exercised subordinate or even antagonistic functions, but was also frequently a collaborator of the Supreme Being. The demiurgic functions ('creative' in a broad sense) of this subordinate Being prevent our identifying him arbitrarily as an adversary of the Supreme Being. In fact, as we have said, there are possible cases of partial, and certainly some of a subordinate, collaboration of the Demiurge with the Supreme Being himself. Nor must this 'trickster' Demiurge, who is often represented as an animal (Coyote in North American mythologies, the Crow in the mythologies of the North Pacific and of Australia) be identified (as we have seen) with the above mentioned lord of the animals, although there are cases of fusion. The lord of the animals is always a lord, a ruler, whereas the Coyote and the Crow are generally creatures engaged (in the primordial time) in a wearisome and frequently unsuccessful quest for possessions and wealth, and are in rivalry with the animal creatures of their own circle.

Other figures to be mentioned are those of the 'Cultural hero', the inventor of the good things of civilization, sometimes identical with the above mentioned 'trickster Demiurge' (for example, figures like those of the Polynesian Maui and the Greek Prometheus, already integrated in a polytheistic system) and the figure of the *Ancestor*, often in a relationship of dependence, or even of a more or less advanced fusion, like that of the cultural hero, with the figure of the Supreme Being.

6. *Magic*

Other typologies, relating to the religions of primitive peoples and also to those of the 'higher' religions, will be dealt with in the chapter devoted to the history of studies and the whole problem of the history of religions. Here what we have already said will suffice for an understanding of the variety of religious typology and of the necessity of typological and specific historical analyses in the study and classification of religions.

But the interesting phenomenon of magic, frequently very hard to understand, deserves a special mention. It is an attitude of the spirit in which Frazer mistakenly saw something anterior to religion (because more 'simple', i.e. not requiring the recourse to superhuman beings), according to a typically evolutionistic criterion, the arbitrary nature of which has already been pointed out. Other scholars arbitrarily confuse religion with magic in the context of a vague recourse to superhuman powers. In reality, magic presupposes the intrinsic efficacy of certain rites and practices, independent of the will of personal superhuman beings, which in fact it sometimes boasts of subjecting to its own will. Magic therefore—in this respect—obeys an inspiration and adopts an attitude, totally at variance with religion, in as much as it believes it can draw upon personal and impersonal powers and use these to its own advantage.

It is also true that magic is sometimes connected with religious conceptions and practices, because it claims to exercise power over gods (or demons) using them for its own purposes and practices, and because it seeks to reinforce, with practices of a magic nature, propitiatory or execratory rites of a religious nature. A typical example of this is found in the Babylonian religion in which the gods themselves, even the great magician-god of the abyss (*Ea*), use magic means to attain their ends. Another typical case of magico-religious association is found in fetishism, in which animist conceptions (the presence of spirits in fetish objects) are combined with magic manipulations of those objects and of the spirits, with the intention of reinforcing their power. In any case it must be pointed out that, even in those civilizations where magic is most deeply rooted, it never supplants religion and never monopolizes communion with the superhuman; on the contrary, there are civilizations, even among the most primitive peoples, in which magic, socially approved, is associated institutionally with the religious system, and even understood as a means emanating from the Deity and placed by him at man's disposal.

Magical practices are based upon the 'sympathetic' principle: imitative magic and contagious magic. In the former case the action is supposed to be that of 'like on like' (for example, in the miming of a hunting event with dances and masks, or the use of drawings or impressions). By the use of symbolic weapons it is believed that it is possible to influence favourably the result of a future hunt, facilitating the abundance, fecundity, capture or killing of animals (cf. many of the prehistoric drawings of animals in caves or on cliffs). With the latter method, as with the former, it is believed that the 'part' can represent and be used against the 'whole'. For example, in a society of hunters, which is by its very nature very sensitive to concepts of fortune and misfortune, we find the practice of 'magical vaccination' that is of the insertion under the skin of the newly initiated hunter, of some ashes from the bodies of animals he will have to seek out and kill. Besides these practices of beneficent or 'white' magic there are those of 'black' or criminal magic, which is harmful to others, a magic socially condemned and feared by primitive peoples but founded on the same 'sympathetic' principles. The method includes, for example, treating in a malevolent manner a man's nails, hair, images, shadows or footprints, in order to cause him harm or even bring about his death.

In spite of all the importance we must attach to the thought, and still more, the practice of magic based on 'sympathetic' principles, we cannot reduce it intellectualistically to the status of that 'false science' of which Frazer speaks, the falseness of which is concealed by the inexperience or misinterpreted experience (and sometimes the bad faith), of those who practise it. The magician often believes he can make use of superhuman powers, and he seeks to penetrate the harmony and energy of a vast 'whole' in order to use these forces to his own advantage (cf. M. Eliade's studies of the alchemist who accelerates the work of nature by abolishing time). Here we have a question not merely of men and of things, but one of superhuman forces and entities, including spirits, ancestors, demons and deities who do not properly belong to the magic world in the strict sense of the term, but to the world of religion. In fact, this participation in the 'totality' of the cosmos, the 'great man' of the alchemists and astrologists, is an expression, although cosmic and sublimated, of the principle of the consubstantiality of man and the cosmos, as well as of the 'sympathetic' principle (cf. pp. 79 et seqq. with regard to 'participation', according to L. Lévy-Bruhl).

7. *Power*

In this context one must briefly mention that concept of energy which some ethnologists are accustomed to call magical, although not so much in the precise sense in which it has been hitherto understood as in a dynamistic sense.

We know that among more or less primitive peoples there exist concepts like those of *orenda, wakanda* (North American), *mana* (Melanesian), *megbe, elima* (among the African Pygmies, according to Schebesta's research), terms which, although they do not express identical concepts, all seek to describe a superior force or efficacy which is not fluid, abstract or universally diffused like an *anima mundi*, but concrete and inherent in persons and things (equipment, weapons, pirogues, etc.). It is more often an emanation from *personal beings* and endows these persons or things with extraordinary power. One must note that these concepts may be found in religious *milieux* of an animistic or, more generically, of an animatistic type, [14] as for example in the case of Melanesia (which is somewhat complex from the ethnologist's point of view) and even in *milieux* open to theistic conceptions. Among the Bambuti Pygmies, studied by Schebesta, a figure of Supreme Being—more or less incarnate in 'hypostases' of a lunar, a sylvan or a chthonic character—is all highest by his very nature, and the rightful ruler and dispenser of energy, which he incarnates *par excellence* and of which he is the source. One must remember also, in this connection, the (Great) *Manitu*, the 'Great Spirit' of the Algonquins, with pronounced theistic connotations. But it would be a mistake in this case to define the Supreme Being as a great magician, since the magician, in the experience of primitive societies to which we must here refer, is not a creative agency, but rather a person who, with appropriate methods, tries to take possession of energy for himself or for his fellows, and to manipulate it for his (resp. their) own purposes. In this he sometimes fails, with catastrophic results for himself and others.

---

[14] For this concept see p. 86 et seq.

Other lesser centres and depositories of energy are frequently the *totems*, [15] or even the ancestors or the progenitor.

8. *The 'holy'*

From certain points of view the concept of transcendent energy has by certain scholars been seen in relation to the concept of the 'holy' which, they say, defines and characterizes religious experience.

Here too one must repeat what has already been said in other connections, that is, that a generic 'holy' does not exist in actual belief, for it is always related to the manifestation of individual divine figures or powers, without which the 'holy' is not so much a religious inspiration (it would in any case be abstract and without importance or meaning) as a *flatus vocis*, without that existential significance which is nevertheless an essential part of the theory in question, characterized by an intuitionism of romantic origin.

9. *Religious institutions*

The historical study of religions is naturally interested, not only in the investigation of superhuman beings, who generally determine the character of the religion in question, but also in the relative ritual and religious manifestations which, although almost universally diffused in the world of religions, nevertheless assume their true and full significance only in their own proper context. Thus a religious rite or custom must be judged in the complex of the religion, that is, of the religious system to which it belongs, and not indiscriminately, as was customary according to the old and discredited method of external comparison.

This kind of comparative method is still seen today, at times, in a 'phenomenology' of religion which does not sufficiently satisfy the

---

[15] The totem may consist of an animal, a plant, a heavenly body or another entity. Totemism, in spite of these possible religious or magical accretions, is elsewhere connected merely with classificatory systems; individuals may have each his own totem, or the group of men and the group of women (in sexual totemism), or the two, four or eight exogamic classes or the clans into which the tribe is divided. It would therefore be mistaken to think that totemism is always associated with exogamy (that is, the law which obliges a man to seek a wife outside his own group). Among many African Pygmy communities, for example, exogamy concerns the progeny, that is, the group of families of the same blood; whereas totemism concerns the clan, a vaster group which includes many progenies, and is not bound by the law of exogamy; the various family groups may inter-marry within the same clan. In conclusion, totemism is expressed in a number of ways, with individuals or with groups, and in various sociological, religious and magical connotations, as the case may be.

exigencies of history, or those of other sciences concerned with religion (see Chap. I and IV). However, one must not deny that the study of religious typology (or, as some prefer to say, of religious morphology) is of great assistance in the historical study of religions—but it must never be divorced from this.

It is enough to refer here to great themes such as sacrifice, prayer, the priesthood, the initiatory practices, religious institutions concerning the family and society, places of worship, times of worship, the connection between ritual and belief, ritual and cosmogony, ritual and existential interests even of an economic and social nature, etc.

To mention some examples of a more general interest: religion tends to endow all that concerns it (persons, objects, places, times) with a 'sacral' connotation which implies a qualification and a separation from the profane. The profane is not absolutely rejected but, with the exception of certain extreme cases, such as cosmic pessimism of a dualistic type, is re-associated with the 'holy', that is, with the world of superhuman beings, of the Supreme Being or of the most significant of these beings, and is thus spared, as we have already said, the final insignificance of all that is merely temporal and worldly. All the interests of the human condition are, or may be, associated with a sacral and religious motivation or guarantee. This is seen in various ways, from the all-absorbing sacralization of many primitive, or other, religions to the strict definition of the holy in monotheistic religions, in their modern forms (compatible with other forms of a lay or secular character) but also, in a manner appropriate to the times, in their archaic forms, characterized by a polemical attitude towards a pagan sacralization of nature. The sacral connotation or seal may thus be applied to a meal, or wedding, the delimitation and foundation of the city, the calendarial organization of the year, etc. In certain cases the qualification 'sacral' is more strict, or even exclusive, as in the case of sacred places and buildings (frequently the object of ritual entrances or pilgrimages, because of being the centre, for one reason or another, of a sacred association or of a more specific sacred manifestation). And there are times, in the context of the week, the month, the season, the year, the lustrum, the century, the 'great year': sacred times which often have a cosmogonical significance because they recall the great events of the origin of the world, and frequently also an eschatological significance because they prefigure the great events of the future: the beginning and the end of history which (together with the 'fulness of time') in Christianity and other religions interested in a *Heilsgeschichte*, have a special meaning.

10. *Sacred periods of time and history. History and 'salvation'*

In this connection we must note that the idea of a 'sacred' periodization may correspond to a precise meaning and intention. Among many primitive peoples we already find the concept that an original close relationship with the Supreme Being, or with another superhuman and primordial hero or other being, came to an end, generally through some fault on the part of man. This relationship may sometimes be restored, not only on the foundation of belief in man's survival in the world to come, with the Supreme Being himself in heaven, but also on an essentially eschatological and sometimes millenarian foundation, sometimes for example, after the return of the primordial hero. Associated with this belief are some of those 'prophetic' movements, or 'expectations of salvation' which often characterize the encounter of primitive civilizations with religious notions of a Christian origin. But elsewhere, especially in India and in Greek thought, the notion of the sacred period is sometimes influenced by specific philosophical-religious conceptions, such as are found in Vedantism, Buddhism, pre-Socratic doctrines, Platonism (*Politicus, Timaeus* etc.), Stoicism, neo-Pythagoraeanism and Orphism, and assumes the form of a cyclic 'return'. On the contrary, the Biblical religions (Old Testament and Christianity and, indirectly, Islam), as well as religions outside the Biblical world like Zoroastrianism, attach a particular finalistic meaning to cosmic periods: a meaning which in post-Gathic Zoroastrianism is caused and conditioned by the pre-temporal presence of Evil which, co-eternal with God, may be eliminated only in the course of history.

Actually it is Christianity which, on the basis of the Messianic doctrine of Israel, introduces the concept of a history which has an appointed end, with Christ as the crucial and central point, a history which, although finalized, may also include repetitions but only, as it were, in the form of an ascending spiral, not in the form of an eternally recurrent cyclic movement.

But sacred times are not only those we find in the 'great history' (history of salvation, millenarianism, *magnus annus*, etc.) but also those which concern the religious and ritual observance of the year, of the seasons, the week, hours, etc. Here also the phenomenology is vast and varied, naturally reflecting the type of religion to which these diverse observances belong. We must make special mention here of the ancient fertility and fecundity rites, especially in the Ancient Mediterranean and Middle Eastern world, all of which are centred in the seasonal renewal of life, the spring. To these belong the well known rites of Dumuzi-Tammuz (Sumerian and Babylonian), Adonis (Syria, Palestine and Phoenicia) and Osiris (Egypt). These 'dying' gods (or, as in the case of Osiris, 'dead' gods) are the tutelary genii of vegetation which, embodied in the king and represented by him, as in the case of the Sumerian Dumuzi or similar figures, return every year from the Underworld to marry the great goddess of nature (Inanna, Ištar or Aphrodite, referred to in the famous Theocritean idyll of 'The Women of Syracuse'). When his work is done the genius returns to the Underworld, amid the lamentations of the women, who will look forward to his return the following year.

As this outline suggests, the gods of these cults are 'dying' gods rather than gods who rise again (they do 'return'): the centre of gravity, so to speak, of this yearly seasonal occurrence is in fact their regular return, which marks the renewal of the regenerating forces of nature and of the life of the community—hence the public and popular character of these rites. The melancholy conclusion of their story, once their work of promoting fecundity or fertility has been completed, is not in contradiction with this positive function: indeed it emphasizes it, giving it the same significance as those agrarian end-of-the-year rites of consumption which are very frequently festivals of the dead.

On the basis of the fertility rites there later arose the 'Mystery' cults, Eleusinian, Greek-Oriental and Roman-Oriental. In the Eleusinian rites the seasonal cycle is associated with (or perhaps merely emphasizes) a soteriological intention, not only ensuring for the soul of the initiate a life of bliss in the world to come, but also enriching him in this life with every sort of good thing given by the 'two goddesses' of Eleusis. In the Greek-Roman-Oriental Mysteries of the Roman-Hellenistic age we even frequently find a *mysteriosophy*, that is, a theory and representation of the deliverance of the initiate's soul from the bonds of this earth, from body and from fate. In this conception, already foreshadowed in the archaic Greek world in that kind of *mysteriosophy* we call 'Orphism', and later on, at the beginning of the Christian era, developed by the Gnostics, the very concept of 'life' was in a certain sense revolutionized. It was no longer exalted by the self-perpetuating renewal of fecund life in the seasonal cycle, but mortified in the struggle of the soul which, though of divine origin, is imprisoned by the rhythms of this world and longs for deliverance: a concept near enough to what Orphism in Greece and

Vedantism in India called the deliverance from the 'cycle of births' and therefore also of deaths.

11. *Persons. Initiations. Ethnical and 'founded' religions; national, mysterio-sophic, cosmopolitic and universal religions*

Even in the case of religious *persons* there is a whole varied typology that must be borne in mind.

One must first of all distinguish between those religions which have an 'ethnic' character, and those which were 'founded', a distinction of primary importance in the typology of religions.

The former have their roots in the pre-history of a people, and it is impossible to ascertain the time or author of their origin. So although in ethnic religions also individual personalities naturally play an essential part, if only in the transmission of the traditions they have received, the complex of the doctrines and of the cult is seen to be inextricably incorporated in the civilization and culture of the group to which it belongs. Thus the religious qualification of a member of the group will generally coincide with his ethnical, cultural and political status. [16]

Therefore, in primitive societies, the *initiation* of the young men, and sometimes that of the maidens also, will serve to graft these new recruits on to the organized life of the group, endowing them with all the necessary notions, skills, functions and duties, on every plane. The religious nature of the initiatory ceremonies of primitive peoples is naturally essential: initiation, with its rules and painful physical and moral ordeals, and its doctrinal content (all of which are guarded under the seal of secrecy from the uninitiated—in this case from those who are not yet qualified to be admitted to this *rite de passage*), is believed by the ancient civilizations of the primitive hunters to have been instituted by the Supreme Being or by one of his representatives. Other rites, some of a magical nature (like the above mentioned 'vaccination' of the hunters), sometimes complete the existential context of these ceremonies. Among other peoples studied by ethnologists, characterized by another type of culture, less archaic and including

---

[16] The concept of an ethnical religion here described—as distinct from a 'founded' religion—may be applied to religious groups like the Hindus, but does not apply to Hebraism, which had strong personalities as 'Founders' or Prophets, in the context of a religion which proclaims a progressive, universalistic and at the same time exclusive message: see below. There is however one point in common, of secondary importance with regard to the question we are now considering, and that is that in Hebraism the 'religious' qualification coincides more or less with the ethnical-national.

agrarian, or merely horticultural rituals, the initiatory rites have as their protagonists spirits or divine beings, and the powers associated with fecundity, and sometimes the so-called *dema* deities who were slain at the beginning of creation and transformed into alimentary vegetables, typical of those horticultural civilizations. This is a theme (see p. 100 et seq.) which some scholars have tried to associate with that of the Eleusinian mysteries, which represent the disappearance into the Underworld of a female divinity in connection with the cycle of fertility. Still in connection with ethnic religions we must bear in mind all those rites, associated with grades and age groups, which also, with frequent religious initiatory connotations, celebrate the introduction of the new citizen into the society of his peers. As for the 'founded' religions, including those which are universalist, they also insist upon the theme of initiation as a prelude to the individual's entrance into the religious community born of its founder's initiative.

Among the ethnic religions the case of the Mystery religions of pagan classical antiquity, already referred to, must be considered apart. These sometimes had a 'civic' character, that is, they were of interest mainly (but, at least in historical times, not exclusively) to the youths of a given city; such were for example the Eleusinian Mysteries for the young men of Athens. The experience of the initiated was esoteric; they could claim special privileges in the world beyond (cf. the end of the 'Homeric' hymn to Demeter; the initiated are called the 'blessed'). Other religions of the Mystery type (sometimes even 'mysterio-sophic' because of the prevalence of an exclusively individual soteriological interest) of classical antiquity which were diffused in a later period, had come from and had originated in national cults of the Barbarian peoples (the cult of Attis, of Anatolian origin, that of Adonis, of Phoenician and, more remote, Mesopotamian origin, of Mithras, of remote Iranian origin which later on, but apparently only in Anatolia, became a mysterio-sophic cult, the mysteries of Isis, of Egyptian origin, and the 'Dionysian' mysteries possibly of Anatolian, if not Cretan, origin, etc.). These cults express a particular form of religion. On the one hand they are ancient ethnical cults, with no trace of any specific Founder and, as we have said, have deep roots in ancient agrarian rites intended to ensure fertility and life, in which the element of magic is frequently present. On the other hand, these same cults become detached from their original ethnical or civic background and assume the character of cosmopolitical and soteriological cults in the context (in the late Hellenistic Age at least) of a 'cosmic' religiosity which tends to introduce the individual initiate into an Elysium which transcends the planetary spheres and is destined to free him from the limitations of this low earthly destiny. In this respect the theology of the Mysteries of pagan antiquity must have more or less closely resembled the dualistic tenets of Gnosticism (already foreshadowed in the most ancient Orphic and Pythagoraean doctrines) whereas elsewhere, as in the Dionysiac mysteries, forms of orgiastic religiosity of the magico-vitalist type perhaps still survived.

One point of extreme historical-religious interest, concerning the Mystery religions of pagan antiquity, is that they must be described as cosmopolitic, which is very different from being universalistic. In fact, although the Mysteries, like Christianity, recruited new members by individual proselytism, they were associated in the same initiate (which never happened in Christianity) with other pagan cults of the most varied nature, that is, with old traditional polytheistic cults as well as with other Mystery-cults. Thus it was no rare occurrence for a man to undergo several initiations, and to enumerate these in commemorative epigraphs. Moreover, the same Mystery manifestation often syncretistically included various cults and deities (as happened, for example, in Mithraism). On the other hand, an essential feature, in fact one of the great novelties of the universal Christian religion (and later on, of Islam) consisted not only in its being open to all, ignoring all barriers of nationality, sex and culture, but also in the fact that it intended to fill completely the space between man and God, in order to exclude the possibility of syncretisms or admixtures of other cults and doctrines.

In this way Christianity created a type of vocation which at the same time concerned the individual alone and yet was open to all men. Addressing itself to all, it demanded of everyone what no pagan religion had ever required: a conversion which was not the adoption of a new cult and a new initiation, but an absolute 'newness of life' which, although recognizing a manifestation of God to man in the natural world (St. Paul, *Rom.* I, 18-21), desired to be ruled by a God who had revealed himself in the Gospel of his Son, Jesus. It grafted itself upon the Jewish religion, which was to a certain extent universalist, because the God of Israel was also the God who had created the world and still ruled over all peoples, whose gods he put to flight. But Judaism was also a national religion. [17] The

---

[17] We use here the term 'national religion' in a different sense from what we

phenomenon, more or less widespread, of proselytism and aggregation did not invalidate this national character. Nevertheless the Jewish religion had a special feature which was to enable it to preach with conviction a universalist faith more easily than the pagan mysteriosophic cults to which we have already referred could have done; it appealed to a positive, historical, factual revelation of God, a revelation granted to Abraham, Moses and the Prophets which had no roots in soteriological-ritualistic cults expressing nature myths (fecundity rites, story of the genius of fertility) but in the idea of a God who entered into personal contact with man by means of a Covenant. Trusting to this Covenant man would sooner or later (and the Messianic hope encouraged this expectation) find the fulfilment of all his highest aspirations.

12. *Qualified 'sacred' persons. The priesthood*

Finally, in this brief summary of the main religious typologies we must mention the fact that the 'sacred' qualification of certain persons may be differentiated even in the same religious group. Among primitive peoples the 'age group', that is, the groups of people who have undergone initiation at the same time, to some extent express this differential qualification; at other times, for example, in the Mystery religions of antiquity, there was a multiform initiatory hierarchy, as in Mithraism. But the most interesting typology is that which one might generically call 'priestly', according to an empirical denomination which must be set in the context of more precise and specific concepts, according to the above mentioned historical method.

The selection and function of priests, that is, of those individuals or groups specially set apart for purposes of worship or sacrifice or, in other forms, for the diffusion of the sacred doctrine and the observances of sacred ritual, and the appointment of those who generally serve as interpreters for the religious practices of individuals and of the community (including at times the State) naturally depend on the type of religion in question. The case of a religion of the ethnical type (in the sense already explained) in which the priesthood is often conferred as a sort of magistrature, will naturally be different from that of a 'founded' religion, in which the priesthood will be ordered according to the person and activity of the Founder.

---

have described as an 'ethnical religion'. In fact, although in both cases the religious qualification implies also a national qualification, Israel had what was more or less lacking in the ethnical religions we have described above: she had 'Founders', from Patriarchs to Prophets, in the context of a revelation of God that was not only primordial but progressive and repeated.

In some ethnological civilizations, and also in others of a more advanced state, especially in Central and Northern Asia, one frequently finds the figure of the *Shaman* who is distinguished by a particular vocation and by particular spiritual qualities. His principal task is, by means of a spiritual 'journey' symbolized by miming gestures, to enter into ecstatic contact with the other world, with the superior Beings, with the Supreme Being, with spirits, and also with the malevolent beings of the Underworld. He usually does this for some utilitarian purpose (reasons of health, etc.) but within the context of precise conceptions of the transcendence of the superhuman beings appertaining to the respective religious creeds.[18] These Shamanic 'transferences' are accompanied by the use of special robes and musical instruments, etc. peculiar to this context. Analogous features, still in primitive societies, are found among the 'medicine men' of North American mythology, who also are familiar with the world of spirits, and especially with the highest spirit, the Supreme Celestial Being. Another ethnological figure is the African *nganga*, dedicated to magico-animist practices which, however, make him something very different from a 'witch doctor' because he attributes his powers to that universal law which is the guarantor of welfare and justice for the community, whereas the witch doctor indulges in anti-social and forbidden practices of 'black' magic. The idea of a relation to the 'energies', or indeed to the whole structure of the universe, is found in the 'priestly' figures of Taoism and of some mysterio-sophic celebrations of classical antiquity. Magic and religious forms were seen mingled in the caste-based priesthood of the *Brahmans*, both as regards the typical sacrifice of that religion—that in some ways repeated the ancient cosmogonic sacrifice which created the world and which therefore exercises an immediate magical efficacy—and, above all, as regards the incantations which already played an important part in the religion of the Vedic age. In Iran the 'magi' were also experts in

---

[18] According to M. Eliade, Shamanism presupposes the concept of a cosmos divided into levels or realms (heavenly, earthly and chthonic), in their turn still further subdivided. Shamanism does not therefore resolve itself in the concept of an 'animist' religion. The descends and ascents of the Shaman (frequently represented in imagery on a 'cosmic tree', the axis of the world) well express, according to Eliade, the concept of a 'breakthrough' (*rupture de niveau*) which is an important and typical aspect of religious experience. Other concepts, which are apparently Shamanistic but have a different substance, are those found in North America which refer to the individual initiation which a youth receives 'spiritually' during a special sojourn in an isolated place, where he receives from superior beings or spirits a revelation of his 'vocation' and soul's capacity.

the technique of offering sacrifice, and they too contributed a category of persons marked by special characteristics, so that they did indeed seem to some ancient classical writers an ethnical group apart. There is still the unsolved question of the origin of this priestly corporation, which some think was instituted by Zarathustra, the Founder of a reformed Mazdaic religion, Zoroastrianism, but which possibly goes back further still. Only in a later age did it adapt itself to the new situation and assume the legacy of the founder: *athravan, zaotar, mobad* were terms which in the long history of the Mazdaic cult were applied to the priests of this religion, dedicated to the worship of fire and to the worship and sacrifice of the *haoma*, a ritual drink originating in Indo-Iranian pre-history (*soma*).

As we have said, the figure of the 'priest', of the expert in the practices of the cult and in relations with superhuman beings (functions which could also be exercised, wholly or in part, by the legitimate representatives of the family or group) is qualified and determined by the type of deity or superhuman power with which a relationship was established and by the nature of this contact. It is therefore easy to understand why a monotheistic religion has a priesthood jealous of the oneness and transcendence of the Deity, and determined to guard the traditions and purity of these; and one understands also why a religion of the 'founded' type associates its own priesthood with the charismatic power transmitted by its Founder. This is the case with the Christian priesthood.

13. *Sacrifice*

Analogous considerations are valid for the most typical of all priestly functions, that of sacrifice, understood as the setting apart (even if only partial and symbolical) of some good thing (vegetable, animal or human) and the offering of this to the transcendent world. This is its 'consecration' or sanctification, which also eventually leads, through the participation of those who have the right to participate, to their own consecration and sanctification. Thus the sacrifice may be understood in different ways, in accordance with the general type of religion in which similar (often only vaguely or apparently similar) practices are integrated. The primitive and propitiatory sacrifice, already found in the most ancient ethnological civilizations of the hunters, is often offered—with varying sentiments and psychological dispositions—to a Being who is the supreme giver of all good things, or to a lord of the animals who concedes the prey to whoever seeks it in the correct way, or to ancestors who are guarantors of fertility. There are also sacrifices or, more correctly, propitiatory offerings, given to exacting and capricious spirits. Finally, there are the complex rites of a magico-cosmogonic type, in which the 'sacrifice', to use a term now generally accepted, has value in itself, being a ritual technique complete in itself and independent of the will of the superhuman beings, as is the case of the above mentioned Brahmanic sacrifice, the validity of which depends above all on its technical precision, which naturally includes not only external acts and circumstances but also personal dispositions. In India the speculation of the Upanishad transcends and at the same time eliminates this sacrifice, and sets in place the *gnosis* of the Absolute and of the Soul. Quite different is the case of those 'founded' religions in which, as in the Old Testament and in Zoroastrianism, the figure of the Founder is all important as the prototype of the perfect sacrificing priest. In the Christian doctrine of sacrifice the priest, Christ, is also the victim and also, mysteriously, one with the Father to whom the victim is offered, in order to realise, through the communion of those who are sanctified by the sacrificial act, a mystical unity with God.

14. *The knowledge of the superhuman*

Similar observations are valid for another activity closely associated with worship and often (though not exclusively) with the priestly function. I mean that type of knowledge which, transcending normal profane knowledge, is particularly desirable and necessary in questions of a clearly transcendent nature, whether in the sense of knowledge of the sublime (knowledge of the invisible superhuman world, of the will of God or of gods or spirits) or in the sense of 'remote' knowledge (knowledge of primordial events at the time of the creation of the world, eschatological knowledge—knowledge of the 'last things'—, or simply of the future), as also in the sense of awareness of existential requirements—concerning problems in the life of the individual or community, on the spiritual and the material plane. In all these cases a superhuman, sacral, oracular knowledge is required, to be obtained by means of revelations, inspirations, ecstasies, divinations and oracles.

Here also the type of religion and the character of the superhuman beings in question condition the nature and meaning of such acts and beliefs. In monotheistic religions a god who can neither deceive nor be deceived, and who controls the course of history and contemplates it with an all-seeing and all-powerful gaze, is the self-revealing source of a knowledge which is at the basis of universal and binding faith. In a more or less organic polytheism, instead, the revelations and oracles share in the diverse natures of the gods from whom they emanate, although some reference is made to a mystical and unitary deity, such as is often found in Greek terminology. In a religion strongly tinted with animism or manism the spirits of nature and of the dead give only fragmentary answers and oracular pronouncements, which are often utilitarian, prejudiced and capricious and may be, at will, cunningly misinterpreted. Analogously, the prophet (interpreter and mouthpiece and therefore also representative) of a monotheistic god, generally has a tone, a style, a field of interests which differ from those of the prophet or mouthpiece of an oracle of a local and polytheistic type, or of the expert in the various forms of divination (observation of signs, of birds, victims' livers, objects like little sticks, dice or small bones). A specific form of the knowledge of the superhuman is *gnosis*, a name which was the object of dispute between the Gnostics who, as we have said, based their beliefs on the gnostic principle of the decadence of divine elements fallen into this world (elements destined to be re-vitalized by a messenger from on high), and the Early Fathers who, clinging to the meaning of the word as used by St. Paul, interpreted it instead in relation to the knowledge of the mystery of the plan of salvation conceived by God and manifested and realized in Christ.

For reasons which are somewhat analogous, the sacred scriptures of a 'prophetic' religion (like the Biblical religions, with Islam) which are considered as the 'word of God' brought to men by inspired persons, are not typologically and historically comparable with the traditional sacred writings of ethnical religions—some of which have a very ancient priestly tradition—like that of the Brahmans. In yet another class must be put those collections of oracular writings which, like the Sibylline books of Republican Rome, were used for divinatory purposes.

CHAPTER THREE

STUDIES AND PROBLEMS IN THE HISTORY OF RELIGIONS

1. *The sources of historical-religious thought*

Like many other specialized historical and philological branches of learning, the history of religions, initiated in the 19th century, may be said to have been already foreshadowed in the 18th century. This was the object of the research of scholars who were anxious to draw conclusions on a documentary foundation, about those problems of a practical and theoretical nature which arose from the ever-increasing knowledge they had acquired of the peoples of non-European continents.

Besides the work of G. B. Vico (a philosopher and theorist in the study of civilizations, and not an ethnologist, but in any case a writer during this initial period who cannot be passed over) it is customary to quote, among the first published studies of religious ethnology, the book by the missionary J. F. Lafitau (*Moeurs des Sauvages Améri-quains comparées aux moeurs des premiers temps*, Paris 1724) which as the title indicates, implies an attempt to compare ethnological data of peoples contemporary with the author with what knowledge was available of the peoples of antiquity (a problem which Posidonius had already faced in the ancient world, and which had arisen in an even earlier period). The book by Charles de Brosses, *Du culte des dieux fétiches, ou parallèle de l'ancienne religion de l'Egypte avec la religion actuelle de la Nigritie* (Paris 1760) [1] was differently conceived. It was a work of erudition and not of direct ethnographical experience and was moreover preoccupied with the extremely difficult problem of the initial forms of heathen religion, but the author also insists on the parallel study of available ethnographical data, as well as data about the ancient world.

With this combination of ethnography and classical studies there arose a tradition of historical-religious research which was to find illustrious exponents in E. B. Tylor, the father of the theory of primitive Animism, N. D. Fustel de Coulanges (*La cité antique*, 1864),

---

[1] Cf. also N. S. Bergier, *L'origine des dieux du paganisme*, Paris, 1767.

J. J. Bachofen, the famous author of the *Mutterrecht* (1861), J. G. Frazer (*The Golden Bough*), E. Rohde (*Psyche* (first ed. 1891-94) and, nearer to our own day and showing a greater methodological awareness, Martin P. Nilsson, Uberto Pestalozza, Raffaele Pettazzoni, Karl Meuli and Karl Kerényi. This classical-ethnological tradition which for good or ill, and more than any other, has provided material and inspiration for concrete comparative research on a vast scale, and has possibly made a greater contribution to this than even the work of students of Eastern religions, in spite of the fame of Max Müller, Robertson-Smith, Wellhausen and Lagrange or even the ethnological experts themselves (with the exception of scholars like W. Schmidt, R. R. Marett and A. E. Jensen) or the religious phenomenologists (here also we must make exceptions in the case of R. Otto, N. Söderblom, M. Eliade and Van der Leeuw).

In our opinion, this sensibility of classical scholars, with a more (or less) adequate training in anthropological research, to the vaster problems of historical-religious comparative studies (with all the risks these studies involve) is a proof that humanistic studies are an invitation to examine the nature of man and of all human manifestations; we say this without in any way wishing to decry the merits of other scholars whose training has been mainly in anthropological, sociological, psychological or philosophical research, from Morgan to Malinowski, James, Wundt, Durkheim, Lévy-Bruhl, Weber, Wach, Lévi-Strauss or even Jung. All these scholars have made important contributions to historical-religious problems, although for the most part they did not belong to the field of the history of religions, properly understood as research into the whole question of the historical and comparative data of religious phenomena.

2. Max Müller and the 'mythology of nature'

Max Müller, [2] a German who had settled in England, a celebrated Indianist and linguist, was heir to a school of thought which had made its name by discovering the Indo-European linguistic family, and was familiar with the *Veda*, the oldest available testimonies of the Indian spirit and among the most ancient writings of all the great civilizations. The archaic nature of the Indian sources and Müller's ability to analyse them philologically and linguistically, led him to use them as a basis for an interpretation of the mythology of Indo-Euro-

---

[2] Author of a long series of works, from the *Essay on Comparative Mythology*, 1856, to *Contributions to the Science of Mythology*, 1897.

pean peoples, as well as for a theory about the origins of religion, and in particular of mythology (or better a theory about the first *manifestations* of religion, which is immanent in human nature): a theory much influenced by his linguistical interest.

For Max Müller the history of words (inseparable from their concepts, even if not a complete expression of these) is also the history of the genesis of religious concepts, in that form of 'natural religion' which is for him the first expression of a religious faith. He believed that religion first appeared when speech acquired a religious or, more precisely, a mythological meaning. According to him, figurative and poetical language led to the personification of natural objects and concepts and so, through a sort of 'sickness' of language and the multiplication of synonyms, to the deification of these objects and concepts and the creation of a pantheon and a polytheistic mythology. In particular the sun and the heavenly bodies, or (especially for A. Kuhn) atmospherical phenomena, led to these personifications, and so gave birth to the 'light' gods worshipped by the primitive Indo-Europeans. The word *deus*, like the Indian *deva* and various other words, is in fact related to a root meaning 'luminous', 'celestial', like the name of Jupiter (Jove the Father), that of Zeus (root: *div*, gen. Δι(F)ός and the Indian word *Dyauspitā* etc.). In this way the myths also arose, myths which frequently described violent deeds and struggles, as violent as the sky-phenomena. Zeus, Heracles, Indra's club, the cloud-cows, the monstrous sky serpent and other monsters, or the heavenly bodies, especially the sun, moon and evening star, became the first gods, or attributes of gods, having been born with religion itself, or rather, with language. [3]

These interpretations of the mythology of nature had a long, although not a lasting success. In any case, they helped to strengthen the tendency, popular even now with teachers of classical mythology, to speak of gods and myths as, respectively, personifications and symbols of natural, frequently meteorological, phenomena and of the heavenly bodies. But another fallacy, apparently more scientific, was to persist in some philological circles, the theory which denied, on historical-cultural grounds, any possible similarity between concepts

---

[3] It is hardly necessary to mention Vico here. As regards the importance of astral bodies—significant for various reasons—we have already mentioned De Brosses, who saw the origin of non-Biblical religions in 'fetishism' (that is, in subjects later much beloved by the anthropological school) and in the worship of the stars which he called *Sabeism*, connected with pagan Mesopotamian cults which were heirs to forms of the 'Babylonian' religion.

and things not linguistically akin. On the one hand this attitude shows a proper caution, and an awareness of the fact that words and ideas are closely bound together, words not being merely abstract 'signs' and conventions to indicate ideas—as if these were pre-existent in an abstract world of their own. But on the other hand it shows very little awareness of the variety and wealth of historical contacts between cultures, peoples and languages.

One must not however assume that Max Müller denied the existence of anything more ancient than the Vedic poetry of the second millenium B.C.; in fact, he freely admitted that absurd and Barbarian elements of Vedic mythology were survivals of a primitive foundation much earlier than the *Veda*, [4] and added that all mythologies, even those of Greece and Rome, contain a thousand survivals or reminiscences of the primitive 'savage' state, and he quoted Vico and Fontenelle in this context; he also wished to make room for something with a more scientific foundation than that found in superficial anthropological comparative studies.

Nor did Max Müller claim that Indo-European mythology was unlike any other, [5] or that the Vedic religion or the Indian *ṛṣi* were present in the very first era of mankind. Whatever opinion we may form of the mythology of savage races, extinct or still living, he observes, one fact is undeniable, that many mythical phenomena took shape in the relatively recent period in which the Aryans had already ceased to be savages, So, he added, just as the Bantu cannot teach us the origin of words like *caelum, sol* and *luna*, so the myths of the Iroquois and the Kaffirs are incapable of shedding any light on the personalities of Zeus, Athena and Aphrodite. Indeed, he doubts whether the savages of today have (or can be shown to have) any gods more ancient than Zeus, and he ironically anticipates the objection (already discussed) to the use of the word 'primitive' by ethnologists. Lang's 'primitives', he observes (he is speaking of the anthropologist we have already mentioned and in particular of the evolutionistic theories which he had adopted before he brought out his new theory on Supreme Beings) belong to the 19th century A.D.; though Müller's own primitives belong, hypothetically, to the 19th century B.C. In fact, he adds, the use of the term 'primitive', applied to Aryan mytho-

---

[4] Cf. *Nouvelles études de mythologie*, Paris, 1898, p. 5. (Translation of the above mentioned *Contributions*).

[5] But here also he admitted, in these comparisons, no particular genetic significance but only some contribution to the explanation of what seems an absurdity in one myth by comparing it with another more intelligible myth.

logy, only means the most ancient concepts we have been able to trace, through philological-etymological research, even if a very long sequence of years and human history preceded it. We agree with him in this, but with the grave reservation, fatal for the most crucial aspects of Max Müller's research, that the means by which he tried to trace the first appearance of the Indo-European gods were too exclusively linguistic and—in accordance with his theory of the 'sickness of language'—too remote from the complexity of generically human, as well as specifically historical, references to religion, or even merely to mythology. It is true that research cannot penetrate beyond language, but this does not always mean 'beyond this particular language'. [6] And this is true not only for language but for culture. Thus, as we shall see later when we speak of the pan-Babylonian hypothesis, a culture apparently as compact and self enclosed as that characterized by cuneiform writing included, in the Near East, cultures and languages frequently of diverse origin. [7]

---

[6] It is curious that modern Indo-Europeists (Devoto and his school) have sometimes arrived at conclusions quite contrary to those of Max Müller, in all that concerns the dynamic of relations between language and religious concepts. At a certain point, according to these scholars, we have a 'secularization' of concepts, shown in the neglect of certain terms of religious contents which express a divine presence (like, for example, the latin *aqua*) and the use of 'neuter' terms (e.g. ὕδωρ) expressing 'things' devoid of sacred personality or contents.

[7] Max Müller sharply criticizes Lang and his anthropological school, or as he wittily dubs them 'agriological' which, he writes, studies the natural races, that is, the most unnatural of men. However, he defends the capacity of these races to evolve abstract concepts, the presuppositions of all language that is not merely onomatopoeic, and asserts the necessity of studying them linguistically and philologically. Let our universities, he says, have as many good professors of Hottentot as they now have of Sanskrit. These criticisms of Max Müller's may now sometimes be verified in actual cases. For example, he rightly affirms that the myth of Kronos who swallows his children cannot be explained by a reference to cannibalism; in fact the theogonic and cosmogonic reference to this myth are obvious: the old God, associated with the primordial chaos of the world's origins, who had separated the Sky from the Earth, opposes the new God destined to bring about a new order in the world. In fact, the ethnological myths themselves, like the well known story of Rangi and Papa, the Sky and the Earth in the mythology of the Maoris of New Zealand, have helped us to interpret this myth; Lang himself had quoted the Maori myth in this very connection. Where Max Müller is mistaken, apart from a certain over simplification of the theories he criticizes, is when in his turn he produces hypothetically naturistic explanations of the name of Kronos, asserting that it possibly expresses a natural entity which 'swallows up' the light gods and re-vomits them.

Another example is offered by Max Müller's criticism of the comparison Lang had suggested between the legend of Daphne transformed into a plant (which took her name) and a myth from the South Seas: two coco-nut trees are born from the brain of a mythical king of the eels, whose head had been buried after being severed at his own request by a woman called Ina [Moon]; as we shall see, we have here

3. *The history of religions, systematically divided into periods*

We have dwelt on this aspect of Max Muller's thought because of the important place he occupies at the beginning of the history of religions, which owes him a great deal, also for having begun the monumental English edition of the *Sacred Books of the East*. But the record would not be complete if one neglected another aspect of his thought, also significant for his age: the tendency to include his theories about the mythology of nature and the beginnings of religion in an interpretation, not historical but systematic and theoretical, of the phases of religion in the general history of mankind. This had been the method used in the well known Hegelian classification of religions in a series of forms which go from that of 'natural' religions to those of individuality and freedom. A philosophizing attitude and a propensity towards abstract systematization in a historically concrete problem is found in the same period also in French positivist and sociological schools of thought and, later on, among the English anthropologists, in spite of the great diversity of their respective cultural roots.

According to these trends, religion, emerging from Savage and Barbarian forms and, evolving later, (through polytheism to monotheism) finally had to give way, in positivistic and scientific civilization, to science and (in the opinion of Auguste Comte) [8] to the 'religion' of humanity which retains very little 'religion' in the technical sense of the term, except in association with morality, with which it merges. [9] Max Müller, like other scholars we shall refer to later on (associated, not fortuitously, with classical studies rather than with anthropological research) sees as a probable religion of the future a

---

the theme of the *dema* deity (see p. 100 et sqq.), the subject of rceent studies, especially by Jensen. The comparison suggested by Lang was in any case neither absurd nor specious. Max Müller's proposal to present the story of Ina as a legend which merely seeks to explain the name of a plant which has become unintelligible cannot therefore be justified: he cites this as the clearest possible example of a 'linguistic sickness'. In his opinion, the term signifying 'coco-nut' came in Mangaia (the island where this myth is attested) to mean 'head', giving in this manner the basis for a myth concerning the decapitation of a fabulous character and the seed of the coco-nut went accordingly to represent the eyes and mouth of the great eel Tuna (the name of the King who was slain). This argument put forward by Max Müller is a typical example of an overthrown explanation, similar to others, both etymological and etiological, put forward by ancient scholars (Atlas as king or mountain, later deified etc.), scholars who were singularly blind to the religious content of the myths and rites studied by their etiologies.

[8] *Cours de philosophie positive*, 1830 et sqq.

[9] The Modernism of A. Loisy was to find eventually expression in this concept.

humanist—immanentist creed not so different from the Romantic—pantheistic propensities of the beginning of the 19th century. According to him, a 'physical' naturalistic religion, characterized by the 'mythology of nature' described above, was to be followed by an 'anthropological' religion based no longer on the great luminaries (and the other realities, far or near, of the cosmos) but on human affections and finally, in the third place, by a theosophical and psychological religion celebrating (as in the speculation of the Indian Upanishads on the *Atman*) the transcendent-immanent Self.

The whole concept was to constitute a natural religion, as contrasted to the notion of historical revelation.

This speculation which came, not by chance, from an Indianist who certainly in his reconstruction attached importance not only to the mythological India of the *Veda*, but also to the theosophical India of the *Vedanta*, [10] is characteristic of the German cultural *milieu* of the beginning of the 19th century and recalls the theory of G. F. Creuzer [11] which, on the basis of an immanentist psychology, emphasized in religion the tendency towards the personification of nature and mystic pantheism, expressed in symbols. [12] For Karl Ottfried Müller instead, it was the 'feeling for the divine', rooted in man's heart, which provided the stimulus for religion. His insistence on the necessity of the philological study of the 'when' and 'where' of the origin of myths is instead more pertinent to the analytical aims of the history of religions. Myths, he maintains, can be understood only if one understands the 'place' (geographical, ethnical and circumstantial) of their birth.

4. *Goblet d'Alviella and the 'Science of Religions'*

We shall dwell no longer on these general interpretations of a 'development' of religion because, although a stimulus to study and to historical research, they are for the most part extraneous to the history of religions in the correct sense of the term because of their postulatory character. But we cannot pass over one of those scholars who, at the turn of the century, theorized about the history of religions. Goblet d'Alviella divided the 'science of religions' or 'of religion', and also his voluminous collection of studies on *Croyances, rites,*

---

[10] India has a role of special importance also in the interpretation of the most recent historians, especially those of the phenomenological school (from Hauer to R. Otto and his followers, and M. Eliade).

[11] *Symbolik und Mythologie der alten Völker, besonders der Griechen*, 1810-12.

[12] Cf. in an epoch much nearer to our own, Cassirer.

institutions, into three treatises covering respectively 'Hierography', (archeology and religious history: descriptive) 'Hierology' (questions of method and of origins: interpretative) and 'Hierosophy' (problems of the present time: philosophical). In this framework the history of religion would probably be classed in the first and second category (the term 'hierology' still survives) whereas the third category is more concerned with interpretations and philosophical arguments on religion, inspired by a polemical attitude towards positive religious belief, an attitude which tends to identify morality and the religious outlook, [13] and has an almost religious faith in progress [14] (the work concludes with a paraphrase, in which 'Energy' is substituted for the Johannine *Logos*).

The writings of Goblet d'Alviella, appointed Professor at the University of Brussels in 1884, well illustrate the spirit and style of the French speaking history of religions at the end of the 19th century and the beginning of the 20th—a history based on philosophical premises and a prejudice against confessional religions, which were to influence the discussion on this branch of learning even more powerfully than the evolutionistic and sometimes materialistic anthropology of the English or the romantic-idealistic theology or learned agnosticism of the Germans and Dutch. Nevertheless, the French history of religions, characteristic of its time, made an essential contribution to the history of these studies, no less valid than the German and Dutch publications which, towards the end of the century, included such fundamental studies as P. D. Chantepie de la Saussaye's *Lehrbuch der Religionsgeschichte* [15] (1897), C. P. Tiele's *Einleitung in die Religionswissenschaft* (1899) and C. von Orelli's *Allgemeine Religionsgeschichte* (1899).

Today, at a distance of time and events, and with new minds at work on this subject, we may say that, within its *engagement*, this history of religions suffered from a methodological disorder resulting from confusing the genuine requirements of scientific autonomy with methodologies (and sometimes presuppositions and purposes) which were not pertinent. Even as late as 1968 a scholar as shrewd and as aware of the necessity of the comparative method and of documentary

---

[13] Therefore along the same lines as the 'religion of humanity' of Comte, and later on of Loisy.

[14] Cf. *Hiérologie*, p. 409, concerning the 'parliament of religions' of Chicago, 1893.

[15] Re-edited, in the 4th edition, by A. Bertholet and E. Lehmann (1924) and recently reprinted.

research as H. Clavier, appealed to the concept of 'free enquiry' in order to illustrate the methodology of the history of religions. This 'free enquiry' is in itself a theological concept (accepted or rejected by the various theologies) and is not the same thing as that methodological and epistemological autonomy of the history of religions which we have tried to formulate in the preceding pages. [16] It is true that, for any science, the understanding of the reasons for its own autonomy implies not an assured privilege but a difficult acquisition of its rigour and coherence.

Concerning Goblet d'Alviella's theory we note that, although on the one hand he maintained the necessity of positive historical research in hierography, and on the other hand the necessity of a comparative method in hierology, his notion of this method is very different from that, for example, of Pettazzoni, a scholar who, in spite of his 'positivist' beginnings, similar to those of these French writers, was more sensitive to the requirements of historical thought. In fact, with Goblet the comparative method proper to hierology is not precisely derived from historical research but is in itself substituted to this. That this is not merely a question of terminology is clear from the fact that the comparative method, as followed by this author, is mainly used to 'formulate the laws of religious evolution'. [17] Goblet lays too much emphasis (with a corresponding neglect of history) on a 'general law, inherent in the very nature of the human soul' (or on a 'certain identity of psychical processes'). [18] This identity, he thinks, is seen 'when the same phenomena, the same institutions and the same evolutions are seen in the same order among peoples who have always lived apart from one another'. Here one clearly sees the limitations of this procedure when contrasted with an authentic historical comparison, which looks for motivations (even if based on historical typology and not on diffusionism) which are specific, and not only generically human, in order to study comparatively and to classify or, when necessary, relate historical facts which are processes and developments, not 'things' which emerge ready made from a vaguely common and 'given' patrimony of the human mind and heart. [19]

---

[16] This sets a limit, at least *de jure*, to the connection asserted by E. Renan between the Reformation and historical and philological sciences.

[17] *Hiérologie*, p. 95.

[18] In practice, the 'elementary thought' about which A. Bastian theorizes to explain the analogies between certain aspects of the cultures of peoples remote from each other in space and time.

[19] Therefore this does not mean that history rejects 'natural' and universal human data and values, but that it 'knows' them only in their concrete realizations.

In other words, Goblet's comparative method, like that of Van Gennep,[20] to whom he explicitly refers, has the grave defect of presupposing human 'institutions' which are supposed to live independently of the course of history. Now, even if we consider institutions of universal diffusion, such as religion or the family, or even institutions which converge towards common forms, like penal law, their universality is always concrete and historical,[21] and open to investigation by an inductive method. Therefore, religion and the family are not a-historical subjects of an evolution governed by their own intrinsic rules, quite separable from any historical context.[22] This is the defect of a naturalistic-evolutionistic presentation, and was later on to be the defect also of the doctrine of 'structures' which some phenomenologists of religion, over anxious to admit archetypes, were to adopt.[23]

As regards what Goblet calls the 'historical' aspect of his research, it can hardly be distinguished from the usual evolutionist position. Quoting the theories of Bachofen, MacLennan and other leaders of that trend, he asserts the need to make up for the insufficiency of information on the historical development of a creed or institution, in a race or a society, by using information culled from other *milieux*;[24] of course, all this has nothing to do with the historical—comparative method.

On the other hand, Goblet quite rightly demands that the comparative method should not be confined, as the Egyptologist G. Foucart wished,[25] to the study of the great religions which have literary texts—but this request, to which M. Müller, as we have seen, added a further request that philological studies should be added to ethnological research, was at least partly answered, at the beginning of the 20th century, by the new science of historical ethnology, with Boas in America and the historical-cultural school in Germany and Austria.

---

[20] *Revue de l'histoire des religions*, vol. LVIII, p. 74.

[21] Concerning the meaning we give to this, see for a fuller treatment *Storia dell' etnologia*, 2nd edit., Rome 1971, pp. 250 et sqq.

[22] So there is no sense in conjecturing with Goblet 'the general laws of the evolution of penal law', admitting that 'local influences' have only advanced, delayed or differentiated this evolution' (*op. cit.*, p. 99). If this law evolves in (or better: towards) analogous forms, it does so in a process or processes which are historic and specific, even if very widely diffused.

[23] See pp. 100, 185 et seqq., 192 et seq.

[24] *Op. cit.*, p. 100, cf. p. 98.

[25] *La méthode comparative dans l'histoire des religions*, Paris, 1909, quoted by Goblet, *op. cit.*, pp. 105 and 266 et sqq.

5. *The anthropological school*

Lang, the target of Max Müller's criticisms, was at that time one of the most characteristic writers of the anthropological school.[26] In this group are usually included writers who were not strictly speaking anthropologists, except in the somewhat vague sense in which the term was then used. Most of them had been trained in other branches of learning.

Thus, Auguste Comte, the founder of the positivist school, and later on Herbert Spencer, the promotor of similar sociological doctrines, were willing to make use of documentary material from anthropological sources to support their theories on the origin of religion, which the former sees in 'fetishism,' with polytheism and monotheism appearing at later stages.[27] By this term 'fetishism' Comte understands, very mistakenly, the veneration of natural objects, including the heavenly bodies (thus constructing a synthesis of the theories of de Brosses) while Spencer depends more largely on manism, the veneration of ancestors, or at least of those dead persons who were very important and treated with extraordinary respect when alive, a conception in which the characteristics of ethnological manism were somewhat influenced by the doctrine of Euhemeros,[28] the object of certain predilections of Greek and Roman speculation on the origins of religion, inherited by some 18th century learned writers. Others, like J. Lubbock, complicate the Comtian evolutionary process by admitting more specific phases with inappropriate denominations or, in order to fill in the lower rungs of the evolutionary ladder, by admitting a primitive atheism understood as the initial absence of religion in primordial human history, an atheism, moreover, which is merely hypothetical because the few cases Lubbock quotes of a-religious primitive peoples were the result of his inadequate information or, in most cases, of too circumscribed a concept of religion, which did not include the exotic customs of the 'savages'.

But the merits of the anthropological school as a whole are much greater than those of these tentative classifications. We refer particularly to the work of scholars like Edward B. Tylor, experienced

---

[26] Cf. *Custom and Myth*, London, 1884.

[27] These ages of religion were, he thought, followed by the age of metaphysics, and this by the scientific or 'positive' age.

[28] The doctrine of Euhemeros of Messene, adopted by scholars like Diodorus and others, explained the gods as great personages of antiquity, acknowledged as divine on account of their good works, or as natural entities, particularly stars, who had been divinized.

investigators 'in the field' and endowed with great ethnographical experience, who have left their mark on research in this branch of study. Among these learned scholars must be mentioned W. Mannhardt, the author of a well known treatise on agrarian and forest cults, [29] in which he discovers, in the characteristic beliefs and customs of European folklore (particularly in Germanic Europe) typical examples of 'survivals'. This term and these discoveries were to enjoy a wide and rather excessive popularity among 19th century ethnologists. He refers to popular beliefs in the spirits of fields and woods, and in other fabulous creatures, as well as to customs observed in the Carnival season, or relative to the 'Maggio', with its leafy tree, or at harvest time with the belief in the 'corn spirit' and vegetable and animal disguises. Mannhardt sought the roots of these beliefs and rites in Indo-European and ancient Germanic sources, rightly maintaining that they were primitive in character, that is, not derived from belief in the great gods of ancient paganism.

Tylor and, later on, Frazer, pointed out the animist or magic nature of these beliefs and cults and emphasized their frequent association with seasonal fertility. Another scholar, already mentioned in connection with his anthropological and comparative studies, Van Gennep, [30] connected many of these cults with the type of 'transition rites' (*rites de passage*), intended to ensure the success not only of the seasons of the agrarian year, but also of every other critical human transition—births, weddings, deaths, inaugurations etc.

6. *Bachofen and the 'Matriarchate'*

We shall refer to Tylor again later on. We must now point out that some of the most classical studies of the anthropological school, although not based on a first hand investigation of the life of primitive peoples, yet brought to light concrete problems relating to the history of religions. This is true of the work of Bachofen [31] (1861) and (more recent, and revised and re-edited over many years) that of Frazer, both of these writers possessing an encyclopaedic anthropological culture and classical scholarship [32].

From a series of ethnographical records Bachofen develops the

---

[29] *Wald- und Feldkulte*, Berlin, 1875-77.
[30] *Les rites de passage*, Paris, 1909.
[31] *Das Mutterrecht*.
[32] A new edition (with some unpublished writings) of Bachofen's works is going on at Basle from 1943.

theory of the Matriarchate, or rather of 'maternal right', that is, of a type of society founded on matrilinear descendence, which he finds already in information given by Herodotus about the Lycians, completed by further information from Nicolas of Damascus, in the light of which he interprets some myths and legends of the classical world. The Matriarchate, he says, was a universal phase, or in any case a historical form of social organisation, which preceded the Patriarchate: numerous survivals remained in the classical world, in mythology (e.g. the story of the Amazons), in ritual, in family institutions, as in the rigid Roman patriarchal system which he thinks was a radical reaction to a preceding matriarchal system, and in religion in general.

In matriarchal religion the 'initial', 'nocturnal', 'material', 'profound', chthonic, Demetriac element predominates, as opposed to patriarchal cults characterized by the spirit of 'perfection' which is solar, spiritual, Apollinian, and diurnal. This was illustrated in Greece, in the myth of Orestes and of his final aquittal and deliverance from the Erinyes, who represented a material kind of justice, with a visceral, instinctive, implacable, material, blind fidelity to ties of blood, whereas a paternal kind of law, rational and enlightened, was represented by the personality of Athena, born of a father only.

In matriarchal societies the youngest child is given the preference over his elder brothers, and there was a certain primitive egalitarianism, very different from the heroic and patriarchal aristocratic system. All this was influenced by the female tendency towards adopting chthonic cults and insisting on the connection between woman and Mother Earth. This, therefore, is the origin of the 'matriarchate' which —in Bachofen's opinion—is not primarily to be sought in economic and sociological-political motivations such as an initial and determinant connection between woman and agriculture in primitive civilizations, [33] or the role of the maternal uncle in family authority.

Whatever may be said about these generical assertions and alternatives, an obvious defect of Bachofen's theory is its evolutionistic presentation (recently discussed [34]) which sees the matriarchate as an ancient phase which universally preceded the patriarchate (see the observations already made about Van Gennep and Goblet d'Alviella),

---

[33] This was asserted by W. Schmidt, but the association is denied by A. E. Jensen and accepted only as one of the possible factors of the 'maternal right' by Murdock. On the other hand a synthesis of the ideo-cultural motivations (ideological-sacral motivation of the practices later found in profane agriculture, and the role of the woman in the origins of agriculture) was included in the researches of Hahn.

[34] J. Dörmann, in *Anthropos* 60 (1965), pp. 1-48.

but it is important to notice that even within these limitations, Bachofen's intuitions are interesting, as they indicate certain feminine and maternal aspects of paleo-Mediterranean religion (Cretan and Anatolian) at least in so far (and this is not clear) as these may be contrasted with patriarchal and Indo-European elements of the religion and mythology of the Hellenic invaders. Other authors, much more recent than Bachofen, have carried this confrontation to excessive lengths (like Walter Otto in his famous book on 'the gods of Greece') whereas it has been reduced to more historically and philologically concrete terms, even if these are at times purely hypothetical, by Martin P. Nilsson with his research into the Mycenaean religion and its connection with the Greek religion of the first millennium. It is also treated by Uberto Pestalozza and Momolina Marconi, in their studies of Greek myths and rites which suggests a cult of the Mediterranean goddess of fertile nature, [35] by Karl Kerényi (for Greek mythology) and by Raffaele Pettazzoni (doctrine of the 'two sources' of the Greek religion and a chthonic and popular explanation of the Greek 'Mysteries', in relation to the former of these two strata, still surviving at the time among the common people of Attic territory).

It is true that the most recent investigations have complicated the problem—both by indicating a more complex cultural stratification in Greek lands and by indicating the significance for Greek (including Hesiodic) mythology of Oriental influences from the Mesopotamian and Syrio-Anatolian regions, already felt in the Greek-Mycenaean age. This is true also of those myths of Zeus and his progenitor gods on whom the above mentioned interpretations are based. [36]

7. *J. G. Frazer*

We owe to Frazer a full anthropological commentary on Pausanias' '*Itinerary of Greece*' (*Periegesis*). He illustrates this with analogies borrowed from ethnology; this work gave encouragement (sometimes even too much) to various classical scholars interested also in Roman law, who were trying to trace 'survivals'. These are treated systematically in a long series of studies which take their name from Virgil's '*Golden Bough*', the key used by Aeneas to enter the Underworld, and used instead by Frazer as a magical clue (like Ariadne's thread)

---

[35] Cf. Pestalozza, *Religione Mediterranea, Vecchi e nuovi studi*, Milan, 1951.

[36] See below, p. 110. Moreover, it is obvious that the non-creationist cosmogonies frequently assign to the beginnings of the world 'nocturnal', chaotic, immense, shadowy and material beings who 'generate' the world.

which leads him on an adventurous and inspiring quest, from strange customs concerning the *rex Nemorensis* of the shrine of Diana at Ariccia to customs of the Near East, Africa, India and elsewhere which concern the figure of the 'sacred king', the patron and guarantor of fertility, which he magically embodies. This is a theme which Frazer extends still further, to the question of the 'dying gods', Adonis, Tammuz, Attis and, to some extent, Osiris, all of whom are also genii of fertility.

Frazer's voluminous treatise, to which he was constantly adding results of further research, [37] is naturally and rightly criticized for its methodology which is devoid of any more specifically historical principle. The various testimonies are compared in accordance with a typological classification and are not framed in the context in which they lived. Nevertheless the work had the considerable merit of presenting an immense range of material and of arousing interest in little known and surprising aspects of the culture of the most diverse peoples. It is also true that in the fascination and suggestiveness of Frazer's work lies one of its chief dangers as regards the reader's training in methodology.

His theories, however, must be taken with much more caution. We do not mean merely the question of the 'sacred king' and the 'dying gods' in which much has had to be revised, or merely his interpretations of exogamy and totemism—nor even the Frazerian notion of a greater antiquity of magic, in relation to religion, based on a supposed greater 'simplicity' of the former in relation to the latter (an evolutionist theory that has no positive value). As regards magic itself, Frazer, in accordance with the thought of Tylor's school, takes a somewhat intellectualist view. Magic was for him a false application of the causal principle which it shares in common with science. Therefore he neglects the emotional and dynamic element in magic (magic seen as the manipulation of a mysterious power). Nevertheless, the emphasis he lays on the 'sympathetic' nature of magical action is a permanent acquisition for our studies. The action may be based on the imitative or, better, evocative principle, according to which like attracts and evokes like, and acts upon it. Hence, for example, the ritual and magical representation of animals by the primitive hunter before he goes hunting, or the masked and mimed actions which imitate the figure and movements of the animal and of the chase. All this is intended to produce and ensure a victory over the

---

[37] 3rd ed. 1911-1915.

animal in question. Or magic may be based on the principle of 'contagion', according to which the part represents (in the etymological sense of the word), and actually takes the place of, the whole. Hence the custom, for example, of maltreating the image, footprint or excreta of a person in the conviction that by so doing the said person will be injured or slain. [38]

8. *Theories on 'totemism' in the general history of religions*

We shall not dwell on other aspects of the research conducted at the end of the 19th and the beginning of the 20th century concerning the subject of 'totemism', because this belongs more to religious and social ethnology than to the history of religions. We mention only that this term has given rise to a variety of acceptations and interpretations of the most varied and surprising nature. The legitimate, if conventional, meaning of 'totemism' refers to an invisible close relationship between a species, generally animal, and a human group, mostly clanic, a group defined by a common mythical ancestry, generally implying exogamy, that is the prohibition of marriage between persons belonging to the group and honouring the same totem. [39] Nevertheless, a series of scholars, who were not even ethnologists, confused totemism with nature worship (e.g. Lubbock) or with the theriomorphic concept of the deity and with the typical Egyptian habit of representing gods with animals' heads. This gave rise to a series of arbitrary judgments pronounced by scholars who, although in other respects trustworthy in their own fields, were disastrously superficial in the field of religious-historical comparative study. This is true of Salomon Reinach, the author of an unfortunate history of religions, [40] who sees totemist survivals everywhere, even in the classical world, and places totemism at the very source of religion, and it is also true of the Orientalist W. Robertson Smith, [41] who sees in totemism the origin of animal sacrifice among the Semites, Arabs and Jews, within the concept of a consubstantiality of race and blood between the totemic animal and the god, a consubstantiality which is shown in the consumption, otherwise forbidden, of the flesh

---

[38] Already in Plato we find that resemblance and proximity determine association.

[39] There is, however, also individual totemism (which relates to a single person) and sexual totemism (totem of the males and totem of the females).

[40] *Orpheus, Histoire Générale des religions*, Paris, 1909, cf. by the same author, *Cultes, mythes et religions*, Paris, 1905-06.

[41] Especially in *Lectures on the religion of the Semites*, which appeared first in 1889.

of the animal on festive occasions. This reconstruction was very soon abandoned because of a whole series of improbabilities and, above all, because it was without any documentary foundation, as well as being extraneous to the religions in question. It also confused the prohibition (frequently found among totemic tribes) of eating the flesh of the totemic animal with the abstention from eating the flesh of bred animals, generally observed among pastoral peoples, who live by the products and services of these animals, as the Bedouin do. [42]

Frazer showed greater critical acumen in his treatment of totemism: He changed his opinion about the origins of this phenomenon more than once and deserves well of all students of the typology of totemism because he rejected the suggestion that it was the original and universal form of religion. Instead he validly maintained its importance in the ethnological study of the social structures of the various peoples. But in recent years Claude Lévi-Strauss [43] emphasized the variety of meanings and of social-cultural realites which come under the general label of totemism, a variety which enables us to question the scientific appropriateness of this term.

It is true that Lévi-Strauss, who gives predominance to the 'structural' criterion in ethnological study, runs the risk of diminishing other aspects of totemism in favour of his interpretation of many totemic forms as the expression of an intention, on the part of primitive peoples, to classify concepts and social groups or to settle conceptual contradictions. In fact, one cannot ignore the consideration of those elements of a mystical 'participation' between totem and group which is proved by so much documentary evidence. [44]

9. *The sociological school*

Totemism, as is well known, was the main object of the research and theories of the French sociological school of Emile Durkheim, Marcel Mauss and Lucien Lévy-Bruhl. Much has been written about, and against, these scholars and this is not the place to dwell upon the objections raised against the tendency of Durkheim and Mauss [45]

---

[42] Other arbitrary judgments of this kind are found in theories about the first forms of religion, asserted even in recent publications in the U.S.S.R. in which any rite connected with sacred objects is described as 'fetishism', any rite or belief involving animals as 'totemism', and all sacred formulas as 'magic'.

[43] *Le totémisme aujourd'hui*, Paris, 1962.

[44] For an account of the whole problem of totemism see J. Haekel, *Der heutige Stand des Totemismusproblems*, in *Mitteil. anthropol. Gesellsch.* Wien, 132 (1953) p. 33 et sqq.

[45] E. Durkheim, *Les formes élémentaires de la vie religieuse*, Paris, 1912.

to identify the origin and essence of religion, in the world of primitive societies, in the absolute predominance of the 'social' over the 'individual' and of collective custom and thought over individual initiative. In primitive societies, these authors maintain, there is a group phenomenon, the aura of prestige which binds the group together and makes it representative of the thoughts and feelings of all its members. Durkheim's definition of totemism as a privileged and peculiar phenomenon of primitive religion was, although not superficial, nevertheless arbitrary from various points of view. The totem, understood as the expression of the thoughts and feelings of primitive people, a 'mystic' collective representative and depositary of the supernatural substance of the group, seemed to Durkheim to correspond well to the sociological requirements of his research into primitive religious forms— forms which he tried to trace by means of a meticulous analysis, conducted according to well defined (even if simplistic) criteria, of the totemistic practices and social groupings of Australian tribes. To his way of thinking, this is the world of the 'holy', of spirits and powers, of the beings who created and founded the world, and in particular of the totem and of the supernatural in general. So, communication, that is, 'con-participation' in this world is ensured by sacrifice, which entails the introduction of the victim into this other world, a 'sacralization' which is followed by a 'de-sacralization', in order to legitimize the profane use of the object sacrificed.

It is hardly necessary to point out the numerous and grave unilateral considerations and improprieties of this method. One must however also observe that the patient and 'single track' speculation of these sociologists has brought to light interesting aspects of the social implications of religion, has clarified some elements of the technique of sacrificial ritual and has illustrated the importance of the savage's concern for classifying phenomena and fostering social solidarity and community feeling—a concern which was at the same time analytical and comprehensive in its outlook. This research (even if founded on different preconceptions, sociological and not psychological) anticipates in some way the structuralist analyses of Lévi-Strauss in our own day. It is significant to note that according to those scholars a geographical and geometrical understanding of the world, apparently as 'profane' as that founded an the cardinal points, is yet closely involved with classificatory instincts and forms which human societies express in their organisations. [46] Moreover, to the extent that magic is not used

---

[46] E. Durkheim and M. Mauss, *De quelques formes primitives de classification*, in

for purely individualistic purposes—which Durkheim considered to be the most obvious contradiction of the religious principle—but implies a use of principles of solidarity based not only on the technique of sympathetic magic but also on a vision of the totality of a universe in which *tout se tient*, the sociological school could boast of having progressed beyond the somewhat intellectualist interpretations of scholars like Frazer (cf. p. 75). Thus were introduced the concept of collective 'representations', as well as that of mystic, affective 'participation', meaning by this term a solidarity between beings we consider to be quite different from one another but which primitive peoples saw as participating in one another's essence and personality.

10. *Lévy-Bruhl and primitive mentality*

These concepts of Durkheim's school are clearly shared by Lucien Lévy-Bruhl, a philosopher of the positivist-sociological school preoccupied with problems of gnoseology. In many treatises, which appeared regularly for several years up to 1939, he presupposes a 'primitive mentality', characterized by 'participation' and by 'pre-logical' thought. His interpretations were much criticized, even after he eliminated the term 'pre-logical' which had become particularly associated with his first successes and with his more numerous failures as a philosoph venturing into the fields of ethnology and anthropology.

In particular his assertion that primitive man does not have our cognitive faculties and feels no need of the logical processes familiar to civilized man was strongly opposed. So was his theory that primitive man was unaware of contradictions (a failing which Lévy-Bruhl thinks must explain the primitive meaning of 'participation' in the sense already referred to) but instead possessed a whole range of representations of reality quite different from our own but compatible with the experiences of dreams, in fact sometimes illustrated by these.

It is true, that Lévy-Bruhl made it clear that this primitive, mystic or 'participating' mentality does not characterize primitive man as an individual, but primitive man in the context of a particular category of his experiences, as distinct from all those other experiences relating to his technical and practical activities, in which his conduct is as positive and rational as that of civilized man. In fact, this primitive

---

L'Année sociologique, VI, 1901-02, p. 1 et sqq. (An Italian translation of this essay appeared in the same volume with other two essays by these authors: Durkheim-Hubert-Mauss, *Le origini dei poteri magici*, Turin, 1951, whose Chap. II considers the calendarial divisions of time, more qualitative than quantitative).

and 'participating' awareness of reality was not, according to Lévy-Bruhl, a faculty peculiar to primitive man but an element of humanity in general, although much more clearly perceptible among ethnological peoples.

'If I look back on what I wrote about 'participation' between 1910 and 1938', writes Lévy-Bruhl in his posthumously published *Carnets*, 'the evolution of my ideas seems to me quite clear. I had begun by presupposing a primitive mentality different from our own, if not in structure at least in its function, and I had found it was difficult to explain the connection between this mentality and the other, not only among ourselves but also among 'primitive' peoples. In fact, I had merely juxtaposed them without succeeding in giving an account either of their co-existence or of their connection'. He thereupon completely renounced the intention to explain participation by referring to any quality peculiar to the human spirit, either constitutional (in its structure or function) or acquired (mental habits). There is no primitive mentality which can be distinguished from the other by two characteristic and peculiar features, mystic and pre-logical. There is a mystic mentality which is more accentuated and more easily observed among the 'primitives' than in our own societies, but which is present in all human spirit.[47] As to participation, it seems to him to be associated with what he calls 'mystical experience'; the essential feature of these experiences in 'the awareness, accompanied by a peculiar and characteristic emotion, of the presence, and frequently of the action of an invisible power, the feeling of a contact, generally unforeseen, with a reality other than the reality of the [particular] *milieu*'.[48] And this experience, familiar to primitive man from his birth, is of an essentially 'affective' nature, so that he feels himself face to face with a complex reality, composed of these two realities, positive and mystical, which continually intermingle to form a single experience, implying a participation between objects belonging to one sphere of reality and objects which belong to the other.

Lévy-Bruhl gives as an example of participation the experience, known to primitive man, of the participation between a recent dead and his corpse. This belief inspires the living to treat the corpse as if he were still alive, and to provide him with the necessities of life, beginning with food. In the first days after death the dead is still thought of as near at hand, in spite of his remoteness in the tomb and

---

[47] *Les carnets*, Paris 1949 (posthumous), p. 131.
[48] *Ibid.*, p. 134.

even in spite of his eventual presence in various places; for example, the dead man is believed to be in the realm of the dead and yet at the same time reincarnate on this earth in another being, human or animal.

With the passing of time, Lévy-Bruhl adds,[49] these participations, already for so long experienced, become more consciously represented and begin to suggest the need for some sort of logical legitimization. This, he says, raises insuperable difficulties, which—he adds—are obvious in the history of religions and in that of metaphysics. At this point there naturally emerges the author's positivist presupposition, and we must at once point out its incompatibility with historical-phenomenological investigation. This makes it quite clear that religious representations, even among primitive peoples, are not without their own logic which functions, every time, on *the basis* of these representations and experiences. That a certain spirit or deity should be inaccessible, mysterious, or even incomprehensible, is the consequence of its mode of being, as imagined and felt but, once the Student has assigned the transcendental being to its proper place, logic reappears, sometimes even expressing itself in a familiar and human way (cf. the capricious spirits of Animism, and the Homeric gods whose *modus agendi* is not merely the result of poetic adaptation). Indeed to understand the logic of the gods, often similar to that of men, is a means of entering into contact with them, surmising their desires or foreseeing their behaviour.

This is true also of myths, in more than one sense, first of all because, for example, a myth of the origins of the world by its very nature presupposes that at the beginning nothing had been created, so that a demiurgic being could, without actual contradiction, 'perceive' that things are yet 'lacking', or could establish himself on a very tiny part of the earth and from this begin to create the earth itself, as it is today. Similarly, the cosmogonic myth expresses the original situation in which things did not yet exist, and it does this frequently by referring to the paradox of the 'world upside down', illustrated with various examples by Cocchiara and Brelich (in the beginning, the sky was below and the earth was above, or else the primordial beings were huge and monstrous), and this is a theme which is allied to the notion that the beginnings of the world were originally formless and defective, or that it was, according to a theme typical of many cosmogonies,

---

[49] *Op. cit.*, p. 136 et seq.

characterized by a negative enumeration of things which were then absent but are now seen to exist. [50] Finally we must mention the aetiological character of many, if not of all, myths, the causal element of which (naturally considered apart from any anachronistic philosophizing) cannot be rejected in favour of the other elements. This is true also in the case of the apparently frivolous 'causes' of minor mythologies. [51]

Nevertheless, in spite of these criticisms, the value of the concept of participation seems quite clear. In fact—as we have seem—Lévy-Bruhl is able, by its means, to transcend the over intellectualist character of Frazer's 'sympathetic' magic, because the relations between things, expressed in participation, imply a communication with their essence—or even a consubstantiality. Thus participation becomes a true ontological category (being = participating), able to express many aspects of the religious feeling, even apart from primitive societies. In these latter it is able, for example, to express that African 'philosophy' which some scholars (like Tempels in his famous essay) [52] prefer to base on the equation, also typically African, 'to be = to have power'. [53] Thus the concept of a participation, and a totality, seems pertinent to these religious, sociological-religious and 'magic' experiences. Here it is not a question merely of the experiences of totemism or of 'nagualism' [54] but also, for example, of many aspects of African 'Manism', like the belief that the individual—whether alive or dead—belongs to the family or clan or tribe, this being a bond which remains valid beyond the variously 'participated' distinctions which separate the land of the living from the land of the dead.

We must note that the mystic and 'irrational' character which Lévy-Bruhl gives to the concept of participation was to be in accordance with the irrationalistic trends of quite another ideological origin (theological, or at least religious, in the context of the Protestant-Romantic tradition) which, as we shall see, found the essence of the

---

[50] The Babylonian *Enuma eliš* begins: 'When the sky above was not (yet) called by a name, nor the earth below...'.

[51] See further on, p. 127 et seq.

[52] *La philosophie bantoue*, Paris, 1949.

[53] Griaule and his followers, however, find among the Dogon of Mali a complex, metaphysical interpretation of the image: things are born from a seed which is also the symbol and image of future things. Cf. M. Griaule-G. Dieterlen, *Le renard pâle*, 1, Paris, 1965 and G. Calame-Griaule, *Ethnologie et langage, La parole chez les Dogon*, Paris, 1966.

[54] This term implies a feeling of comparticipation, or almost of identity, between a human being and an animal.

'religious' in the superhuman power of the divine and (like R. Otto) of the 'holy', that is, of the numinous (*tremendum* and *fascinans*), and of the 'totally different'. As we have seen, Lévy-Bruhl also speaks of 'the awareness accompanied by a peculiar and characteristic emotion, of the presence, and frequently of the action of an invisible power...'. This explains why scholars like Maurice Leenhardt and Gerardus Van der Leeuw have eagerly accepted Lévy-Bruhl's presentation of the problem, Leenhardt even denying any presence of causality in the 'lived' myths of primitive peoples whereas Van der Leeuw, in *Structure de la mentalité primitive* (1928) and *L'homme primitif et la religion* (1940), considers 'primitive' from a very favourable point of view, and, like Lévy-Bruhl, makes it a perennial element of man's nature. Lévy-Bruhl himself, in spite of the general trends of his philosophy, plainly rejected the evolutionistic dogma of the 'simple' character of primitive peoples, and even criticized the habit of 'considering as absurd or grotesque, or in any way inferior, anything which is not in accordance with our own customs...'. [55]

11. *Tylor and the theory of Animism. The notion of spirits and of the soul among primitive races*

We must now return to our account of Tylor's research. Since his book '*Primitive Culture*' [56] was published in 1871 the religious phenomenon which this scholar called 'Animism' and which he defined as a 'belief in spiritual beings', has been given great prominence. At the root of this phenomenon, which Tylor describes analytically and in great detail (the details being drawn, as was customary at that time, from the most diverse peoples and cultures), is the idea of the soul, or rather a particular idea of the soul, one that Tylor called a shadow soul or image soul. He believed that primitive man had succeeded in conceiving the notion of the soul (or, as we shall see, *this* notion) through experiences like dreams, trances and ecstasies, natural or artificially produced. The image seen in a dream, especially that of a person physically remote or dead, was understood by primitive man to be a 'double' of the physical person in question, a 'double' able to move about and even to cross the profound abyss which separates the living from the dead. Such a soul is also an 'image' soul because it exactly reproduces the person's features. Nevertheless, it has not the

---

[55] *Les cahiers*, cit., p. 209.
[56] *Primitive Culture. Researches into the Development of Mythology, Philosophy, Religion, Language, Art and Custom.*

physical body but only the etherial agility of this person and this characteristic, together with the twilight scene of its usual appearances, makes it also a shadow soul and a ghost soul. This image of the soul resembles a number of conceptions which survive today even among civilized peoples: we remember the characteristics of the *psyche* in the Homeric poems, the *psyche* which in fact appears as an *eidolon* or image, or as vapour, as an impalpable silhouette, agile and tremulous, always ready to withdraw to its vague and shadowy Underworld. This *psyche*, as in many primitive concepts, issues with the breath of a swooning person and returns to him when he recovers—although it must not be forgotten that Homer apparently perceives the *psyche* after it has left the body or in the very instant of this leaving. [57] With this ecstatic soul, sometimes subject to metempsychosis, which can be separated from and reintegrated with the body, are associated certain concepts of the Barbarian peoples of classical antiquity, people like the Thracians—and this capacity for separation and reintegration perhaps recurs in some 'divine men' of Greek lore, figures like Hermotimus, who were later on integrated in a more advanced, ideological system like the Pythagoraean, which still had some surviving primitive elements. Among some primitive peoples this ecstatic soul may also be described as an 'external' soul. This theme is well known, even in modern folklore: the vital principle, the soul of a personage, generally hostile or endowed with particular privilege, is hidden in a peripheral part of this person's body, in an external place or object or in an animal organism. Generally speaking, this external vital part of the person in question is found by the hostile action of someone who in one way or another has discovered the secret, and when this vital part, the seat of the soul, is discovered and attacked, its owner dies.

At other times, instead, some of the spirits attain the rank of local

---

[57] Erwin Rohde affirmed in his famous book *Psyche, Seelenkult und Unsterblickkeitsglaube der Griechen* the animist presuppositions of the most archaic Greek conceptions concerning the soul, and the Greek cult of the dead. It was published 1891-94 and reprinted several times; it had great influence over subsequent researches. See below, p. 143. Jane Harrison's book, *Prolegomena to the Study of Greek Religion*, was equally fond of anthropological references. It first appeared in 1903. Cf. also various studies by A. Dieterich (*Mutter Erde, Nekyia*) and by Murray, who supposes hypothetical evolutive phases of the Greek religion, basing his theories on the somewhat untrustworthy foundation of the hypotheses of the anthropological school. More recently, ethnological aspects of the Greek religion have been brought to light by Meuli ('Shaman' influences of the Balkan and Northern populations, which Dodds also has studied, in the context of a psychologistic methodology: see below, p. 143).

deities. They may be distinguished from the authentic deities of the polytheistic system by their localized character—the fact that they belong to a specific place, even when venerated far and wide. A polytheistic deity, instead, although having his own shrine or, more frequently, shrines, has in his own right a cosmic range and a 'national' cult.

Moreover, Tylor's animist theory concerns neither the shadow-soul alone, as a constituent element of the human person, nor the shadow souls of the dead alone. Animists believe that spirits people all nature, especially wild nature; their natural home is in the bush and the forest, the river or the lagoon, or in general the areas which surround or interrupt the cultivated lands. This, more than dreams or ecstatic states, is the true realm of the 'spirits', here primitive man enters with fear in his heart, or refrains from entering, because it is a place haunted by the spirits who own the water, vegetables and fruits found therein. If he enters he is careful to pay a sort of toll, which may serve as a ransom paid to the spirits, owners for whatever object (even if of little value) he presumes to take away. And the power of these spirits, frequently confused with the spirits of the dead, is very great. They inflict the most dreadful punishments on all who fall into their power and generally, after terrifying the invader, they slay him. They act invisibly, mysteriously, even if at times they are said to wear animal or phantasmogoric forms which the sacredness of the locality makes even more impressive and horrifying.

Already, a few years after the publication of Tylor's book, the limitations of the animist theory, even in an evolutionistic context, became obvious and for a two-fold reason. On the one hand it was found that Animism was not capable of covering the whole varied, complex and sometimes contradictory range of concepts relating to the soul, or to what corresponds more or less to this in primitive notions. On the other hand, Animism was not even able to explain those primitive conceptions which, based upon an experience of the 'power' animating nature (or better, of powers animating individual natural objects and phenomena, even phenomena of a majestic order) seemed incompatible with the Tylorian concept of a 'double' soul. We shall briefly indicate these two directions in which, still within the evolutionistic context or already outside this, Tylor's theories were contested.

As regards the soul, one of the founders of the historical-cultural school, Ankermann, pointed out the variety of primitive conceptions, which he divided into two clearly distinct possibilities: the image soul, more or less the same as that of Tylor's animistic theory, and the life soul (breath-soul or power-soul) associated with the breath and even more with the life force, warmth and the heart. Moreover, the notion of several souls or of several aspects or, better, hypostases of the soul, all of which after death have different destinies, is characteristic of primitive races. These destinies are either a sojourn with the Supreme Being in heaven (or, alternatively, in cases of grave unworthiness, in painful conditions elsewhere) or a return to the totemic 'reserve' of souls, or even a reincarnation in a new being, by means of the breath transmitted from mouth to mouth by the dying father to the son who bends over him.

12. *The theory of 'animatism' and dynamism. 'Power'*

But Tylor's animistic theories were to show their inadequacy also because they did not pay sufficient attention to beliefs in superhuman entities and powers which cannot be reduced to the concept of a natural soul or of a soul understood in the manist sense. In fact, R. R. Marett observes the presence of religious beliefs relating to divine manifestations in nature, or more precisely in individual natural occurrences, especially in the most impressive of these which had no need to depend on animistic presuppositions. For example, the divine presence animating a powerful whirlwind does not necessarily imply the notion that this phenomenon is the seat of an invisible and menacing soul in the animistic sense of the term; from the point of view of religious psychology it seemed to Marett possible, and often even probable, that the impressive and marvellous superhuman power seen in the whirlwind was thought to be inherent in it, and animating it. He therefore elaborated, in opposition to the theory of primitive animism, the theory of *pre-animism* or *'animatism'* which sees powers (or, according to E. S. Hartland, personal superhuman beings characterized by certain powers) [58] where Tylor saw spirits. Strictly speaking, animatism, which Marett thinks was typical of the beliefs of primitive races, although he does not exclude the presence of animistic conceptions also, does not imply the concept of a general or universal power animating all nature equally. Such a conception is rarely found among primitive peoples—not, for example, in some beliefs of the North American Indians, sometimes expressed by the terms *orenda, wakanda*

---

[58] Söderblom (see below p. 96) and J. W. Hauer, as well as R. Otto, shared some of these views.

or *manitu*.[59] Primitive people usually believe in superhuman phenomena animated by powers which reveal themselves individually, mysteriously and unexpectedly, in manifestations of particular violence or force which strike their imagination. This theory of animatism was supported by another series of observations which began with the well known discovery by Codrington (preceded in this by T. Cook, the famous navigator)[60] of the notion of superhuman power (*mana*) conceived by the inhabitants of Melanesia. Here, as we have already said, persons, animals or things, whether superior beings or mere tools and objects made by hand, which seem to possess a superior power, are considered to be vehicles of a force which dwells within them but comes—and this is significant—from personal beings, spirits or souls.

13. *Supreme Beings and the idea of God among primitive peoples*

During the same period a student of the Tylorian anthropological school, A. Lang, made a fresh contribution to this line of research with his book *The Making of Religion* (1898) in which he pointed out certain primitive conceptions much neglected by preceding scholars, conceptions which, after careful analysis, were seen to be irreducible either to pre-animistic or animistic beliefs. These beliefs were in beings which from that time on were to be called Supreme Beings, that is, divine figures that, in most primitive religions, represented a deity who, in his essential characteristics, did not differ much from conceptions of a monotheistic type. These Supreme Beings, conceived as creators of the world, sometimes referred to as 'Father' and generally associated with moral and tribal institutions (for example, with initiation ceremonies) were found among ethnological peoples of a fairly high degree of evolution (peoples that evolutionist ethnology classified as 'Barbarian') as well as among the most primitive 'savage' peoples, like the very ancient hunting tribes of Australia, Southern Africa, Far Eastern Siberia, peripheral South Eastern Asia, etc.

Lang had to engage in a memorable rispute to defend the originality and greater ethnological antiquity of these concepts concerning the

---

[59] This last term however indicates also the Supreme Being, or supernatural Beings in general. For a comparative study of these three terms, of which only the first signifies 'supernatural power' (the other two, like *wakan*, signify chiefly 'supernatural') see Å. Hultkrantz, *Les religions des Indiens primitifs de l'Amérique*, Stockholm, 1963, pp. 15-20.

[60] Cf. F. R. Lehmann, in *Festschrift W. Baetke*, Weimar, 1966, pp. 215-40, with a new linguistic analysis of the meanings of *mana* and an account of relative studies.

Supreme Being against the objections raised by the exponents of animism, from Tylor to Hartland. He pointed out that a spiritual, or rather an etherial character was by no means one of the characteristics of the Supreme Beings, who differed from the spirits (in the Tylorian sense) not only in their creative function, but also in their reality (which does not mean mere material reality) which made them very different from the phantom spirits of the animist world. Moreover, the Supreme Beings, who had clearly defined personalities, differed in this from the impersonal or vaguely discerned 'powers' of pre-animism. The differences were equally marked on the moral plane, as soon as the vigilant and coherent ethical quality of the motives for the behaviour of the Supreme Beings was seen to be in strident contrast with the unforeseeable irresponsibility of the 'powers' or the multiform contradictory and capricious variety of the spirits and 'souls'. This discovery dealt a mortal blow at the evolutionistic theory of the different origins of religious, as opposed to moral, concepts. Lang made further important contributions concerning the function which, in the evolution of religious thought, had been exercised by Animism and by what he called the monotheistic concept of the Supreme Being, each in its own way. The latter, which according to Lang might be of greater antiquity, was the source of the idea of God, fundamental for the whole successive course of religious history; to the former he attributed the merit of having given rise to speculations and conceptions relating to the soul, its nature and its destinies, that is, to another fundamental element in the religious experience of mankind. Once these two centres of interest, God and the Soul, had coalesced, religious thought would be able to fulfil, in the course of its complex history, the greatest aims of religious experiences.

But the study of the Supreme Beings and of their chronological and, more generally, historical connection with other types of religious belief was to be the principal though not the only task of the most eminent scholar of the Viennese 'historical-cultural school', Wilhelm Schmidt, who in 1912 initiated the series of *Der Ursprung der Gottesidee* with a lengthy treatise on the Supreme Being, in the context of the new methodological orientation of ethnology, in vigorous opposition to the generic theories of the evolutionists. [61] The historical-cultural school rejected that *a-priori* schematic interpretation of the

---

[61] Some years previously Schmidt, originally trained in linguistics, had founded the review *Anthropos*.

evolutionary processes which presupposed a straightforward and homogeneous evolution from the rude and 'simple' to the complex and 'superior' and tried to reconstruct the effective and multiple historical processes from which, they thought, were derived (in different times and places) the various cultures. The belief in a Supreme Being, characterized by the above-mentioned attributes of morality and creativity, was found by Schmidt and his collaborators in the most ancient civilizations, those of hunters and collectors, in all four ethnological continents. The Supreme Being was found also in other civilizations and almost universally in the ethnological world (except in the case of the '*Zweiklassenkultur*'). Nevertheless, Schmidt found that it was in the most primitive civilizations that the figure of the Supreme Being was most clearly delineated and had a marked monotheistic character. Schmidt's conclusions, developed and collected in his vast work on the origin of the idea of God, were later supported by the results of ethnological research undertaken under his guidance by Gusinde and Koppers among the most primitive tribes of the Tierra del Fuego, by Schebesta among the Pygmies of equatorial Africa and Far South-Eastern Asia; cf. also the research by Lebzelter in South Western Africa. All the ethnological studies relating to peoples who were already extinct or fast disappearing in Australia, Tasmania, Southern Africa, California, the lands of the Eskimos and the Algonquin Indians, of the peripheral Asiatic zones and the great nomadic civilizations of Asia, etc. were subjected to a most careful re-examination. But, as we have already observed, this enquiry, on the part of Schmidt and Koppers, was sometimes marred by over schematic (even if technically elaborated and consequent) analyses and forced interpretations of the available material.

The problems raised by the research of Schmidt and other members of the 'historical-cultural school' were treated by other students of religious history from more or less divergent points of view and were at times the subject of heated debates. One of the most eminent of these scholars was Raffaele Pettazzoni, who in 1922 dedicated a whole book to the problem of the Supreme Being (*Dio. L'essere celeste nelle credenze dei popoli primitivi*) in the context of a historical-religious research which, beginning with the religions of primitive races, set out to study also the polytheistic religions of the ancient world and the great monotheistic creeds. Pettazzoni proposed to trace the vicissitudes of the notion of God, in order to discern the dynamism of this concept in the history of the various civilizations and situations of mankind. In fact his research ended with the first of the three books which he had planned, that is, with the volume concerning the Supreme Being in primitive cultures. In this first phase Pettazzoni insisted on the celestial character of the Supreme Being, as conceived by ethnological peoples. In his opinion, this notion of a heavenly Supreme Being was founded not on aetiological speculation about the origin of things but an a mythical apperception of the sky, in its immensity and, in particular, in its all-seeing power, associated with its diurnal and nocturnal illumination. The ethical qualities of the Supreme Being, understood as observer, judge and castigator of moral and social transgressions, were also explained by Pettazzoni in relation to the luminous, heavenly and all-seeing power of the Celestial Being. During the years that followed Pettazzoni continued his research concerning the Supreme Beings of primitive peoples and their connection with the notion of divinity in the polytheistic and monotheistic religions, as well as concerning a particular attribute of the Supreme Being and of other divine figures, an attribute of a 'luminous' nature: omniscience (*L'onniscienza di Dio*, 1955 and *L'essere supremo nelle religioni primitive*, 1957).

As regards the primitive notion of a Supreme Being, Pettazzoni revised his earlier interpretation (which was too exclusively uranistic) and tended to distinguish several types, conditioned by varying cultural situations. In his opinion, among the most primitive civilizations of hunters the Supreme Being was thought of mainly as a Lord of the Chase and a lord of animals, and sometimes coincided with that figure which was so typical of many primitive mythologies, the 'trickster'—Demiurge, a morally ambiguous personage, connected with the animal world. Later on—according to Pettazzoni—appeared figures of Supreme Beings which were closer to the description of these personages found in Schmidt's historical-cultural ethnology. But the idea of these beings also were essentially conditioned by the type of civilization into which it was integrated, and in them the uranian element gradually became more and more pronounced. This affected, mythologically, some of their principal attributes, like that of omniscience and their association with ethical principles. There were also—in Pettazzoni's opinion—some Supreme Beings who were feminine and maternal, like the Eskimos' Sedna, the Mistress of marine animals and of that watery world which determines the nature of fishermen's civilizations whereas, in *milieux* culturally affected by agricultural activities and chthonic interests, Mother Earth became the Supreme Being. [62]

14. *Myths about the origins of the world, in the most ancient civilizations*

Another point of extreme importance in the question of the Supreme Beings is that of their connection with myths, and in particular with myths about the origins of the world of man and of society. In this connection the historical-cultural school, and other scholars too, like Söderblom and Radin, [63] tend to insist on the aetiological motivations which may have inspired the concept of the Supreme Being as creator (in the absolute sense—sometimes even as creator *ex nihilo*, as in certain North American beliefs—or in a relative sense) [64] as well as

---

[62] With regard to this amplification and cultural-historical relativization of the figure and concept of the Supreme Being, one must, however, observe that it produces objections and difficulties, because it renders more generic and indeterminate that phenomenological and religious-historical category of what ethnologists have until now, with good justification, agreed to call 'Supreme Beings'. In other words, the Supreme Being, as Lang and subsequent scholars have found him in primitive beliefs, is not just any divine or superhuman Being, who, for one reason or another, and with varying characteristics, may be described as 'supreme', or most important in this or that primitive religion or mythology. There are a number of beings, or even of divine entities, some even abstract or potentially impersonal, who are supreme in their own way, but who do not present that typical figure which, with substantially analogous characteristics, is found among many primitive peoples, beginning with the most ancient, and to which has been by general accord given the name of 'Supreme Being'. This term is certainly conventional and anyone may use it or discard it at his will, or attach new meanings to it, but this does not alter the fact that the Supreme Beings, in the sense used by Lang and his followers, especially those of the cultural-historical school, and by most of the others, like, for example, the North American ethnologists, have a physionomy that cannot be confused with figures like those of the 'trickster' Demiurge (of which we shall have more to say later) or Mother Earth. These latter present a totally different *ethos*, type and history, even if one admits the possibility of reciprocal influences. As regards the 'lord of the animals', it is doubtful whether this personage is sufficiently unitary and coherent to be able to represent the religious experience of the primitive hunters. One can, in fact, distinguish a 'lord of the animals' who has an autonomous personality and is distinguished by his pre-eminence in the world of nature and of animals over which he rules (but in this case he generally rules in one way or another also over the world of human beings)—and so we have a figure who may be comparable with the Supreme Being in the specific sense already described. But there is also a 'lord of the animals' who is only a 'divine' hypostasis of the animal species in question, or of several species grouped by a common association with hunting (like the Eskimo Sedna). In more recent civilization a 'Destiny-God' or 'Cosmic-God' is also quite different.

[63] *Monotheism among Primitive Peoples*, 1st ed. 1924; 2nd ed. 1954.

[64] As, for example, in the widely diffused theme of the Earth diver in the primordial sea (or of the Flood). The Earth diver was a collaborator (sometimes even

insisting on the primitive races' elaboration of a cosmogonic mythology. Primordial men, looking around them in the world, must all have asked themselves the 'why' and 'how' of things and given substantially the same answers about the creation, at least in those civilizations (and that means most) which had already conceived a Supreme Being who was the creator, or a Demiurge. Other scholars, taking a different view, insist upon the emotional, even irrational, mythological or existential character of religious experience among primitive peoples. For some of them, especially those most influenced by positivist and evolutionist theories, primitive mythology is fundamentally illogical, erroneous, fantastic and arbitrary—in fact an expression of 'primitive stupidity' as was once observed by Preuss, who nevertheless contributed much to our knowledge of primitive psychology and mythology.

Others consider that primitive mythology, even in its irrationality, is the living and sentient, and therefore authentic, expression of a way of perceiving, or rather understanding and making contact with reality, and above all with that decisive phase of all being, the time of the origins of the world, when all those things were created which are now inseparable from our lives and condition it, giving it a meaning. In this line of thought are the studies of Adolf Jensen, [65] who follows the interpretative trends of Leo Frobenius, [66] for whom, however, the mythology of primitive man was to be understood more as cosmological (that is, as a mythical interpretation and vision of the real world) than as cosmogonical, that is, as an interpretation of its origins. This latter position, according to Frobenius, already shows the influence of a way of thinking that seeks to find explanations, a way of thinking which would be alien to mythical thought. It is true that Jensen accepts explicitly, as regards the primitive concept of a Supreme Creative Being, the viewpoint of Lang and Schmidt, that is, that it expresses the answer to a question 'why'? put by primitive peoples about the first beginnings of things, and that in fact this is an amythical concept, in the sense that the process by means of which the Supreme Being creates the world is generally marked by simplicity, immediacy and a detachment very different from the complicated, sometimes adventurous, forceful and, at least to our eyes, grotesque procedure

---

a rival) of the Supreme Being who created the great earth itself from a few grains of mud the diver brings to him.

[65] *Mythus und Kult bei Naturvölkern*, Wiesbaden, 1951; *Das religiöse Weltbild einer früher Kultur*, in various editions.

[66] *Die Weltanschauung der Naturvölker*, Weimar, 1898. *Das Zeitalter des Sonnengottes*, I, Berlin, 1904.

of other primordial beings associated with the origins of things (for example, the 'trickster' Demiurge, or the *dema* deities of whom we shall speak later on).

As regards Mircea Eliade, [67] we have already mentioned his theory about the world at the time of its origins. According to him it was a world full of plenitude, integrity and sacred powers, the *illud tempus* in which are placed the persons and actions of primordial beings, beginning with the Supreme Being. One cannot say that this interpretation, in spite of its mainly existential significance, implies really a criticism of the attribution to primitive peoples and their cosmogonies of an aetiological way of thinking: there is an ontological causality (rooted in the actively creative period of the origins of the world) of all that belongs to primordial times and to their indescribable sacredness and richness, a causality which ritual periodically re-enacts in order to re-charge the world and to restore its activity and life, which would otherwise disappear, leaving it impoverished and inanimate. [68]

To a certain extent Pettazzoni follows both these tendencies: the tendency to reduce primitive thought to a 'mythical apperception' conditioned by the historical and psychological circumstances of primitive humanity (although it expresses a universal and essential human sense, the 'religious') and the other tendency to confer an 'existential truth', quite different from the truth of reason, on primitive mythology, because this latter, according to Bronislaw Malinowski, contains the motivation of certain ways of behaviour, ways of living and ways of facing the world on the part of individuals and societies that believe in it. Pettazzoni criticizes an anti-mythological mentality characteristic of all those scholars who in one way or another decry myths, seeing in them only childish imaginings. On the other hand it is undeniable that he himself sometimes adopts this way of thinking, when he makes an absolute distinction between the two truths, existential truth and the truth of reason. In conclusion we may say that the most prudent position seems to be that of viewing all primitive mythologies, and particularly all cosmogonies, as the result of a total human activity which includes emotional attitudes, rational motives

---

[67] *Traité d'histoire des religions*, 1st ed., Paris, 1949, and various other works, including *Le mythe de l'éternel retour*, 1st ed., Paris, 1949; *Aspects du mythe*, Paris, 1963 and, concerning initiatory rites, *Naissances mystiques*, 4th ed., Paris, 1959.

[68] For some objections to the general validity of this scheme see the Author's *Teogonie e cosmogonie*, Rome, 1960, pp. 153 et sqq. and below, pp. 184 et seqq.

and existential elements determined by our common human nature, as well as by specific historical, cultural and social circumstances.

15. *The question of monotheism*

Another theme which has lately come to the forefront of our discussion of these studies on the Supreme Beings is that which concerns the question of monotheism, with its relation to primitive beliefs about these beings, and polytheism. As we have said, the attitude of the evolutionist schools to this problem was clear: whereas primitive religions were in turn classified under the terms Animism, Manism, Fetishism and pre-Animism, variously combined and listed, polytheism, typical of the great civilizations of the ancient world, was said to have appeared at a later stage, and monotheism was said to have evolved from this at the culminating point of the religious evolution of mankind. In other words, the spirits, 'souls' or ancestors (in which the 'powers' were concentrated) became transformed, with enriched personalities, into the gods of classical polytheism, and from these, by a process of selection, came the exalted single god of monotheism.

This presentation received a double blow, from Lang's research and from the historical school. The Supreme Being, believed in by many primitive peoples, could not be reduced to the 'souls', or the ancestors, or the 'powers' and therefore introduced an unexpected element which had not been considered in evolutionist theories. Moreover, historical thought discerned, and distinguished from one other, periods, cultures and religious forms in the thought of 'savage' peoples, and so necessitated a reconstruction of the genesis and development of religious phenomena which was historically differentiated and very dissimilar to that resulting from evolutionist studies. The upholders of the historical-cultural method, moreover, believed they could find, in the most archaic cultures, a particular pre-eminence of the figure of the Supreme Being, in which all the other beings and superhuman powers became essentially reassumed or to which they appeared subordinated. For this reason, first with Lang and later on with Schmidt, many of those scholars did not hesitate to describe the religious beliefs of the most archaic civilizations as monotheistic. The rise of Animism and Manism, like that of polytheism, came at a later phase. This interpretation was opposed by Pettazzoni who, while acknowledging a partial typological and historical continuity between the Supreme Beings of primitive thought, the 'high gods' of polytheism and the one God of monotheism, nevertheless maintained that monotheism was only to be found in the great religions of the Old Testament and Judaism, of Mazdaeism, Christianity and Islam, and that the attribution of a monotheistic character to primitive religion would imply an error of historical perspective. Monotheism, for Pettazzoni, presupposes a pre-existent polytheism, not because it evolves from this but because, on the contrary, it appears as a revolutionary movement whenever a prophet or a religious leader rejects all other gods in order to affirm the One.

The discussion about the 'monotheism' of primitive peoples, especially in the most ancient civilizations, seems to have suffered more than its due from terminological confusions and obscurities, inherent in the too systematic and 'civilized' aspect of the term, which therefore lends itself to objections on the plane of historical realities. This does not mean that we must agree with Pettazzoni's assertion that monotheism *always* presupposes a revolution against polytheism, for such a theory tends to assimilate two elements which are quite distinct from each other, that of a revolutionary character in monotheism and that, more compatible with a prudent interpretation of the facts, of a latent and explicit presence in monotheism, from the Old Testament and Mazdaeism onwards, of a critical attitude towards other religious of the world, which moreover are not always only polytheistic but may also be any religious cult or magic practice, which seems to rival, or to be incompatible with, the 'true worship' of God. In short, it is not merely the arguments against the 'many gods' which form the subject of the preaching of the great exponents of monotheistic religion. For all these reasons it is inopportune to restrict monotheism to a monotheist-polytheist dialectic like that set up by the revolutionary theory of monotheism proposed by Pettazzoni. Still worse is the interpretation presupposed by those scholars who believe that the antithesis: monotheism-polytheism excludes every possible religious alternative, as well as other eventual complications. On the other hand it seems prudent to renounce a term which seems too rigid when applied to the religious studied by ethnologist. This does not alter the fact that the Supreme Being tends to subordinate to himself other beliefs and conceptions. These even include, in various civilizations, that lively and chaotic world of spirits and fetishes which, as in the religions of the Guinean and Congolese regions, people the lives of individuals and groups and seem, for this very reason, to have little in common with monotheism.

16. *The Supreme Being and his Sitz im Leben*

These considerations lead us to the question of the significance of the worship of the Supreme Being in every day life (which however must not be considered as being something quite apart from the modules of that time of the origins of the world, in which our present day realities were created). In other words, what is his *Sitz im Leben*? One of the characteristics of the Supreme Being has apparently been a certain inactivity, or at least a certain distinterestedness in the actual events of this world, and this remoteness seems reflected also in the rarity of organized religious manifestations in honour of this figure, whereas other manifestations of a more spontaneous nature are very frequent. Söderblom [69] and Van der Leeuw [70] have both insisted on this aspect of the Supreme Being among primitive peoples. Söderblom sees the Supreme Being as a 'Primal Cause', a Creator, able to satisfy aetiological requirements but not a suitable subject for worship. Van der Leeuw sees in him a feature which distinguishes him sharply from Yahweh in the Old Testament, who shows instead supreme activity and initiative during the whole course of history. This contrast is certainly exaggerated, but is nevertheless to some extent valid, especially if we bear in mind the effective discrepancy between a religious experience so strongly coloured by historicity and eschatology (even if the eschatology is 'earthly') as that of the Old Testament and the static (or non-existent) view of history and its evolution held by primitive peoples. Their religious interests, while not completely devoid of eschatological values, were above all in the realities of daily life and in those 'origins' from which, as we have said, derive the motivating and propulsive force of our world today.

Having said this, one must admit that there are some intimate historical and phenomenological links between the Supreme Beings of primitive man and the God of monotheism. One must therefore try to understand this detached, sometimes inactive, character of many of these Supreme Beings. This is not true of all, or even perhaps of most Supreme Beings, since it is well known that among the most ethnologically ancient peoples, as well as among some of the most advanced, the Supreme Being at times intervenes forcefully, either to punish

---

[69] *Das Werden des Gottesglaubens*, Leipzig, 1926. He sees the Supreme Being as the Cause, the Creator, who satisfies the requirements of causality, but is not a suitable subject for worship.

[70] *La religion dans son essence et ses manifestation*, Paris, 1948 and in particular *Die Struktur der Vorstellung des sog. Höchstens Wesens*, in *Archiv für Religionswissenschaft*, 29 (1931), p. 79 et sqq.

transgression of the tribal laws or for reasons which primitive man found mysterious and inexplicable, and which are not unconnected with the sublimity, transcendence, sovereign power and mysteriousness [71] of the Supreme Being himself. On the other hand, where a detached and eventually inactive nature of the Supreme Being is evident, this may be explained in various ways. First of all, it may depend on the importance eventually assigned to beliefs and practices of another type, which relegate the Supreme Being into the background. Or it may happen that his figure suffers from assimilations or syncretic associations with extraneous figures, like the Ancestor. It may also be that his very sublimity tends to set him apart from the events and needs of common life, which however often inspire prayers addressed to him or even, especially in the event of the death of someone dear, recriminations or, on the contrary, expressions of resignation, sometimes of a vaguely fatalistic character. At other times his very goodness will make the people feel sure of him and so, to a certain extent, render his cult superfluous, whilst capricious spirits or even, in primitive religions of a dualist kind, cruel and malign beings who have power over life and death, need to be propitiated by a cult. Finally, another motive, on which Pettazzoni has rightly insisted, although in the context of a doubtful 'magical' interpretation of the creative powers of the Supreme Being, derives from the belief that any further intervention by him, in the affairs of a world ordered according to certain valid and acknowledged principles, could only be disquieting, or even imperil the stability of the cosmos itself, as dangerous as the disquieting intervention of a magician in every day life.

One must set aside the 'magic' aspect of this interpretation, since the creative power of the Supreme Being is not to be compared with the power of a magician in our world, who does not create or evoke anything from nothing, but rather magically manipulates or transfers what already exists (see above, ch. II, p. 48). Therefore the creative and primordial character of the Supreme Being, which forms the foundation of reality, may be partly responsible for his remoteness from every day life, as also for his apparent inactivity. One must add that this theme, so frequently found in primitive myths, of the

---

[71] It has been pointed out that in certain cases (for example, in West Africa) it is the most extraordinary events that are attributed to the Supreme Being, just because they can be attributed only to the most sublime and mysterious Person; the most customary events also which express a natural law of which the Supreme Being is the source, are attributed to him.

withdrawal of the Supreme Being after the events at the time of the origins of the world, contains two elements, first of all the creative and transcendent nature of this Being as a Founder of the world and secondly certain ethical motivations regarding a primitive failure or sin on man's part, which caused the withdrawal of the Supreme Being. This detachment of the Supreme Being does not imply a total withdrawal from our world, and so is very different from the withdrawal of other primaeval Beings, such as the 'cultural hero', the founder of civilized life, sometimes identified with the Ancestor, or the Trickster-Demiurge, often animalesque (cf. the Coyote of North American myths or the Crow of the myths of the North Pacific peoples). These figures (especially the last named) emerge at the time of the world's origins, sometimes as collaborators of the Supreme Being, sometimes as his rivals, in order to organize or, more often, to transform and 'complete' (and often to damage) the world. Anyway the activity of the Trickster-Demiurge is entirely restricted to the time of the world's origins. For these reasons, to appeal today to the Coyote (or, worse, to worship it) would be senseless, whereas to appeal to the Supreme Being, even in a spontaneous and informal way (which does not mean a manner without traditions or rules) is a custom still very much alive in primitive civilizations. It is found also in the form of that 'first offering' which—although with varying psychological *nuances* or motivations—represents an acknowledgment of the valid sovereignity of the Supreme Being, or of the lord of the forest or the lord of animals (when offerings are made to them and not, as elsewhere, to the dead) over all things, life itself and the means of life. On the other hand, rites performed in spirit cults in animistic civilizations are very differently conditioned and involved, in accordance with the particular nature and power of the intervention required of these beings. We shall speak later on of other aspects of the worship of the Supreme Being, connected with prayer, sacrifice and initiatory rites.

17. *The primordial dema divinities and their mythology*

The particular trend of contemporary ethnology which is called 'cultural morphology' shows a special propensity to study the inferior world of primitive cultures. Its chief exponent was Adolf Jensen [72] who, through his theory of the *paideuma*, returned to the interpretations of Leo Frobenius. The latter, at the beginning of this century,

---

[72] See above, p. 92 n. 65.

after a series of studies conducted according to the then new historical-cultural method, was dissatisfied with what seemed to him an exaggeratedly statistical procedure, in the definition of areas and cycles of culture, and turned towards a dynamic, organic, psychological interpretation of the various civilizations and of their way of viewing the world, according to their own *paideuma*, that is, education, which meant an ideological complex or a conception of world different in each case. Spiritual life, as revealed in ritual, art, ideology, and especially in mythology, is therefore the source and supreme expression of a culture. The analysis of the interior world of what Frobenuis considered to be the two chief African cultures is well known. There was the culture he called 'Ethiopian', partly corresponding to that formerly known as West African, and the 'Camitic' culture, two types which he contrasted with each other almost symmetrically, under diverse aspects—from the shape of their houses to their type of economy, their way of perceiving space and human settlements and even their *ethos* and art—a characterization which however is based on the interior spiritual life, their own *paideuma*.

Jensen also insists on culture being a 'way of looking at the world', that is, a spiritual phenomenon which reveals or, to use a key term of his interpretation, 'expresses' itself in a complex, or cultural cycle (an expression which he continues to defend). The elements which express a civilization and its fundamental intuitions are for Jensen above all the elements of its spiritual culture, since these are more likely to correspond to the innermost factors of a civilization and show a greater stability as well as a lesser degree of communicability—this view being held also by our contemporary ethnologists. On the other hand, objects and customs relating to material life (and also, according to other scholars, social institutions and structures) may more easily become confused and descend to the level of pure 'utilization', devoid of any meaning truly expressive of a civilizations' peculiar and inspiring values. It is also true that even in the sphere of the spiritual life, Jensen finds no lack of periods when the expressive power of the cultural elements is reduced to a mere utilitarian and profane function. All this prompts Jensen to seek, in the constant elements of a *paideuma*, a cultural tradition, an idea or myth that has inspired it.

Jensen's analysis is directed with particular attention, and in harmony with these principles, to a culture, or cultural cycle, which in some ways corresponds to what, at the beginning of his historical-ethnological research, Frobenius called malayo-nigritic' culture, and which Jensen proposes to call 'lunar'. The *paideuma* of this culture has a characteristic vision of the world, in which there is a special class of superhuman beings who existed at the time of the origins of the world and of mankind. These are the *dema* deities, which Jensen thus describes by a name drawn from the Indonesian cultural *milieux*. They are gods, or, better, primordial figures, partly human in appearance, who in a remote past, at the beginning of man's history, suffered a peculiar fate. They had been treacherously slain or sacrificed (cf. the famous myth of the maiden Hainuwele of the island of Ceram, Eastern Indonesia) and their buried bodies turned into alimentary plants, especially those tuberose plants which, according to Jensen, are indispensable to the economy of the civilizations of primitive agriculturalists. The myth of Hainuwele refers to this belief. The 'way of looking at the world' of these primitive agriculturists of the tropical zones was then founded on the recognition of a profound connection between death and life: primordial death produced the alimentary plants which are in a certain sense the 'life' of the farming community. Consequently man, when he takes hold of life, that is, of the alimentary plants which support life, becomes at the same time capable of generating more life while he himself is destined to die, with the prospect of entering an underworld realm of the dead still ruled over by that deity, or one of those deities who were the protagonists of the primordial episode of slaughter.

Jensen proposes to call this mythology, supposed to explain the concept of life and the fundamental rite of the religion of primitive agriculturists (or better 'planters') a 'lunar' religion, because of the connection between the *dema* divinities and the moon, and he believes he can find it, in scattered survivals, in the American, Asian and African continents. Jung has sought to explain it psycho-analytically. He thinks the myth of Hainuwele expresses one of the archetypal elements present in the psyche, that of the 'divine Maiden', an archetypal element to which Jungian 'depth psychology' does not assign any historical origin and which, although the moment of its introduction into the psychical inheritance of mankind remains mysterious, even today constitutes—in Jung's opinion— a recurring element of mythology, as in that referred to by Jensen, and of the imagination and dreams even of modern man. Jensen keeps well away from these psychological explanations and, as we have said, explains in a historical-cultural sense the ideology based on the *dema* deities and their savage myth, connecting it with the 'lunar' culture of the primitive cultivators of tuberose plants, that is, with an economic activity and also, and even more, with a conception of life very different from those expressed in later cultures characterized by different interpretations of the world. These expressed themselves in myths like the 'Promethean' story of the theft of seeds from heaven by a primordial Demiurge. Jensen suggests that this last concept may be found in truly agricultural civilizations, founded on the plough and cereal crops.

Naturally, in accordance with what we have already observed, these interpretations of Jensen's differ from presuppositions based on the determining influence of a natural *milieu* or of an economy. On the contrary, Jensen believes it is spiritual culture, with its coherence and interior life, which best expresses the soul of a civilization, including also those economic activities, like agriculture itself (and, for Hahn, the breeding of livestock) which originally had a function which was not utilitarian or productive but ritualistic. It is true that this theory, sometimes tinged with a certain irrationality (Jensen is rather unwilling to accept this term) and presenting a civilization and its mythology as to some extent incommunicable and monadic, seems somewhat exaggerated, provoking the criticism of other scholars who, although by no means influenced by economic determinism, are perhaps more aware than Jensen of inter-cultural communications and inter-minglings, and of the variety of those factors, also economic and sociological, which intervene in the history of civilizations. But these civilizations do not thereby cease to be human phenomena, bound together by the inventiveness and variety of eventual human options. [73]

---

[73] Other, partial, criticisms of Jensen's interpretation have come from other scholars (such as Schmitz) who have pointed out that the theme of a violent act performed to obtain the means of life appears also in civilizations different from those of the tropical cultivators of bulbous plants, and that among peoples practising this form of economic activity there are also different myths (for example, of the Promethean type), whereas the types of agriculture dependent on cereals and the planting of tubers co-exist among various peoples, making it difficult to classify them by simple cultural-economic criteria. These objections, on the other hand, are exposed to the possibility of being criticized for over generalization, as for example when they claim to identify the two myths, of Prometheus and of Hainuwele, because the theme of the violent (or cunning) act performed for the acquiring of economic wealth (and even cosmic benefits, like rain or sunlight or a moderation of this) or of immortality or fire, etc. is an archaic theme (one must remember the myths of the 'trickster' demiurge or of the cultural hero we have already referred to) and nothing authorizes us to confuse it with the theme of the *dema* divinity, whose dead body nourished the alimentary plants. Jensen was right to point out the importance of this theme, even if he himself probably exaggerated it, not only by making it the exclusive theme of a specific culture but also by connecting it substantially with phenomena like head-hunting and ritual cannibalism, which perhaps have many and various motiva-

18. *Polytheism and cosmological speculation in the more 'advanced' civilizations*

The civilizations which are generally called 'higher' or 'superior' cultures are very different from those studied by ethnologists. Most of them are characterized by typically polytheistic conceptions, by speculations of a systematic type (cosmogonies of a pre-philosophical nature, a propensity for chronology, genealogy, dynasties and history), by specific social institutions (monarchies based on territorial possession, specialized priests, officials, classes and corporations, sometimes feudalism and slavery) and at times by specific economic activities (agriculture of a more advanced type). All these elements seem to conspire to create a kind of civilization which is not unlike those primitive eneolithic cultures which (at the dawn of the great civilizations of Near Asia, and later on in India, China and Egypt) constitute an essential stage in the development of our cultural history. [74]

As regards the spiritual life of these peoples and cultures we must pay special attention to polytheism, with its fondness for the proliferation of temples and priesthoods, its presentation of doctrine and cosmological speculation, and an organization which extends from the cosmos and the 'departmental' and hierarchically ordered gods who rule it to the territory itself, represented and parcelled out by the king, and to the city, wherever it exists, with its sacral, sociological and urbanistic organization (cf. the cities of ancient Mesopotamia and Egypt).

Polytheism is therefore not a very archaic phenomenon in the history of mankind; it has a two-fold historical role: in the multiplication of the cities and their numerous particular gods, and in the development of a cosmic concept which organizes the various divine 'departments' of the world. Other functions of polytheism, still on the political-cosmic plane, are seen in the specialized organization of society (divine patronage of special activities, capacities, etc.). In any

---

tions and cultural associations. Moreover, Jensen refuses to connect primitive planters' activity (and the ideology of the lunar civilization, or the myth of the *dema* deity) with the 'matriarchate', whereas Schmidt, even in his last work on this subject, links together the matriarchate, cults of a feminine and chthonic type and the feminine invention of agricultural activity (that is, of elementary agriculture).

[74] Ethnological regions interested in this type of culture are instead Africa (the neo-Soudanese and 'Rhodesian' cultures), Polynesia and above all Central America, where one may even speak of 'literary' civilizations, and Peru. These last named cultures, together with those of the Sudanese Kingdoms, are, even if for different reasons, on the periphery of the properly so called ethnological sphere.

case, the central characteristic is that of a divine and cosmic system which confers upon polytheism, even when most chaotic and most conditioned by its origins in complex events, the character of a pantheon, in which a supreme god, *primus inter pares*, supervises, with the collegial assistance of the other gods, the correct 'departmental' ordering of the world. Polytheism has also a cosmological and cosmogonic character, because of which the gods, without of course being what the old naturistic interpretation of natural mythology presupposed (i.e. personifications of natural events), are associated with the various spheres of reality, not in an exclusive way but consistently with their clearly defined individual anthropomorphic personalities.[75]

The cosmic nature of the polytheist gods, and of polytheism itself as a system, explains why, in these more advanced civilizations, cosmogony is at the same time a theogony and a theomachy. One must remember the theomachic version of the old theme of the violent separation of the sky and earth (understood as a primordial pair), and the myth of Rangi and Papa of Polynesian cosmogony,[76] or of Odudua and Obatala of Yoruban myths. These stories are very different from the primitive cosmogonies of the type to which we have already referred.

In the course of history (which sees religious and cosmological speculation develop in diverse and complex forms, with the elaboration of a pantheon and of a mythology) an evolutionistic interpretation would certainly be out of place. We must admit that the Supreme Being of primitive peoples shows a certain partial historical and phenomenological similarity to the Supreme Being of polytheistic pantheons. In these we recognize the special privileged status of this figure of religious belief which has accompanied men through the most diverse phases of their cultural history and so shows a chronological as well as a geographical universality (with some well known exceptions). There are also traces in polytheistic periods of a survival of the typical figures of Animism, or Manism, or of the *dema* deities, etc. even if elements of these figures are perhaps integrated in polytheistic figures. We see this in the 'trickster' qualities of a Prometheus or a Hermes, the latter being a polytheistic god known to history and not a Being active only in the beginning of the world. And we remember the animistic qualities of minor figures such as nymphs. As

---

[75] Cf. A. Brelich, *Der Polytheismus*, in *Numen* VII (1960), p. 133 et sqq.

[76] This myth, in the struggle of the young gods against the Sky-God, prefigures the Hesiodic myth of Uranus.

regards the survival of the *dema* deities, Jensen seems to have been over eager to recognize them in divine figures of more recent polytheistic cultures, figures like Persephone, subjects of myths very different from that of the buried *dema* and of the maiden Hainuwele of the Ceram myth. In short, the polytheistic gods are very far from being the continuation or evolution of the former spirits of nature, or of the dead, enhanced in status and importance.

On the other hand, an important role in the formation of the ideological-spiritual character of the most advanced cultures, and of polytheism itself, as well as of cosmogonic speculation, may be seen, at least hypothetically, in the so-called 'megalithic' cultural system, the special object of the research of Heine-Geldern. We refer to that series of primitive 'monumental' remains (*dolmen, menhir*, mounds, etc.) which seem to denote a cultural system extending from Northern and Western Europe to Northern Africa, Near and Southern Asia, the South Seas and the Far East. These megalithic monuments, the 'seats' or 'supports', of the souls, were intended to ensure the immortality of the dead and also the perennity in efficacy of the sacrifices of animals and hecatombs offered in that place, all associated with the cult of the dead and—perhaps—the promotion of agrarian fertility. Their funerary, chthonic and fertility associations are often difficult to discern but perhaps less difficult to understand, for they show a particular sensibility to cosmic and mythical genealogical elements; there are even megalithic monuments which bear some reference —as it would seem—to the fecundity of the sky and earth, those cosmic progenitors already present in the most ancient cosmogonies but destined to form the foundation of the theogonies and cosmogonies of advanced civilizations. These monuments in which an astral reference may sometimes be traced (for example, in calendarial and commemorative stelae) are often monuments in the strict etymological sense of the term, 'records', and so testify to a new perception of time, of chronology, of history and even of genealogy (with which is associated their funerary and 'fecund' character, because of the well known connection between ancestors and human and vegetable fertility). They tend to express a dynastic way of thought and a regal ideology, combined with a regal love of monumental records, in the two-fold sense of being a lasting and commemorative record and a grandiose structure. So, this regal ideology appears to be one of the primal causes of the primitive perception of history, understood as a division into dynastic periods. Moreover, this dynastic sequence is connected, through genealogical speculation, with cosmogonic events, from which is derived, as we see in well known Polynesian examples, the antiquity of the dynasties, descending from the cosmic and divine Beings of primordial times.

To return to the 'High Cultures', cosmogony, with its polytheistic associations, receives much attention in these cultures and incorporates a number of more ancient themes which it develops along a line of its own. We have already referred to the myth of the sky and earth, progenitors of the gods and of the world, a myth already present, in anthropomorphic and highly mythologized forms, in some ethnological cultures (even if not the most ancient) and which apparently came from a centre of diffusion in tropical Asia. This concept is however different from, and less archaic than, that of the sky which is conceived as a person or as a cosmic element, detached and exalted above the earth in order to make room for vegetable life and life of man. Another characteristic theme of the cosmogonies of the 'higher' cultures is that of the 'cosmic egg', which opened to let out the sky, the earth and the sun—in fact, the world itself. This theme, sometimes referring to analogous objects, is found in Polynesia (a shell) and in the Soudan (a gourd). A similar theme is that of the primordial cosmic giant. These mythical themes or *motifs*, not necessarily whole or complete myths, are re-adopted in the higher civilizations and interpreted by philosophic-mythical speculation, which covers religious and human interests in a vaster field than that covered by the scientific cosmology of more recent thought. They are found in Greece (Uranus and Gaia, and the cosmic 'orphic' egg), Mesopotamia (An-ki, sky-earth of the Sumerians and Babylonians), India (Purusha, the primordial man of ancient Indian speculation,—and again the cosmic egg), China (Yin-Yang, the two metaphysical and cosmological principles of Chinese speculation), Izanagi and Izanami (in the Japanese myth), right up to the Germanic Ymir: [77] Some of these themes where interpreted in a pantheistic and cosmosophical sense. On the other hand, among the entities named above, the earth, with its various hypothases, mostly female, holds pride of place in ethnological cultures and in some neolithic cultures which used to be called agricultural-matriarchal. All these were fused, in neolithic times, as it were, in the figure of Mother Earth, or better in the various goddesses who express the concept of fecundity, from the Mesopotamian Inanna-

---

[77] Regarding these cosmogonical personages and myths see U. Bianchi, *Teogonie e cosmogonie*, Rome, 1960 (Series *Universale Studium* No. 69).

Ishtar to the Anatolian goddesses and those of Minon Crete) and were later transfigured in the great Mother Nature.

One must note that this transition from an archaic theme and an archaic mythology to a type of speculation which is cosmogonic, or even at times frankly cosmosophical and philosophical, is already found, in more or less embryonic forms, in those ethnological cultures we have mentioned as being more advanced (through their own endogenous capacity or external influence) on the way to 'higher culture'. The frankly polytheistic myths of various Sudanese peoples also contain elaborate cosmogonic speculations (for example, the Yoruban myth of Olokun and Olurun, deities of the sea and sky respectively, and of Odudua and Obatala, a primordial couple, or of the holy city Ife as the centre of a cosmogony, just as the holy cities of Egypt and Mesopotamia also were believed to be cosmogonical centres. According to the interpretations put forward by the school of Marcel Griaule, the complex symbology of other tribes, further in the interior of the Sudan, like the Dogon, Bambara, etc. contain even more of these speculations about the cosmos. In Polynesia the development is even clearer with the local speculation centred in local shrines or directed by a specialized priesthood, a speculation concentrating on the high gods Tangaroa, Tane and Vatea, on the infernal entities of the time of origins (the Po as primordial chaos and the other 'abstract' entities endowed with a well defined cosmic meaning: the Void, Smell, Night, etc.), on the primordial cosmic couple, Rangi and Papa, already mentioned, and above all on that mysterious figure $I(h)o$ which, in the speculation of some Tahitian priestly circles, assumes the dignity of a primary and mysterious cosmic principle, according to a line of thought which India, with her *Brahman-Atman* and China, with her Tao, were to render famous. Ethnologists, as well as historians of religions, must study the relations between these primordial entities and the more ancient and, for the most part, different representations of the Supreme Being. As regards the higher cultures there is no need to dwell on the complex polytheistic-cosmogonical system illustrated (with traces of European influences) in the *Popol Vuh* of the Maya, or on other testimonies from the same *milieu*.

19. *Religion in the 'higher cultures'*

Obviously it is impossible to given here even a summary account of all the principal subjects for study in connection with the religions of the 'higher' cultures, meaning by this term those civilizations which possess their own writing, and often their own literature, and have an organized urbanistic life. It is true that an exaggerated insistence on the religions of primitive peoples might strengthen the erroneous impression that it is these which constitute primarily, if not exclusively, the object and inspiration of the history of religions, especially as it has been chiefly the task of students of the ethnological schools (evolutionistic and historical-cultural) to decide, on a scientific basis, questions of the origin and essence of religion. On the other hand, students of the phenomenology of religion, like R. Otto and M. Eliade, avoid seeking to base their theories merely on materials provided by ethnology, and in fact identify the essence and origin of religion, respectively, in the sense of the 'holy' and the experience of hierophany which they think are found in all forms of religion. Nevertheless they have shown less interest in the historical study of the forms and developments of religious phenomena, declaring themselves agnostic, like Eliade, about the problems of origins.[78] In any case, the students of the history of religions best furnished with historical records have warned us of the urgency, and at the same time of the difficulty, of problems relating to those elements which are common to the various religions, and of the problems relating to their development, chronological order and mutual attraction and repulsion. This urgency is all the more evident if we consider that specialists in the study of religions of the more advanced civilizations have been much less concerned than ethnologists and anthropologists with the typology of religion and its periodization—contenting themselves, with rather rash humility, with hypotheses offered by anthropologists of the evolutionistic school or by ethnologists of the historical-cultural school, when they did not prefer instead to have recourse to the theory of the 'holy' and to other theories more connected with phenomenology than with historical development. Two exceptions, not very satisfactory ones, are represented by the pan-Babylonian school and by what may be called, by analogy, the pan-Egyptian school.

20. *Pan-Babylonianism and pan-Egyptianism*

The students to whom we refer are of no great importance in the study of the history of religions and cultures. In keeping with the

---

[78] In spite of a similar judgment on various questions of religious typology (for example, on the question of the archaic and specific nature of the Supreme Beings among primitive peoples) Eliade takes a different view from that expressed in W. Schmidt's work entitled *Der Ursprung der Gottesidee*, 12 vols., Münster, 1912-1926.

philological character of their studies, in Assyriology and Egyptology, (but they formed in minority even in these circles) they had recourse to 'diffusionistic' hypotheses, in order to be able to assert that many religious elements in the various civilizations, including those studied by ethnologists but excluding the lowest and most primitive forms, (such as beliefs in spirits or genii of nature, etc.) could be explained by reference to Babylonian or Egyptian influences.

These hypotheses refer to the great antiquity of cuneiform or hieroglyphic records, as well as to the well known diffusion of the Mesopotamian culture, and take into account the philologist's natural objection to depriving of their title to the greatest antiquity famous records of civilization which go back thousands of years, in favour of civilization which philologists have proved to be more recent or even, like those studied by ethnologists, are contemporary with us. Nevertheless these theories arouse grave objections. In fact, they are incapable, not only of revealing the lines of this cultural diffusion which they presuppose, or even its possibility but, even worse, of distinguishing the precise object of the diffusion.

H. Winckler, A. Jeremias and in particular E. Stucken (within certain limits A. Deimel also) tried to show the almost universal influence of Babylon (with the usual reservations concerning the 'savage' peoples) from the third millennium B.C. onwards. The chief factors in this influence were, they supposed, the concepts of astral religion and astrology (myths and calendars connected with the Pleiades or the Zodiac), conceptions which seemed peculiar to the Mesopotamian religion and corresponded also to a sort of pan-Babylonian mythology of nature which seemed capable of replacing Max Müller's linguistically based mythology. But the technical bases of Winckler's hypothesis were at once attacked by Fr. Kugler who demonstrated that the Babylonian astrological concepts were of a much more recent origin than was supposed by those scholars who based their theories upon their antiquity. [79]

The pan-Egyptian hypothesis was put forward by G. Elliot Smith and W. J. Perry, who resorted to daring diffusionist theories rejected by ethnologists. The Egyptologist G. Foucart is in a class apart. Instead of seeking in Egypt the historical source of religious concepts (as did the pan-Egyptians who however, as we have said, excluded

---

[79] Note however, that recent research by Griaule's school show the presence of highly developed and specific astral concepts among various Sudanese tribes.

primitive concepts peculiar to illiterate peoples) he proposed to choose the Egyptian religion, because of certain of its characteristics, as the type or model to be used for identifying and classifying religious forms. [80] In fact, Egypt seemed to him to have expressed a very special type of civilization, archaic, rich in religious manifestations and yet, because of its cultural isolation during the Pharaonic Age, unmarred by historical admixtures. This was a very strange claim and certainly failed to satisfy the most elementary requirements of historical methodology.

Another theory, very different from the pan-Babylonian or pan-Egyptian suppositions, is that of an original diffusion, from proto-historical Mesopotamia, of the impulse to found superior civilizations of an urban type, such as those to which we have already referred. [81]

21. *Historical-religious and comparative aspects of the 'cuneiform' area and adjoining regions*

Champollion's deciphering of hieroglyphic script, on the occasion of the Napoleonic expedition to Egypt, was a decisive contribution to the study of Near Eastern religions, and the same may be said of Grotefend's deciphering, begun in 1802, of cuneiform lettering, on the basis of the trilingual inscriptions of Persepolis. The Babylonian, Assyrian, Sumerian and Hittite texts with, later on, the Ugaritic texts, were to be the objects of generations of research, as a source of first hand knowledge of these religions and mythologies, some of great literary and religious value. Their scattered remains (fortunately, as was later verified, still recognizable and substantially unaltered) were found in the work of ancient erudite scholars like the Babylonian Berosos, the Phoenician Philo of Byblos and the Egyptian Manethon.

These investigations gave rise to the concept of a cuneiform cultural

---

[80] *Histoire des Religions et méthode comparative*, 2nd ed., Paris, 1912.

[81] Henri Frankfort, *The Birth of Civilization in the Near East*, Garden City, N. York 1956, p. 1 (1st ed. 1951), writes: 'It is true that the transition from primitive to civilized conditions has happened more than once; but the change has mostly been induced—or at least furthered—by contact with more advanced foreigners. We know of only three instances where the event may have been spontaneous: in the ancient Near East, in China and in South and Middle America. However, the genesis of the Maya and Inca civilizations is obscure, and for China we must count with the possibility—one would say the likelihood—of a stimulus from the West'. (To similar views point the diffusionist hypotheses of Heine-Geldern). Frankfort even demonstrates a Mesopotamian influence over Egypt towards the end of the IVth millennium B.C.

area, stretching from Mesopotamia to Anatolia, Syria and Persia, and characterized by the use of this type of writing, the records of which provide an almost inexhaustible source for historical-religions or comparative research relating to the last 3,000 years B.C. In fact, the diffusion of certain particular myths, such as the Churrite myth of Kumarbi, the 'Churrite Kronos', of Ullikummi, the stone monster, a sort of Typhon *ante litteram*, and of Telipinus, all preserved in Hittite texts, could be traced even beyond this area, to Cyprus and Greece, [82] thus re-opening the question of the sources of imported elements in Greek mythology, at first too glibly 'explained' as an expression of the hostility of the old Mediterranean pantheon to the new Indo-European gods, or too closely assimilated to the sky-earth myths of a 'universal mythology'. In the same way, comparative interest was aroused in figures like that of the hero of the Babylonian epic, Gilgamesh, [83] and of earlier Sumerian poetry. Archeologists combined with epigraphists to reveal the forms of this extraordinary cultural development, in these and adjoining areas, in a series of discoveries. The most sensational, after those of Persepolis, Nineveh, Babel and other cities, [84] were those of Mari with its famous palace and archives, of Tell-el-ᶜAmarna in Egypt, with its collections of documents in cuneiform lettering, of Jericho, 'the most ancient city of the world', of Ugarit in Syria, with a collection of palaeo-Canaanite myths and, recently, of Çatal Hüyük, in south western Anatolia, where the remains of sacred buildings show traces of a very ancient life and fertility cult.

We have already mentioned comparative studies of Graeco-Anatolian mythology. An even vaster perspective, which must however be treated with caution because of an over-hypothetical Semitic interpretation of archaic Minoan writings (in the so-called linear A) [85] is found in the comparative studies of Cyrus H. Gordon, who believes

---

[82] Forrer, Güterbock and Otten.

[83] See Luigia Achillea Stella, *Il poema di Ulisse*, Florence 1933.

[84] Centres of very ancient traditions, like Uruk, the city of Gilgameš, and Nippur, the city sacred to Enlil the God of the atmosphere and of storms, in which was traditionally found the *Duranki*, or 'union of sky and earth', in which the sky and earth were severed by this god, meaning that our present world, in which sky and earth are clearly separated and opposed to each other was created; here too, in the *Uzumua* ('the producer of flesh'), mankind had emerged.

[85] See the Preface (p. 7) to *Il Vecchio Testamento e i popoli del Mediterraneo orientale*, Brescia, 1959, revised and enlarged edition of the American and German editions (*Introduction to Old Testament times*, Ventnor, N. J., 1953 and *Geschichtliche Grundlagen des Alten Testaments*, Einsiedeln, 1956). Jean Vercoutter, *Essai sur les relations entre Egyptiens et Préhellènes*, Paris, 1934, instead insists on Egyptian influences.

that in the middle of the second millenium B.C. Israel and Mycenaean Greece were members of a kind of cultural international *koiné*, sharing the composite culture of the Eastern Mediterranean, the Mycenaean civilization being just as much a part of the Biblical world as were the civilization of Mesopotamia, Egypt or Anatolia. As regards the Old Testament, Gordon particularly insists on the 'epic' elements and naturally also on the 'sapiential' ones which belong to a kind of international literature of that time.

22. *'Myth and ritual'*

The question of ancient Eastern epic poetry is not the same as the question of a mythology but is frequently connected with this, especially in some narratives with a heroic and adventurous subject.[86] Much material was contributed to this argument by the discoveries at Ugarit in Syria (1928-1939), which brought to light tablets of the second half of the second millennium B.C. (XIVth century) containing a whole series of narratives, some relating to late Phoenician mythology attested by Philo of Byblos and by his acknowledged 'source', Sanchuniaton, who was said to have lived 'before the Trojan war'.

The discovery of the Ugaritic myths led to discussion of a more general historical-religious interest, regarding the connection between mythology (or at least narratives with super human protagonists) and ritual. In fact, while the first scholars (Virolleaud and Dhorme), who were studying the Ugaritic texts, presented them as texts of a definitely mythological and legendary character, or as literary documents, other scholars, like Pedersen, saw in some of them a liturgical drama,[87] a description of fertility rites, characterized by the typical yearly cycle of life, death and return (we refer to the texts which relate to Baal, the god of fertility, who conquers Prince Yam, (Sea) and is defeated by Mot (Death), the god of mortality and drought —only to return later for the good of the fertile earth). According to these scholars the Ugaritic myth ritual expressed a septennial cycle.

Apart from this last hypothesis, which seems incompatible with what we know of the annual ceremonies in honour of Adonis in Phoenicia in the first millennium B.C. (although these have a certain similarity with the Baal myths) it is still clear that the dramatic

---

[86] Regarding connections between myth and epic, from the sociological point of view, see Dumézil, *Mythe et epopée*, Paris, 1968-71-73.

[87] The connection between myth, ritual and drama is treated by Th. Gaster, *Thespis*, 1950.

character of the Ugaritic texts makes it improbable that they were of purely narrative interest, or merely literary.

The question of the connection between myth and ritual has in recent years been one of those most discussed in the field of historical-religious studies, involving not only the interpretation of old and new texts but also more general questions—these two aspects of religion having sometimes been considered as terms of a unitary religious experience. This is seen in the Essays published by Hooke under the titles of '*Myth and Ritual*', and '*Myth, Ritual and Kingship*'. But before we speak of this myth-and-ritual school and of another closely connected with it, that of the 'mythic-ritual pattern', we must note that the question of the connection between mythology and the religious life has received full treatment in anthropological circles also, with the researches of Malinowski, and a more general historical-religious treatment in the work of Pettazzoni and Eliade. We refer to the theories elaborated by these scholars respectively on 'the truth of myth' [88] and on mythology as the expression of the totality and sacredness of the origins of the world. The myth, as the foundation of actual reality, of the customs and beliefs of men, is, they say, not a fable but an experienced, binding and valid reality. Indeed, the mere recitation of the myth can be itself a rite, that is, an action to be performed at a certain time, on certain occasions, with certain dispositions, and with very concrete, even utilitarian, intentions. [89]

This is demonstrated by the results of ethnological research, and not by these alone. There is the classical example of the Babylonian New Year's Day, the famous feast of *akitu* which included in a series of celebrations (for example, the humiliation and re-enthronement of the king, who is co-protagonist of these rites of the year's renewal) [90] the recitation of the *Enuma eliš*, the Babylonian epic of creation. Thus the creation of the world and the new beginning represented by the New Year, when the particular destinies of the coming year are decided at Babel (just as the general destinies of the world were

---

[88] Cf. above, p. 93.

[89] M. Leenhardt even speaks of a myth 'lived before it was narrated', and of the decadence of a myth reduced to a *fecit* that is, to an etiological story. Unlike Eliade, who sees in the 'time' of the myths about the world's origins (to which in fact —according to him—all myths refer) a time of primordial fulness and creative activity and, in contrast with Pettazzoni who sees in the 'time' of the myth of creation a period now concluded (just as creation is now concluded), Leenhardt distinguishes the 'living myth' lived and inserted in the very time of being, from a 'dead myth', or mythological story.

[90] G. Furlani, *Riti babilonesi e assiri*, Udine, 1940, pp. 119 et sqq.

decided in the beginning by Marduk after his victory over the powers of chaos) were closely connected.

It is true that the recitation of the *Enuma eliš* was mainly intended to be a glorification of Marduk, the hero of the narrative; but it was perhaps also an appeal to the god to perform another great work for the benefit of his worshippers, [91] and this implies a connection, through the person of the god himself, Demiurge and lord, between the story of the first beginnings of the world and the renewal of the year's life. This connection—although very differently motivated in the different instances—is obvious in all liturgical typology, even outside Babylonia, and is found also in the typology of the Easter liturgical tradition which includes the re-lighting of the fire and the recitation of the beginning of the Book of Genesis before that of other Biblical texts concerning the story of redemption and regeneration.

23. *The 'myth-and-ritual' pattern*

But the associations conjectured by the theory of 'myth-and-ritual' were more specific: according to them the myth must be understood as the sacred text accompanying the sacred action, so that 'true' myths are only those which have, or at least had, a place in cult manifestations (Widengren). So the 'myth-and-ritual' school presupposes, at least for the Near East, the scene of most of its research, a true 'myth-and-ritual' pattern, implying a particular content and protagonist. The link between these two corresponding aspects, mythical and ritual, is the king, the hero of a ritualistic narrative which culminates in his marriage with the great goddess of nature, a culmination already to be found (in the opinion of those scholars) in the myth. A pattern of this type is said to be found in the seasonal rituals of the ancient Near East. [92]

On the other hand, Henri Frankfort, in *Kingship and the Gods* (1948) finds, in this notion of a pattern, an element which destroys

---

[91] G. Furlani, *Il poema della creazione*, Bologna, 1934, p. 3: id., *Miti babilonesi e assiri*.

[92] Cf. the volumes edited by S. H. Hooke, *Myth and Ritual*, Oxford, 1933; *The Labyrinth. Further Studies in the Relation between Myth and Ritual in the Ancient World*. London, 1935; *Myth, Ritual and Kingship. Essays on the Theory and Practice of Kingship in the ancient Near East and in Israel*, Oxford, 1958. Cf. concerning this school, S. G. F. Brandon, *The Myth and Ritual Position critically considered*, in the third of these above mentioned volumes, p. 261 et sqq and the methodological reservations programmatically expressed by E. O. James, *Myth and Ritual in the Ancient East*, 1958. See also Th. Gaster, *Thespis*, 1950.

the possibility of a useful comparison. Egypt, he argues, is without the concept of an Earth Mother, for it believes that life proceeds from a male god, even if chthonic, whereas the Egyptian king being divine, could not have been humiliated or deposed or replaced by a substitute king, of the type seen in certain examples, found in ethnological studies, in folklore and even in history, which Frazer collected. [93] Moreover, while the Mesopotamian king may in certain cases (in the third millennium B.C.) impersonate the spirit of fecundity, Dumuzi, the cult of the 'seasonal' god Osiris had no ritual representation of a sacred marriage, and the king did not impersonate the god while he lived, but only after his death, to ensure his own immortality. And Osiris is a 'dead' god who remains in the Underworld, whereas Dumuzi is a 'dying' god who returns. [94]

It is true that, as is proved by recent research, [95] there is no 'resurrection' of Tammuz or Adonis, since their departure, accompanied by the prospects of their 'cyclic' annual reappearance, was the conclusion and not the beginning of the god's annual story. In spite of this, the myth has a positive content because the spring wedding of the spirit of fertility has meanwhile guaranteed the renewal of the life of nature. [96]

But, if this is true of the Near East (we shall refer later on to some questions relating to Israel) is it equally true of an eventual myth-and-ritual pattern, or rather of a specific pattern like the one we have already mentioned, in other regions of the ancient world? Greece has Eleusis, the home of Mystery cults connected with the theme of seasonal fertility, in which the connection between myth and ritual is certainly closer than H. J. Rose is willing to admit, in spite of his classical and ethnological erudition. The myth of the rape of Kore-Persephone (perhaps also the myth of the origins of agriculture, taught to Triptolemus) were central in the Eleusinian Mystery rites, which moreover included the sacred wedding of the priest, perhaps also the union of the Sky and Earth which promoted fertility.

---

[93] As for the humiliation of the Babylonian king, some arbitrary links were traced with the fate of the god of Babel, Marduk, in myth and ritual.

[94] Thus, according to Frankfort, there is in both systems the Egyptian and the Mesopotamian, a preoccupation with the same annual event, the seasonal fertility cycle, which results in resemblances in myth and ritual, but not in unitary pattern.

[95] Cf. U. Bianchi, *Initiation, mystères, gnose*, in C. J. Bleeker, *Initiation*, Leiden, 1965, pp. 154 et sqq., and the bibliography on pp. 160 et sqq.

[96] See also further on, regarding the subsequent history of these myth-rites, in the mysteriosophies of the Roman-Hellenistic Age.

In other civilizations the question is complicated by the apparent or real absence of myths. This is true of Rome, [97] of Zoroastrian Iran and of the religion of Israel, [98] to mention but three of the great religions of the ancient world. It is not by chance that all these, though in different ways and for different reasons (political for the first and religious and political for the second and third) are interested in history. This history is an end in itself in Rome, although set in the gloomy light of the *saecula* which are destined to come to an end (according to the Etruscan *discipline*) but is incorporated in the great cosmic and human story of the creation, of the Messianic hope and of eschatology in Israel and Iran. In Iran however the manner and extent of history are very different, because the Mazdaic texts, for the most part, deal with a historicization of cosmic myths describing the struggle between the two Principles whereas, on the contrary, in Israel the primary reference is to a human history guided by God.

We must therefore consider these three cases separately. As regards Iran and Israel, certain Scandinavian scholars are eager to find in them religious traces of the ancient seasonal rites, as well as a complex ritual centred in the person of the king. [99] Engnell interprets in this way the Hebrew feast of Pæsaḥ and the narrative told in Exodus 1-15, although he points out (in relation to the essential historical content of Hebrew tradition) that this does not invalidate the historicity of the Mosaic exodus. In a similar way S. Mowinckel distinguishes elements

---

[97] Naturally, we are referring to the indigenous Roman religion. The Greek mythology introduced into Rome provides only cases of *interpretatio* between deities (or of philosophical-mythological motivation of the Roman Etruscan traditions about the *saecula* and the *magnus annus*: IVth Eclogue, Horace, Ovid, Tibullus, etc. [Sordi]) and is usually reduced to a literary theme. For Bayet the re-mythization was a corruption of the Roman religion. The Germanic myths of the Edda are of doubtful local authenticity and are now merely literary narratives; however, they include the myth of Balder, the slain hero whom Frazer numbers among his 'seasonal' gods.

[98] Concerning which see further on, paragraphs 30-32.

[99] Mythical, semi-divine or human personages of the Mesopotamian world (Gilgameš and Adapa, respectively) have, however, been cited as cases of a historicizing of myth; inversely, historical figures like Sargon and Semiramis have been cited (Fr. M. Th. Liagre Böhl) as cases of a mythologizing of historical figures. Semiramis has assumed the aspect of the Great Goddess. Gilgameš, in his turn, is associated with the story of the sacred marriage with the goddess although, in the well-known narrative, he rejects this marriage, which would 'crush' him, and so in a certain way he, the King, leads in a paradigmatic manner a sort of personal 'revolution' against the old notions of the rite which was believed, with the king as intermediare, to promote life and collective 'salvation'. It is true that the context of the story is now only mythical, legendary and folkloristic. Cf. p. 159, note 1, and p. 163 of the article by Ugo Bianchi, *Initiation, mystères, gnose*, in *op. cit*.

of a general Oriental character, and a specifically Israelitic element, in the Israelitic concept of sacred kingship, especially because of the particular nature of Yahwism, of its idea of God and therefore of man, and also of the king, and because of Israel's patriarchal tradition. Mowinckel excludes the possibility of Israel having a rite like that of the 'cult drama', in which the king acts in the name of a god, or in which there occurs the death of the god or his sacred wedding (*hieros gamos*).

As regards Islam, although G. Widengren admits that the myth-and-ritual pattern is conditioned by the general pattern of the civilization in which it is found (thus combining, at least in theory, the theories of this school with the prudence of Frankfort's attitude) he maintains, perhaps with somewhat forced argumentation, that the myth-and-ritual pattern in the Indo-Iranian civilization concentrates on the feast of the New Year: a divine hero slays the dragon who is holding the rain in bondage, so that the rain waters may again fertilize the soil. At the same time he frees the dragon's two wives and marries them, thus integrating the theme of the sacred wedding (*hieros gamos*), which Widengren connects with the theme of the seasonal myth-rite, in the Indo-Iranian system.

In this context therefore one would set also the Indian-Vedic myth of Indra, the slayer of the serpent Vṛtra—we shall refer later to its more direct cosmogonical meaning—and the Iranian (Avestic) myth of Faridun (Thraetaona), the conqueror of the three-headed serpent tyrant Aži Dahaka and the husband of his two wives (alluding, it would seem to us, to a double, that is, to a complete lunar figure): the monster is slain by the hero (or rather, chained and rendered innocuous until at the end of time he is to be killed by the other hero Keresaspa). In this we see the eschatological presentation typical of the Iranian religion, differing from the cyclic representation of the Syrian-Anatolian-Egyptian rites of a seasonal character. But the transformation of a cosmic myth into a historical narrative is made still more clear in the Iranian story by the fact that Aži Dahaka and Thraetaona appear as two of the kings [100] who succeeded one another in the history of primitive man, [101] and they appear as such also in the final, completely literary and no longer religious (at least in the sense

---

[100] According to Widengren, the king represents in the annual rite the hero who promotes fertility.

[101] See however below, p. 117 n. 103 for a different though not incompatible, interpretation of these same figures.

in which it was originally religious) version of this 'history', that is, in the *Shahname*, the 'kings' book', by the Persian moslem Firdusi, the masterpiece of post-Zoroastrian Persian literature. [102]

Another student of comparative mythology, of whom we shall have more to say later, Georges Dumézil, had, in connection with these myths, drawn attention to the Iranian ritual and folklore relating to the feast of Nauroz, the spring equinox (a season in which light and fertility return triumphant over the powers of darkness which in Iran are demoniac and the sign and substance of death). In these spring rites of the renewal of life Dumézil notes the evocation of Aži Dahaka and of other personages of the 'historical' narrative about him, that is, the significant presence of monstrous animalesque figures, with legends of huge swallowings, of wild cavalcades, of ephemeral 'triumphs' on chariots drawn by demons: carnivalesque features which, as we learn from folklore, generally accompany the pre-spring or spring rites of fertility and life (or in any case the fertility rites, like those of the Greek Dionysiac cult). The monster Aži Dahaka is thus presented also as a typical mock king, or as the intermediate and substitute king, destined to be eliminated at the beginning of the new cycle.

It is obvious that an indispensable condition for accepting these interpretations (in spite of some reservations about details and presuppositions) [103] is that one should not discourage but stimulate the

---

[102] In this connection we note Bausani's observation of the marked Mohammedan tendency to historicize mythical or legendary themes which, however, as he rightly points out, results in quite original narratives, not merely new versions or survivals of an-Islamic stories.

[103] So we must remember that the myth of Thraetaona has been also differently interpreted, even in the course of researches in comparative mythology not unlike, in their methodology, those of Widengren. The Swede, Stig Wikander, sees in the succession of the first three legendary Iranian Kings (Yima, who is also the first man, Aži Dahaka and Thraetaona) a pattern identical with that of the succession Uranus-Cronus-Zeus in Hesiod's theogony (a pattern which, as we have seen, has been in its turn compared with that of the Churrite theogony, in which an 'atmospheric' god succeeds Kumarbi, the 'Churrite Cronus', who has dethroned the Sky-God. Here then we have an amalgamation (visible also in the Babylonian *Enuma eliš*) of the theogonic concept of the old gods being replaced by new gods with the cosmogonic concept of the violent 'opening' of the universe ('from chaos to cosmos') through the intermediary action of a god, Cronus (or a similar figure) who still shows the cruelty and selfishness of the powers of chaos (he was said to have swallowed his children) but also prefigures the greater personal differentiation of the young gods as compared with the primordial divine entities, like Uranus, the Sky-God, or rather the God-Sky. As an example of the possible variety of interpretations of the same myth, Dumézil has included the figure of Uranus (whom he, like Max Müller, identifies with Varuna) in the pattern of the three functions, to which we shall refer later.

investigation into the peculiar elements of those religions to which the various testimonies refer, without presupposing an archetypal, 'phenomenological' and non-historical pre-existence of these 'structures' —for their universality, or at least wide diffusion, should be demonstrated case by case as a historical fact. Widengren rightly observes that the Iranian religion, with its dualistic character, presupposes a vision of the relations between good and evil, life and death, which cannot be identified with the Phoenician- Mesopotamian pattern, with its dying god. In fact, Thraetaona is a conqueror, as are, in heroic fashion, all the 'saviours' (*saošyant*) of Iranian eschatology. This must be related to the particular dualistic beliefs of the bellicose Zoroastrian religion (see the following paragraphs), and to its eschatological nature, i.e. the belief that a final and total victory, at the end of the nine historical millennia, will put an end to the struggle between good and evil: now, a personage like Thraetaona prefigures this victory. [104]

24. *Death and evil in some ancient religions of Near Asia*

In a parallel case we note the difference between the concept of evil in the Iranian context and the same concept in that of the Syrian-Anatolian-Egyptian pattern, and the very different connection not only with the seasonal story but also with the cosmogony. (As we shall see, the meaning of the seasonal renewal cannot be separated from the cosmogonical meaning of the myths in question).

In the Zoroastrian religion evil is essentially something extraneous to the Creation, which it seeks to corrupt and destroy by a process of paralysis—which is why the first victory over evil was won when the world was set in motion. Ahriman and his acolytes are essentially destructive and negative entities, because they are absolutely false. In the Syrian-Egyptian cultural area, instead, the various adversaries of the fecund gods Baal, Adonis and Osiris are Mot and Seth, who are

---

[104] This explains the meaning, in Zoroastrian religious tradition, of 'suffering' personages, like Gayomart, the first man, slain by the principle of evil, and the primaeval and cosmic ox, who suffers the same fate, or even Yima himself, another primaeval man and king. These are all victims of evil (destined to be liberated) and not themselves liberators, for these form a group apart. A partial union of the two types in the figure of the *Erlöste Erlöser, Salvator salvatus* (or better, as Colpe suggests, of the *salvator salvandus, der zu erlösende Erlöser*), is to be found in Gnosticism, which in fact asserts the consubstantiality (even the fundamental identity) of the heavenly being who has fallen a victim to material force and the heavenly messenger who awakens him to *gnosis*, that is to the knowledge of the divine life which is intrinsically his.

certainly destructive (*Mot* means Death) but only in what may be called a dialectical sense, because they are essential elements in the seasonal cyclic drama and are themselves a means of promoting fertility. In fact, in the Ugaritic myth, Mot's body is finally chopped into little pieces, and the birds nibble it as if it were corn: this seems to be reminiscent of the role played by a puppet called Death or other effigies of the same in some popular fertility rites, and in general of the trial, slaughter (hanging or decapitation), burying or incineration of the 'Carnival' (or of related characters). All these are customs recurring in popular tradition, in which 'Death' and the Carnival King at times resemble each other, the final elimination of this personage being at the same time tragic and burlesque.

In the case of the 'dying gods', Tammuz and Adonis, and of the 'dead god' (this useful distinction was proposed by Frankfort), Osiris, the differences between the Near Eastern and Iranian contexts are fundamental. In fact, as has been already observed, and in contradiction with what is generally admitted, Adonis and Dumuzi-Tammuz (as well as Attis, who however belongs to a different *milieu*) are not properly speaking resurgent gods, but dying gods, since their cycle concludes with the lamentation, which is the *punctum saliens*, and the characteristic feature of these myths and rites. [105] The return of Adonis and his triumphal union with the goddess of fertility form the initial act of the drama, at the end of which the god 'departs' for the Underworld and the goddess and all the worshippers begin a long lamentation for him. Finally, at the end of this dirge, it is announced that he 'lives' in the world beyond, and will return the following year. This is also the meaning of the Mesopotamian myth of Dumuzi and Inanna; as we learn from the new fragments, the god is kept a hostage in the underworld and will remain there intermittently, so that the goddess of life may be saved for ever from death. [106] The same theme is very clearly seen in the texts concerning Adonis by Theocritus and Bion: the Theocritean idyll (the 'Women of Syracuse') describes the feast of the god's wedding with Aphrodite and ends with the prospect of his departure to the sea, whereas Bion's lament, full of grief for the death of Adonis, ends with the exhortation to

---

[105] For more details see the Author's *Initiation, Mystères, Gnose*, in C. J. Bleeker's *Initiation*, Leiden, 1965.

[106] In fact, she once 'died', causing the mortification of life (properly, of animal fecundity), as is told in the Akkadian myth of the descent of Ishtar to the Underworld. Compare with this the theme of the earth's sterility caused by Demeter's grief in the Eleusinian myth.

Aphrodite to cease her lamentation: 'You will have to weep again in the coming year'. The funerary character is therefore so all-pervasive that the poem, besides lamenting the drama of the present year, predicts also that of the year to come. The same meaning results from other texts relating to the rites of Adonis in the Hellenistic Age, alluded to above, especially that of Lucian (*De Syria dea*, 6, cf. Cyrill, *In Isaiam* 18, 1, 2 [P. G. 70, 440]). [107]

25. *Iranian-Near Eastern syncretism: Mithraism*

A link between the Iranian and Near Asian world, probably to be found in their respective 'life' rituals, is attested by the 'Mysteries' of Mithras, which—as it seems—began in Anatolia and spread widely, especially in the Roman world of the West, but was also present, in the Roman Age, in the Eastern Mediterranean (for example in Phoenicia). These Mysteries, a favourite subject for study by Iranists and classical scholars, from Bidez and Cumont [108] to Widengren and Vermaseren, [109] perpetuate some elements of Iranian mythology and theology, especially in all that concerns the nature of evil, which seeks to destroy life, and the beneficent and solar role of Mithras. They also seem to owe much to the fertility rites of Anatolia, endowing the god Mithras (a celestial and solar god in Iran) with chthonic characteristics, more similar to those of the Anatolian Attis. Mithras was 'born of a rock', not, it seems to us, of that stone element which was meant to be the sky, or of the mountains on the horizon, but—as it were—of a 'maternal' rock, a characteristic feature in the Anatolian religious world.

---

[107] Quite secondary to this is the 'historicizing' process which Widengren sees at work in Near Eastern myth and rites of the seasonal cycle, in which the protagonist of the story is the hero founder of the city. The city is in fact ritually equivalent to the cosmos, or at least to the 'inhabited cosmos', the 'cultivated land' or, using the Mesopotamian term, the land itself, 'country', the human settlement. Another feature of a 'minor historicization' of the vicissitude of the god of fertility is the very human and episodic character of his story.

[108] The chief works of F. Cumont, *Les religions orientales dans le paganisme romain* (4th ed., 1929); *Textes et monuments relatifs aux mystères de Mithras* (a repertory of Mithraism, to which is now added Vermaseren's *Corpus*); *Lux perpetua* (1949), dedicated to the concepts held by the world of late antiquity about death and the life beyond, and *Les Mages hellénisés. Zoroastre, Ostanès et Hystaspe d'après la tradition grecque*, by J. Bidez and F. Cumont (1938) are all classics of religious-historical research about the ancient world. As regards the interpretation of Mithraism, Cumont seems, at least from an Iranist's point of view, to have exaggerated the importance of Zoroastrian elements in this.

[109] Who is now editing a collection of studies relative to Oriental religions in the Roman world.

Concepts of a mysterio-sophic kind about the sky, the celestial bodies and other cosmic hypostases, derived from Babylonia or rather from the Chaldaeans, must have given to the Mithraic Mysteries that soteriological and gnostic character (with the soul's flight above the planetary spheres) which was found in late antiquity also in other ancient cults of the Ancient East, including the cults of Adonis and Attis, transformed into Mysteries or indeed (because of the development of doctrines about the divine soul being imprisoned in the material world) in 'mysteriosophies', that is, in centres of a speculation which was in one way 'naturalistic' and in another way (and in a qualified sense of the word) 'spiritualist' (as in the theme of the divine soul imprisoned in the world). These two aspects were later on to be united in some systems of gnosticism.

26. *Indo-European mythology and the ideology of the 'three functions'. Classifications and structures in myths and in society*

The questions relating to the 'non-mythological' religions like those of Rome and Iran do not however end here. G. Dumézil (with a group of scholars under the influence of his indefatigable research work, culminating now in *'Mythe et épopée. L'idéologie des trois fonctions'*) discern, in the pantheons and legendary traditions of Rome, Iran and even of India, as in those of other Indo-European linguistic groups, from the Celts to the Caucasians, the remains of an ancient mythology closely linked with sociological structures which he considers typical of these races (if not necessarily exclusive to them) and capable of investigation by comparative methods of study which must be concerned not only with linguistic but also with functional matters. Dumézil, who is obviously here following the tradition of French sociological research (but independently from Lévi-Strauss' structuralism), believes that a tripartite social structure (royal and priestly function, warrior function and producer function) was typical of Indo-European Society, as it is to a certain extent typical of post-Vedic India, with her three castes, brahmans, nobles and warriors, and producers, and is reflected in the pantheons of the respective peoples who ordered and grouped the gods according to this criterion. For example, in India Varuna and Mitra represent respectively the 'magical' and 'juridical' aspects of kingship, Indra represents the warriors, while other male and female deities represent the third category of the producers, sometimes in groups, because they are associated with the various aspects and resources of fecundity and production.

The myths relating to these gods were characterized by their respective functions. In the Roman world, and in the world which, in Iran, reflects the Zoroastrian tradition, both these words characterized by the disappearance of the mythology of gods (but not of the gods themselves), the relative myths were transferred to figures presented as historical personages, protagonists of a history or of a primordial legendary world. Thus, in Rome, whereas the triad Jupiter, Mars and Quirinus reigned in the Pantheon, the two first kings impersonate respectively a) the royal-powerful (warlike and magical) aspect of kingship in Romulus, the head of the *celeres* and *luperci*, b) the priestly and juridical aspect of kingship in Numa, the wise man and first law-giver. The second function of the triad, that of martial activity, was represented by Tullus Hostilius, and the third by Ancus Marcius.

Dumézil's hypothesis, of which the theory relating to the transference to human beings of qualities and functions belonging to the gods of the three functions is only a secondary element, may seem somewhat forced and at times is indeed arbitrary. But it cannot be denied that it brings to light an impressive number of indications which are, to say the least, most curious, and include the famous tripartite division (philosophers, warriors, producers) of society in Plato's ideal city, and also the tripartite division of the levels, or 'parts', of the human soul (rational, passionate and vegetable) according to the same philosopher, as described in his '*Timaeus*'. The two Platonic tripartite divisions, of the society and of the soul, are fused together when Plato extolls (in his *Republic*) the corresponding virtues: wisdom and courage belong respectively to the first two categories of the ideal city while temperance (involving the harmony of the State) is assigned to all three categories and not only to the third, as one might have expected. [110]

Dumézil has amply extended this interpretation to include Iran, and not only its pantheon (which—in his opinion—had already been re-ordered by a reform preceding that of Zarathustra) but also those *Ameša Spenta*, 'Immortal Beneficents', expressions of divine qualities

---

[110] For a comparison (which, given the anti-cosmic presuppositions of Gnosticism, does not imply identification) between these two tri-partite divisions and the Gnostic groups 'pneumatic', 'psychic' and 'hylic' see the Author's *Razza aurea, mito delle cinque razze ed Elisio*, in *Studi e materiali di storia delle religioni*, 34, 2 (1963) p. 167. A significant tri-partite structure, reminiscent of that of the gods of the three functions, has recently been discovered in a Gnostic text of Nag Hamadi, in which are similarly presented the three pairs of archons who rule this world.

and powers, in which we generally see, if not the fruit of the creative thought of the Iranian prophet—since they may have existed before him—at least the instrument of his perception of the divine. Thus, of the six *Ameša Spenta* of the post-Gathic *Avesta*, the first two, 'Good Thought' and 'Order-Truth', represent the two aspects of the priest-kingly function, and the third, 'power', represents the second function, i.e. the noble-warrior function. The other three *Ameša Spenta*, 'Devotion' (feminine), Immortality and Health, represent the fecund, rich, productive and healthy aspects of the third function. We must note in passing that the complex of the *Ameša Spenta* provides, already in the Gathas but also in successive Zoroastrian speculation, a key to the interpretation, not only of the divine power but also of the human faculties and the elements of the cosmos as this theology sees it, divided into Man, Beasts, Fire, Metals, Earth, Water and Vegetation.

Other Iranian research conducted by the Belgian J. Duchesne-Guillemin and the Swedish scholars G. Widengren and Stig Wikander follows the lines laid down by Dumézil. While Widengren studies Iranian notions of kingship and feudalism (finding in them themes for the religious history not only of these peoples but also of the area in which their influence was felt), Wikander concentrates his research on the 'priests of fire' and on the *Männerbünde*, associations of men founded on the principle of age groups, resulting from the participation of its members in a common initiation; these associations were known also in Spartan Society. [111] The *Männerbünde* exercized certain particular functions in ancient Iranian society, especially in the promotion of certain aspects of social life, which experienced their powerful intervention: this was rather like what Roman tradition saw in the *celeres* or even in the *luperci* of Romulus, or what Indian mythology saw in the *Marut*, companions of a no less energetic and violent Indra. Other aspects of the 'triad' sociology were analysed by Dumézil himself in his research into *Aspects de la fonction guerrière*; a sociology relating to war which the Italian scholar, A. Brelich examines from another point of view (but still associated with initiations) in an investigation into ritual wars and competitions, which seem to have constituted what seems to us a strange form of association or integration (or of cathartic alliance) between cities of the ancient world, as in Greece. This is a principle analogous to that of functional competition

---

[111] The Latin use of the *ver sacrum* has also sometimes been interpreted as referring to the initiatory age groups (Piccaluga).

in the *milieu* of integrated communities, seen most clearly in various primitive societies, founded on the two matrimonial classes (elsewhere these are subdivided into four or eight)—classes said to derive sometimes, conventionally, from an ancient legendary hostility between two races or two ancestors (for example, in Australia, the race of the Eagle and that of the Crow) [112] a hostility which only later was ended by marriages, without the two 'halves' thereby losing their individuality, because the distinction between them remained the prerequisite of social organization. An organization of this kind, said to go back to an original pair of twins, [113] was classical among the Bororos of Brazil, where it was reflected in the topographical division of the village, in the distinctiveness of the roles of the various members and also in ritual prescriptions. This is a principle which, even if one does not read into it particular historical associations, is, as it were, grafted on to the classifying structures of the most diverse human societies, from European Medieval city-games and inter-ward rivalries to the trend to bi-partizan organization, more sociological than political, in the traditional European sense, in certain modern American societies.

27. *Cosmic and cosmogonic rituals*

But the connection between myth and rite may be seen in other 'patterns', as the Indianist J. Filliozat points out. So the Vedic sacrifice, to which Sylvain Lévi has devoted a famous treatise, is to be understood as a truly cosmogonical act.

Certain significant myths refer to this. The well known Vedic hymn to Purusha (the First Man) shows that he was sacrificed by the gods at the beginning of the world. It was a cosmogonic sacrifice, not only because of the victim himself, but also because of the ingredients used. 'When the gods prepared the sacrifice with Purusha as the offering, the spring was the melted butter, the summer was the firewood, the autumn the oblation'. From this sacrifice, offered in its entirety, the melted butter sprayed (with lactic acid) was scooped

---

[112] These personages, however, have other religious-historical associations, the former resembling a figure of the Supreme Being and the latter, like the Raven of paleo-Siberian mythologies, a figure of a 'trickster'-Demiurge (see pp. 45.87 ff.).

[113] The comparative research of Alföldi, concerning ancient Rome and the Central-Asian Turkish tribes, are connected with comewhat analogous conceptions, with the presence of twins and of animal nurses (bibl. in the Author's *Il dualismo religioso* Rome, 1958, p. 206). It is well known, moreover, that the two bands of the Roman *luperci* recalled according to some authors the story of the Twin Founders of the city. But the mythological (and ritual) typology of twins is much more extended than is here indicated.

up and from it he made (the subject of the phrase is not clear) the animals of the air, the forest and village...'. And the hymn goes on to say that the mouth, arms, ankles and feet of Purusha became respectively the four social classes, the Brahmans, warriors, producers and the members of the lowest caste. From him also were made the moon, sun, fire, wind, atmosphere, sky and earth. This text then shows the enormous expressive possibilities of a cosmogonic myth centred in the person of the *macranthropos*, the 'great man', who is at the same time man's prototype and primordial man himself, from whom were created the parts of the cosmos and the cosmos itself, in a 'productive' sacrifice, of a type very different from a sacrifice intended as a means of honouring or pacifying the god. And this cosmos is also the human cosmos, formed of the whole articulated complex of human society; all this is founded on a mythical-ritual and cosmic-human integration.

Myth and ritual of this kind have been widely explored by the Scandinavian historical-religious school, which was particularly involved in this type of research. K. Rönnow supposes the myths of a primordial sacrifice to have been connected with an ancient rite of human sacrifice: the primordial man sacrificed was, he thinks, the mythical counterpart of an actual human sacrifice, understood as promoting in the highest degree the Creation or periodic re-creation of the world: a highly efficacious sacrifice, because of the nature of the victim offered. One must however point out that this hypothesis is not really acceptable because it seems probable that the sacrifice of a human victim was, in Indian speculation about sacrifice, a theoretical or mythical example, put forward as the consequence of a general theory about sacrifice, held by the authors of the texts called *brahmana*. In the actual rite, in fact, the most solemn sacrifice was always that of a horse. This is of course mentioned here without any intention of denying the presence of the human sacrifice in other cultural *milieux*, epochs and ceremonies. [114] Moreover, the concept of cosmic man does not necessarily depend on the concept of a sacrifice of a

---

[114] Nevertheless, the notion that the sacrifice (or death) of a man may be of efficacy for some extraordinary undertaking or necessity tends to re-emerge almost by its own intrinsic force, and not only in the religious context of the offering to a deity (as in the sacrifice of the Phoenician *tofet*). There are in fact numerous cases, in folklore, of people slain (deliberately or otherwise) in the course of an enterprise, and as part of this enterprise (for example, buried in the foundations of a house; one remembers the legend of the Turk buried in the bridge over the Drina, in the romance of that name).

primordial man. There are other possible references, as we shall see later.

The concept of the *macranthropos*, and the man-cosmos link (the cosmos being either a 'great man' or made from the limbs of a 'great man') and *vice versa* the notion of man as a 'little cosmos', was to linger a long time in the history of religions, even if scholars, especially those most interested in this field of research, did not pay enough attention to the distinction between myth and the mythical theme (or even, simply, symbol or image). A myth is composed of a minimum of plot and narrative, and is quite different from a mythical theme, or simply an explanatory image, a conceptual representation which consists merely of a statement. Thus, the concept of the *macranthropos*—or the representation of the cosmos or of any other whole, as a 'body'—does not necessarily correspond to a myth, when it is adduced merely to give the idea of the organic derivation or organic coherence of a whole, (as, for example, in the case of certain Iranian speculations about the world being derived from the body of Ohrmazd, the Zoroastrian god or, still less, in the absence of naturistic content, in the case of the Pauline image of the mystic 'body' of Christ, or of Christ as the 'head' of a 'body' which is the Church). Reservations must also be made concerning the resemblances, pointed out in certain Swedish comparative studies, between the Indian concepts and the Platonic concepts of the *Timaeus*, although both contain the organic concept of the world as a great 'living' entity. Similarly, objections may be raised (on the typological, rather than on the historical plane) to the tendency of this school to give too indiscriminate a content to the concept of the High God, the Supreme Being, with reference to such a typically personalistic and creative deity as the Ahura Mazda of the Avesta, and to certain semi-personal hypostases of cosmic entities or principles, such as Time (Zurvan, in the Iranian tradition) who appear in cosmogonic and theogonic myths of a very different type from that of the Creationist myths. One must however add that recent studies tend to emphasize the presence, in Iranian theological tradition, that is, in the doctrines of the Magi, of speculative developments of the concept of germinal. Moreover, the theoretical and practical elements (whether sublime or utilitarian) of a cosmography, and of an anthroposophy which present the cosmos in the form of a *macranthropos*, emerge in a vast Hermetic, alchimistic, [115] magical and astrological tradition already present in

---

[115] Cf. also the concept of the *homunculus* and, in the *Cabbala*, the creation of that strange creature, the *golem*.

late antiquity and coinciding in part with certain aspects of the gnostic tradition. Here, as we have said, converge naturalistic and spiritualistic elements in an association which seems strange from the point of view of religiosity of a Biblical type, and which therefore appears, in contrast with this, to be typically pagan (that is, founded on a 'cult of the material elements and their divine substance'). This appears also in the 'Faustian' and magical tradition of a part of the Renaissance teaching about the cosmos.

28. *From the myth to the 'logos'*

We must now refer to studies relating to themes of religious thought, ideology, and mythology. We have already said something about this in connection with the French sociological school and Lévy-Bruhl, besides our references to Max Müller's theory about myths, and about primitive religious thought being a 'sickness of language'.

The theory that thought, and religious thought originated in mythical speculation is put forward by various authors, with different connotations and at times exactly opposite conclusions. For example, Cassirer, the famous author of the 'Philosophy of symbolic forms', points out that it is absurd to describe as a 'sickness of language', that is, as a pathological phenomenon, a human, mythical and generically primitive-religious phenomenon which has had such a powerful and widespread influence in cultural development. This conclusion of Cassirer's in some ways resembles the reassessment of the myth by ethnologists and religious historians like Malinowski and Pettazzoni. Indeed, Cassirer's reassessment goes deeper, far beyond the mere recognition of the myth as having a functional role in the cultural *milieu* in which men believe in it, and make it a basis for their thought and action. The German philosopher's interpretation seeks to study mythical speculation in relation to the whole history of thought, and the development of the human cognitive faculties as such.

The theme of the 'intellectual adventure of ancient man' and of the transition from *mythos* to *logos*, was the subject of two well-known works, written respectively by the Americans H. and H. A. Frankfort, J. A. Wilson, T. Jacobsen and N. A. Irwin (1954), and by the German W. Nestle (1941). The former of these two books affirms that Eastern thought is mythical and myth-creative, because it animates and personifies the cosmos and its history. It is imaginative and fantastic and therefore very different from rational thought, such as we find in Greece. The theses of this volume were criticized by other Orientalists, like S. N. Kramer, who pointed out the vast numbers of rational acquisitions in the ancient East, in the field, for example, of the exact sciences, or of medicine or metaphysics.[116] Moreover, as we have already seen, the myth does not imply an absence of logic. The most prudent solution, however, seems that proposed by S. Moscati, for whom 'the mythical character has value, not because it eliminates rational thought but because it integrates it in a superior unity. The ancient Orientals were not incapable of rational thought, but were not interested in, and did not see the need to set reason apart in its own autonomous system and then to theorize about it'.[117] This is what happened in Greece, with its autonomous rational reflections about the universe which in certain cases begin (or, more often, conclude) with mythical references (as in Plato), which are however included in the context of these reflections as their limit, and also their inspiration.

The fact that the first Greek philosophers studied 'nature' and were 'physiologists', Werner Jaeger justly observes, is because the study of the *physis* and *genesis* was pursued purely for love of the *theoria*. 'The problem of man was only conceived theoretically by the Greeks when, with regard to the problems of the external world, chiefly problems of medicine and mathematical intuition,[118] there was formulated a sort of precise *techne*, [or pattern] to serve as a model for the study of man's interior life ... The Greek Spirit, accustomed as it was to the consideration of the regularities of the external cosmos, soon discovered also the interior law of the soul, and so arrived at the objective consideration of an interior cosmos'. In fact, 'the process my which rational thought grasped the world was to develop as a gradual penetration of the outer spheres in order to reach the most profound inner depths, and finally, with Plato and Socrates, to reach the centre, the soul'. The problems of the cosmos then became once more the object of study, until classical philosophy merged into neo-Platonism. Thus, 'the Platonic myth of the soul was strong enough to

---

[116] *Journal of Cuneiform Studies*, 2 (1948), pp. 39-70.

[117] Silvio Accame sees another aspect of the 'Greek miracle' in the origin in Greece, of historical scientific methodology (*La formazione della civiltà Mediterranea*, Brescia, 1966, p. 225 et sqq). This does not mean that only the Greeks were interested in historical narratives (cf. S. Moscati, *Le origini della narrativa storica nell'arte del Vicino Oriente Antico*, in *Memorie dei Lincei*, VIII, X, 2, 1961) or in the meaning of history (so characteristic of Israel).

[118] Therefore of spheres in which the East had already been involved in activity of a rational nature, although not with a purely theoretical purpose.

oppose the total dissolution of Being in the rational and, moving from the interior outwards, was able to re-penetrate the rationalized cosmos and progressively to dominate it'. [119]

These considerations must be borne in mind when confronted by others put forward by a distinguished classical philologist, E. R. Dodds, who in a recent book on 'Pagans and Christians in an age of anxiety', sees in a certain period of Greek history, that is, in the second Hellenistic Age, fro mthe IInd. and the Ist. century B.C. a retreat towards the inner life, towards anguish, alienation and the irrational, and the interruption of a progress towards conquest, knowledge and technical skills, a progress which was to recommence in the modern world. This interpretation which, as we have noted elsewhere, lends itself to certain objections and may even be accused of anachronisms, is in open contrast with another, also based on psychological arguments, put forward by Marcuse, according to whom the Ancients decided deliberately to reject technical skills and machines because of the dangers of alienation which these presented. The other well known work by Dodds, *'The Greeks and the Irrational'* is also open to objections, especially where it sees in primitive Greece, on the plane of moral concepts, a 'guilt-conscious civilization' (showing Northern mystical influences) following a Homeric civilization characterized more by the feeling of shame. This also is a psychological over-simplification. Homer is well aware of the concept of ethical responsibility —although it is combined with concepts and beliefs about a complex divine world which is present to man and makes itself known to him—and of the concept of the conditioned, but vividly experienced, autonomy and freedom of human conduct. Nevertheless, Dodd's theory is a useful corrective to a unilaterally rationalistic and illuministic interpretation of the Greek spirit.

In all that concerns the history of religions it is certainly most important to take into account the rise in Greece of a way of thought destined to influence all successive development. A theology which was a theory of the divine, a theory or a criticism or even both together, [120] appears in Greece and represents something different from the sacred chronicles, the theogonic, calendarial and ritual treatises and the preachings of the various founders, reformers and prophets. But on the other hand there is also a Greek theology which

---

[119] W. Jaeger, *Paideia, Die Formung des griechischen Menschen*, vol. 1, Berlin-Leipzig, pp. 209 seq. and 208 seq.
[120] Cf. Xenophanes' questionings, or the Platonic *Euthyphro*.

expresses itself entirely in mystical and kerygmatic terms; in fact, the term *theologos* in classical (already Aristotelian) use, concerns also those writers, mostly anonymous, who adopted or were given impressive and semi-divine pseudonyms, like Orpheus, Musaeus, Linus, etc. and who composed in verse the ancient history of the gods in a style and with a religious character *sui generis*, very different from the epic-narrative or erudite style of poets and mythographers like Hesiod and his imitators.

These doctrines of the Orphic 'theologians' contained *in nuce* a mythical-symbolical interpretation of the world and of its divine origins, an interpretation which, with its naturalistic themes—cosmic egg, primordial darkness, Time as the progenitor of the world, hylozoism, cosmic elements, etc.—was already present in Phoenician cosmogonies and theogonies, no less ancient than the Orphic system and possibly the original models of these. It is true that the ancient Orphic theogonies and cosmogonies, like the Homeric and Hesiodic systems allegorically interpreted, gave an impulse to the new philosophy of the 'physiologists'; in fact, the Orphis theologians certainly contributed more to these because, as we see in the subject matter we have already mentioned, they themselves were already engaged in speculation on the origins and essence of the gods and of the world.

The significance of Orphic speculation or in any case of these theologians,[121] in the development of Greek religious thought, although certainly minimised by Lobeck's strictures and by the inadequate interpretations of philologists, from Gruppe to Cornford, who were influenced by a typically positivist depreciation of the content of mythical thought and of archaic Greek mysticism, nevertheless gave rise to developments, theories and constructions sometimes obviously exaggerated or wrong, especially in authors like R. Eisler, who depend too much on their 'combinatory' method which seeks resemblances and contacts in the most diverse aspects of the religious thought and practice of the ancient world, although they are not to be rejected before examination merely because they seem surprising or, to our way of thinking, bizarre. Eisler's ample treatise, *Weltenmantel und Himmelszelt* (1910), starting from a study of cosmic symbolism reflected in divine and royal iconography, is a typical example of this kind of procedure, in which the comparative method, sometimes too arbi-

---

[121] For the debate on 'Orphism' see, author's contribution to the *Festschrift* in honour of H.-Ch. Puech.

trary in its search for analogies and its endeavours to reconstruct forms of mythical speculation insufficiently authenticated from available sources, shows some of its most obvious dangers. A research study by Onians, on 'the origins of European thought' (Ist. ed. 1951) provokes the same criticisms. It attempts to distinguish more or less subterranean connections between a verbal style and a way of thought, examining the history of terms, expressions and concepts which at first seem irrelevant but which do in fact express a symbolic-conceptual content. Some of the most remarkable of these expressions refer to 'spinning' as a mythical and concrete image of the notions of destiny, from the spinning of the goddesses of Fate down to humbler examples. Here also there is a series of comparisons, sometimes chosen arbitrarily, but none the less of great interest to all who do not wish to exclude the possibility, or rather the necessity, of studying ancient thought in its actual origins. The reader is referred to what we have already said about the origin in actual experience of certain abstract forms of classificatory thought, such as for example, the divisions of time and space which seem to us obvious and natural.

In this connection we note that there are interesting and unexpected references to this type of thought, still with the characteristic images of 'spining' and 'weaving', in the testimonies of religious-metaphysical speculation based by Griaule and his followers on research among the Dogon of Mali (living in the bend of the Niger). This tribe or rather, their wise men, seem to hand down from one generation to another a metaphysical explanation of the 'Word' which evokes and creates. All things, like embryos, are born from the womb, but also from the thought and word, of a primordial Supreme Being, and they grow according to patterns, or signs, of which there are four classes (from the most embryonic but most potentially rich to those nearest to concrete realization) and in fact from 'words', which however are themselves entities and are grouped in essential categories. These categories, in their turn, cover all the possible, apparently extrinsic, connections between the realities of creation, including those which at first sight seem to have least in common (for example, the connection between a certain type of cereal harvested ritually, *fonio*, and birth).

These testimonies of Dogon ideology suggest delicate questions of a philological and historical-cultural nature, regarding their origin. Thus, certain aspects of the complex cosmogony and theogony which they contain, in spite of the typically African-Nigritic form in which they are expressed, have been likened to the way of thinking and the cosmogonical system of Egyptian gnostic speculation of the IInd. century A.D. On the other hand, as regards the symbology thought-word-seed-thing (see also the introducing lines of the Hermetic *Poimandres*!), and the typically metaphysical way in which it is very imaginatively expressed, and as regards the tendency towards a metaphysical interpretation of numbers, a comparison might be made not only with the Gnostic Systems (characterized in fact by the transformation into metaphysical and creative entities of psychic sentiments and experiences) but also with the most ancient Egyptian thought of the theology of Memphis, in which 'every divine word [of Atum] came into being through that which the heart thought and the tongue commanded', so that the God Ptah 'was in every breast and in every mouth, of all gods, all men, all beasts, all creeping things, while he [Ptah] thinks and commands what he whishes'.[122]

Other similar comparisons could be adduced. There is a Sumerian concept (the object of particular study by G. Castellino) of the 'patterns' or original designs of things,[123] the 'projects' used for their creation by the gods, which are now preserved in heaven, patterns which however are material things and can be handled by the gods, who can steal them, recover them, etc. On a more metaphysical plane there is the Persian concept, typically concrete-abstract like all this trend of thought, of the *mēnōk* as an ideal, or rather a 'seminal' state of visible concrete things, of which the *mēnōk* is, as it were, an essence, or even (though this seems paradoxical) a 'raw material' from which the specific entity is created.[124]

From the historical-religious point of view, it is clear that concepts of this kind are integrated in a certain type of cosmogony, sensitive to metaphysical ways of thought and to the stages in the genesis of things (which was generally effected though intermediate stages and intermediary or mediatory entities, as in neo-Platonic philosophy)[125] and differed from the Biblical concept which is centred in the one deliberately creative God.[126]

---

[122] These last texts are quoted by W. F. A. Albright, *From the Stone Age to Christianity*, Garden City, N. Y., 1957 (1st ed. Baltimore 1940, 2nd ed. Baltimore 1946), p. 180. Concerning the Dogon conceptions see author's remarks *Liber Amicorum* (Festschrift Bleeker), p. 27 et sqq.

[123] In Sumerian: *me*.

[124] Cf. also G. Gnoli, *Osservazioni sulla dottrina mazdaica della creazione*, in *Annali Ist. Univ. Orientale di Napoli* N.S., XIII (1963) pp. 180-192.

[125] As in Plotinian doctrine of the One, the Mind, the Soul, and the souls.

[126] As for some Platonic aspects of Philonian cosmogony, they express anyway a dynamism of a personalistic type, not of a cosmic-panentheistic type like that of the

29. Concrete nature of the symbol. Symbology of the king

In archaic religions one often finds an awareness of symbolism which is much more vivid than its conventional use in modern cultures. Archaic symbolism often implies a total and mutually shared homology, or even a consubstantiality, between the representative symbol and what it represents. We see an example of this in the symbol *par excellence*, the mask, among primitive peoples and, to a different extent, in the classical world. One must also consider many of the customs relating to royal insignia, the throne as a cosmic symbol (referred to in J. Auboyer's Indian research) and the royal robes, also endowed with cosmic symbolic meaning (see above). In fact, even the physical person of the king is often immediately understood to possess healing power (cf. belief in the 'royal touch' which healed certain types of illness). This belief persisted through the Middle Ages.

Among these priest-kingly personages must also be numbered, still in the context of this symbology, priests like the Chief Roman flamines, especially the *flamen Dialis* (priest of Jove) who is at the same time the official and the symbol, in the very concrete sense we have already illustrated, of the forces which guarantee the survival of the community (he is *cottidie feriatus*, the object of symbolical taboos). K. Kerényi observes [127] that these personages of a religion like that of Rome, which fashions divine images not from marble but from life itself, so that they are like living sacred statues (cf. Plutarch, *Quaest. Rom.* III) are personages of a myth which is not seen in a timeless and ideal aspect but is concrete, repetitive and operative. This is true also of certain sacred African regal figures, or even of certain priests, like the *hogon* of the Dogon of Mali which we have already mentioned, with his symbolical taboos, his regal dignity and cosmic symbology, expressed in his attire and in his dwelling.

But regal ideology is not merely a mythical or ritual phenomenon, the re-evocation and perpetuation of archaic symbolism; it tends to re-emerge with the historical re-emergence of certain forms of authority, as we see in the case of the regal ambition of Julius Caesar, proclaimed (it does not matter whether directly by him or by his supporters) with references to the legend of Romulus and the myth of the *gens Julia*. This was clearly seen also in episodes like that of the *Lupercalia*

Egyptian, Gnostic and African and, to a certain extent, Iranian concepts already mentioned. Instead, these have something in common with the Late-Judaic gnostic trends of the *Cabbala*.

[127] *Die Religion der Griechen und Römer*, Munich-Zurich, 1963, S. 240.

in the year 44 A.D. when Caesar was acclaimed with expressions of homage full of references to Romulus and royal status, references which were well understood by many whose indignation was thereby aroused, because of the traditional Roman hostility to royal power. Almost the same hostility may be seen in Hebrew history, in which the dislike of regal ideology is shown in many ways, and variously explained as being inspired either by motives derived from historical-cultural tradition, or by religious and religio-political objections against most of the characteristics that marked regal ideology and ritual in the Syrian-Palestine world. The Scandinavian scholars believed they could identify in the Hebrew world—on the basis of psalms interpreted in a ritualistic sense—certain rites accompanying the king's accession to the throne: the king's figure, however, is strictly conditioned by the religion of Yahweh, as was ascertained by the above mentioned researches of Mowinckel.

30. *Non-mythical religions. The God of Israel*

We have already alluded several times to the very special case of two religions, the Israelitic and the Zoroastrian, as regards problems relating to mythology.

First of all we pointed out their characteristic attitude towards a history which is not merely a chronicle or a glorification of kings and dynasties and of their achievements, but also an interpretation of their story, told retrospectively, or sometimes prophetically, in the context of the history of salvation. The Old Testament describes a people who follow their God through the most diverse places and in the most disparate historical situations and circumstances, thus testifying to their own awareness of sacred history; this by far surpasses even what we find in Zoroastrianism, which also was deeply involved in complex and diverse events (from Alexander's invasion to the Arab conquest and later still) but which was firmly established, until the arrival of the Arabs, on a land which was uncontested by other peoples.

Hebraism and Zoroastrianism however both suggest another order of observations. Both are firmly anchored to their respective theologies (which even in the case of Zoroastrianism was in some respects strengthened by monotheistic faith) and faithful to their respective creationistic cosmogonies, as well as to their respective and precise ethical and ritual systems, all these aspects depending on, or at least associated with, the concept of a personal God, Creator of the world. They have something else in common too, which suffices to set them in a class apart from the religions of the ancient world: they still exist are religions, the Jewish faith being today more alive than Zoroastrianism, and they both survive as religious minorities (if we prescind from the state of Israel) and in scattered communities.

They both have their prophets, who left their mark on all their subsequent history: Moses and Zarathustra, so that the religion of Israel may legitimately be called Mosaic and Mazdeanism (from the name of the god Ahura Mazda) Zoroastrianism.

It is true that this parallelism to which we have drawn attention is, when studied more closely, not perfect because there are a number of significant divergences. The Zoroastrian religion, with its prophetic and theistic (when not monotheistic) character, is nevertheless still bound to ancient experiences and to ritualistic doctrines taught by the Magi; these had become typical of Zoroastrianism and are quite alien to the religious spirit of Hebraism. The Hebrews preserved some references to ancient Canaanitic ritual customs, which were however transferred to the worship of the God of Israel. But certain aspects of the Zoroastrian cult, particularly that relating to fire and the 'elements', seem typically 'pagan' to a Biblical mentality. On the cosmological plane this finds expression in the central importance assigned to doctrines like those of the *mēnōk* and *gētīk* in late-Zoroastrian theological treatises, doctrines concerning the substance of the universe, the material of creation. This speculation is associated with those speculations on the First Principles (*archai*) and the 'elements', typical of non-Biblical cosmogonies, whereas the Biblical Book of Genesis, and indeed the whole Old Testament, concentrate exclusively ond the action of God, presenting the elements of creation as an empirical series, as they appear to the ordinary observer, who finds in them a religious meaning.

Finally, on the mythical plane, Zoroastrianism is strictly conditioned (except in its Gathic form) by an ancient Indo-Iranian mythology of fecundity and life. But this is never included *in toto*; those gods which had been most characteristic of its heroic myths were excluded or transformed into demons, as happened in fact to the god of exuberant fecundity, Indra, who is always a demon in Zoroastrian belief, Hebraism shows a similar hostility to the Canaanite gods and goddesses of fecundity, the Baals and Astaroths of Palestine. This polemical attitude in both religions (but especially and typically in the Israelite, because of the polytheistic tendencies of classical Zoroastrianism) rests, not so much on theoretical monotheism or anti-polytheism, as on faith in God's creative and saving power, in a supreme and unique representative of a divine transcosmic, instead of in divine powers immersed in the cycle of fecund life. But here also there is a difference: the Zoroastrian tradition is always anchored to a theology of life, a *'magic'* (in the etymological, that is, Iranian sense) of life, whereas the Old Testament expresses a theology of God, and only the Cabbala was to represent the growth of a 'magic' speculation and practice centred on life and on the 'elements' of the cosmos, that is, of being.

Naturally it is impossible here to give even a brief account of the problems of religious history that concern Israel and its historical *milieu*, treated in the studies of Wellhausen (which gave a decisive impulse to the *Quellenforschung*), of Delitzsch, with the dispute over *Babel und Bibel*, and of Gunkel, with his *religionsgeschichtlich* researches (we come later on the historical significance of this expression) down to contemporary Biblical archeology.

All these studies, especially those of genetic and comparative interest, have shown the influence of views prevailing in their respective epochs. For example Wellhausen (*Prolegomena*, 1878) accepts many of the presuppositions of the anthropological school (as did Robertson-Smith later on) but pays particular attention to the Hegelian doctrine that history proceeds by thesis, antithesis and synthesis, thus following the example of the Biblical scholar W. Vatke, and proposes hypothetically a whole evolutionary process to explain the progressive development, from forms of primitive belief, of henotheism and finally of monotheism. This procedure, combined with a method based more on comparative philology than on comparative history, gives Wellhausen's reconstruction an 'academic' aspect, but leaves him the merit of being the first exponent of a criticism of sources which still influences our studies today.

The deciphering of the Babylonian texts, during the last century, opened up a vast field to the comparative-historical study of the Bible, both as regards its narratives, like that of the Flood, and as regards particular themes. The greater antiquity of these Babylonian texts, as compared with the text of the Pentateuch, suggested as the first and most natural solution a pure and simple borrowing on the part of Israel, which would imply that Israel's learned men had appropriated for themselves and for their religion an unwarranted authority (Delitzsch). But naturally the truth is more complex, in fact quite different. It is not a case of pure and simple borrowings, and even less a case of tricks played by a clever priestly class, but rather of great historical events, in the light of which the stories in the Old Testament should be situated, by the comparative method (Gunkel) and by sociological and psychological analyses (M. Weber, A. Alt, J. Pedersen) as well as by archeological research (W. F. Albright and others) which contributes extra-Biblical elements for the reconstruction of the history of Israel and its comparison (positive and negative) with other cultures, elements no less precious than those of the literary texts. The derivation of important elements of the 'patriarchal' religion from North-Western Mesopotamia, before the Middle of the second millenium, and the exodus from Egypt of an important Hebrew group (XIIIth century?) with other episodes of the Jewish tradition, decisive also for the religious experience of the race (in particular the Exodus) thus emerge from a series of researches as the specific historical context of a unique religion, peculiarly attached to history. On this concrete foundation should be studied (as Albright attempted to do) the genesis of Hebraic monotheism. [128] This is, in any case, at least initially very different from a systematically philosophical position. It is an experienced reality and therefore, as the same author points out, [129] the anthropomorphic concept of Yahweh is fundamental in the most ancient Israelitic religion and is deeply rooted in the Mosaic tradition. Thus, we observe, what is today commonly thought of as a negative aspect of the God of the Bible, the anthropomorphic concept which is sometimes 'justified' by not very cogent arguments, is in reality one of its great merits and characteristics. The God of Israel 'in the image of man', [130] nof of animals or realities of Nature, nor even of First Principles as in the cosmogonies of the East and of Greece, expresses through his very anthropomorphism his own singularity and essentially 'anti-mythical' character, because the human, even passionate, feelings attributed to him are all of a superhuman grandeur or, as the American archeologist says, 'heroic' (he cannot be seen by human eyes). The God of Israel, moreover, is not submerged by human existentiality, for he is unique in his attributes and sole creator of the universe (and God of all peoples in the world) without a wife or children or ancestors; yet at the same time he is the God of every Israelite and the God of the whole people. Moreover, the God of the Old Testament cannot be reduced to a 'great man', the product of the exaltation *ad infinitum* of positive human qualities

---

[128] *From the Stone Age to Christianity*, Baltimore, 1946^2.
[129] *Op. cit.*, chapt. IV C, 3.
[130] But see end of this paragraph.

because, even apart from his name Yahweh, which is probably associated with the concept of creating or 'calling into being', he has a nature, a personality and a 'place' which set him for ever above all mankind—for from certain points of view he is *the very opposite* of man,[131] and was never his Ancestor—and above the earth, for he was never its mythical inhabitant.

31. *The question of myth and the Old Testament*

These reflections on the characteristics of Hebraic monotheism set in a clearer light a question which has always been confused: that of mythology and the Old Testament. This confusion arises from the diverse meanings and connotations always attached to the word 'myth'. Sometimes it has been understood as a fictitious, or even false and indecorous, narrative about the gods: this is the sense in which the term is used in ancient Christian (and Hebrew) polemical works against mythology, that is, against the forms of Greek-Roman-Oriental religion in existence at that time, exemplified not so much in its living forms (although at times in these also—one must remember the attacks on the theology of the Mysteries) as in the mythology of the poets or of the ancient Roman religious traditions.

In their criticisms of the mythology of the poets the Christians and Jews of late antiquity make use of arguments already elaborated by Greek philosophers, from Xenophanes onwards; nevertheless, in the cultured Greek pagan world, there soon appeared a more benevolent interpretation which allegorized or even, in certain cases, idealized the myths. The Christians, for obvious reasons, restricted themselves to some symbolical interpretations, for example of the figure of Orpheus.[132] The poetical-mythological tradition, of Platonic inspiration, was also confined to the 'gentile' and non-Christian world, for obvious reasons, because both the Hebrew religion and Christianity were founded on Biblical narratives, with regard to which a philosophical interpretation, if any, was used, including a tendency to allegorize, but within very precise limits, by Philo of Alexandria. In fact, it was believed that the Greeks, even Plato himself, were inspired by the Mosaic revelation, according to an account of the relations between Greeks and Barbarians which had long been familiar to

---

[131] See for example Isaiah, 55, 8-11.

[132] When they do not prefer to have recourse to Euhemeristic explication, in which the gods are ancient deified men, or to daemonistic speculation, in which the gods are manifestations of demons or raised by demons.

the Greeks, always willing to acknowledge their supposed borrowings from the East. But, *vice versa*, with the intensification of anti-Christian and anti-Hebrew polemics, there was a tendency to level the accusation of 'mythology' (in the negative sense of an unacceptable fable) against the Biblical narratives. This was done by neo-Platonic philosophers and scholars, in the disputes which lasted from Celsus to Porphyry.

All this goes to prove that, during the first centuries of Christianity, the dispute about mythology and polytheism (often traditionally linked together) goes much further than a theological argument about the unity of the divine, which even the pagans, or at least many of them, accepted in their own way, that is, in syncretic, gnostic, neo-Platonic or Stoic-pantheistic forms. It concerns also the 'quality' of the narratives in question, and of the divine, angelic or human figures involved. Those Pagan stories in which the Deity demeaned, or seemed to demean, himself in situations that were indecorous or inadmissible were either rejected or explained allegorically. The allegorical explanation could be used (but with very different aims, i.e. respectively 'philosophical' or 'spiritual'-soteriological) for Greek narratives as well as for some Biblical episodes (Origen), and could apply also to the 'anthropomorphic' (but anyway not indecorous: see above) characteristics of the God of the Bible—but this God himself was challenged only by the Gnostics, who identified him with the inferior Demiurge. In short, whereas the pagan gods, as personal figures, faded away, and their mythology with them, accepted only symbolically or reduced to the status of fables, the God of Bible, and all the events associated with him, did not suffer this fate. His strong ethical character, and his pre-eminence as the only protagonist of creation and history, and also, naturally, his followers' belief in him, protected him from this. The Greek gods, instead, involved in theogonies and theomachies which showed them being born, and fighting among themselves, could only be re—absorbed in an order that was more real and sublime than their own. The same sort of fate, although in an diverse way, was prepared by the Gnostics, the 'Hellenizers' of Christianity, for the God of Israel, who was not rejected but de-moted and disfigured.

This characteristic of Biblical monotheism and of Biblical anti-mythology, is reflected also in another stage of the religious disputes of the ancient world, to which we have already alluded, the stage in which the Hebraic religion of Yahweh opposed the fecundity cults of the Phoenician-Canaanite world, and their claim to be able to control life [133] and the renewal of nature.

Here also it was essentially religious argument which characterized the attacks on a pantheon which the Hebrew tradition considered unworthy of the divine name, in fact blasphemous. So we see an attack which was substantially directed against idolatry and at the same time against polytheism struck at the heart of the religious life and of fundamental religious faith, which in Israel was so different from that of her neighbours the Canaanites. Idolatry and polytheism were associated together in all Hebrew-Christian tradition and remained instead rather distinct from the disputes about the divine hypostases (disputes which were also in existence, in their own realm).

32. *The meaning of the term 'myth'*

When the question of mythology and the Old Testament is thus correctly presented one can see how mistaken are those other meanings of the term 'myth' which are sometimes used, not so much by historians of religion as by philosophers and students of cultural anthropology (or even by theologians) who in practice consider the two terms 'mythical' and 'religious' as being synonymous, because they identify in myth, or in mythical characteristics, a religious content, as distinct from philosophic or scientific knowledge. At other times, as in the famous example of Bultmann's 'demythization', they describe as 'mythical', which to them means unacceptable, the concept of the appearance of divine manifestations in human, temporal, historical and eschatological forms. At other times they see (as did the Frankforts to a certain extent in the above mentioned 'intellectual adventure') in the will of God of Israel or the will of the God of Mahomet the only mythical element in these religions. Or sometimes, like the 'death of God' theologians, they claim that in a modern civilization a God who does not fully express himself in a worldly 'incarnation' is inconceivable. This is not the place to dwell on such discussions, which are for the most part extraneous to the history of religions and instead concern the philosophy of religion. We merely note how profitable it would be for everyone concerned if all were to use these terms in a clearly defined sense, especially the term 'myth' in the meaning, very concrete to historians of religion, of a *narrative*, not a system or a

---

[133] Coppens sees this argument already present in the Genesis story of the Fall of Adam.

theory, *about the gods as personages belonging to the age of the world's beginning, or to the last age of time,*—a narrative moreover in which *the gods themselves are set in a milieu which is vaster than themselves and which in various ways transcends them and in which they are not only the subjects but also the objects of events.* Instead, 'mythical characteristics', which may eventually be attached to other divine figures (or to the same figures in another context) will be understood as meaning all the aspects which resemble those most organically and legitimately incorporated in myths. Myths will either be believed in by their respective peoples and therefore held in supreme honour as the source of life and of the final meaning of things, or they will be rejected, by those who once believed in them but believe no longer, or by those who have never believed in them because they are strangers to the various religious traditions to which they belong. These persons will point out their inconsequence and inadmissibility, or they may subject them to a radical re-interpretation. In the case of the God of Israel, his fundamental non-mythical character derives from the fact that he is neither the object (passive, as it were) of a story (theogonic, theogamic, theomachic or based on the seasonal cycle) [134] nor absorbed into one. Among the mythical characteristics which may adhere to some scenarios in the Genesis, his 'anthropomorphic' (see above) nature may not, for the reasons already given, be included. On the contrary, this characteristic, understood *per viam eminentiae* (which does not mean in a symbolical, allegorical or even a 'spiritual' sense, but in a heroic [see above], transcendental sense) has done much to ensure for the God of Israel a transcendence, an aloofness from the world of nature and of natural relationships.

Of course, from the point of view of terminology, one may instead accept the myth as being similar to other narratives about transcendent personages and events (for example, about primordial beings), narratives which are not verified because they are incapable of verification except, eventually and indirectly, by signs and traces left by these primordial beings themselves. But in that case we must take care not to generalize too much and not to lose sight of the diversities in the type of narratives, personages and events, because the historical-comparative method will find conclusive evidence in the specific character of these various typologies and their diversities (for example in the difference between a God, like the God of Israel, who is not

---

[134] As in the fertility rites.

made the passive object of a vicissitude and a deity like Adonis or like the divine protagonists of the Babylonian theocosmogony).[135]

33. *The VIth century B.C.: an 'axial epoch'*

A very important theme for comparative-historical studies is offered by certain events and personages of that VIth century B.C. which Jaspers has rightly called an axial epoch of our history.

The VIth century, and the two which preceded it, saw the development, in India, of the speculations of the Upanishads, and in this same century there began the preaching of Buddha, which led this speculation, that taught men to transcend the illusory visible world which perpetuates itself with the succession of re-birth, to a drastic conclusion, which was nevertheless in some way consistent with the premises. In the West, the VIth (or, at least, the Vth) century provided the first documentation of a way of thinking, Orphic and Pythagoraean, which also, in certain forms of pre-Socratic philosophy, tended to theorize about an eternal cosmic process, of a combined Dualist and Monist character. In connection with this were elaborated soteriological concepts that were still founded on a belief in metempsychosis, like that of the exile, in this world of change and growth, of a spirit of divine origin. To the same century is generally assigned the activity of Zoroaster, the prophet of Iran; the part of the Avesta that is attributed to him, the *Gatha*, is on the one hand clearly averse (like all the *Avesta*) to anti-cosmic trends of Orphic or Indian thought, but on the other hand itself implies a vision of the cosmos as the object of a secular process in which divine presences and powers are engaged.

All this presents a series of problems concerning typology and historical diffusion. To what extent did the tendency towards a 'spiritualistic' interpretation, with a particular fondness for dualist concepts,[136] prevail in this epoch and spread across the world between the Mediterranean and India?[137] To what extent and in what way could analogous circumstances produce analogous developments? To what extent did this kind of soteriological-mystical speculation, expressing itself in anti-cosmic forms, react against a ritualism that was

---

[135] For recent studies of the myth, see G. Lanczkowski, *Neuere Forschungen sur Mythologie*, in *Saeculum* XIX, 2-3 (1968) pp. 282-309.

[136] See above pp. 41ff. and p. 155ff., for a definition and typology of 'dualism'.

[137] And even further afield, if Chinese Taoism, in its speculative form, was due to Indian influence.

also prevalently symbolical and mystical, like that of the Indian treatises of the *brahmana* which theorized about the cosmic symbolism of sacrifice and the supernatural efficacy of the rite? To what extent was this reaction due to 'lay' personages, outside the priestly caste (as in fact was the case with Buddha himself, and, it seems, with many of the Upanishad thinkers)? This series of problems is complicated by others which concern the relations between the various historical *milieux* and the peripheral *milieux* and regions which, hypothetically or according to legend, exercised considerable influence. How far was Greece in the VIth century influenced by the Balkan world and Eastern Europe, especially by Thracian-Getic notions, through the intermediary action of mythical or real personages like the 'Thracian Orpheus', or Abaris, Aristeas, or Hermotimus of Klazomenai—or at least through the use the Pythagoraeans made of these? [138] May we agree with Meuli and Dodds about 'shamanistic' influence in the Greek world, resulting in trends which implied a new awareness of 'spiritualist' phenomena, of the powers of the soul and of its 'detachable' nature? And how much could this affect the rise of the soteriological concepts already mentioned, which in fact distinguished in the soul a divine element, destined to be subjected to the body for a time, but later on to free itself with a cathartic movement of renewal and restoration? It is true that Shamanism and in general all the ethnological techniques about soul are directed more towards worldly interests: even those of which we learn from Herodotus and other authors, about the Thracian-Getic concepts of the immortality of the soul, do not really imply concepts of purification, but rather a search for the means of attaining immortality. But even in the Orphic world, how much was this concept of purification [139] based on ethical concepts comparable with those which we associate with the concept of purification, or did it instead not mean the liberation of divine powers, the 'immortalization' of man, the 'refining' and protection of the soul, certainly not in an identical sense but yet in some way, and significantly, akin to modern psychological healing techniques? (A healing, anyway, in those conceptions, surely connected with the world of the holy and the piety).

This theme is not confined to the Greek and Thracian world: a

---

[138] Cf. a text like the beginning of the Platonic *Charmides*. One reads therein that Zalmoxis taught the Thracians to cure the soul, and not only the body, like the Greek doctors.

[139] These concepts are comparable, and not identical, given the diversity of the ideological (metaphysical) premises.

people of great significance in the ethnical and historical events of ancient Europe, the Celts, had a priestly class, the Druids, whose doctrines, certainly with some practical applications, contained the notion of immortality, and also that of reincarnation.

34. *'Salvation'*

The central theme of religious thought and experience is salvation. In primitive civilizations it mainly concerned the safeguarding, through ritual observances, of life itself; for example, there were the seasonal festivals of renewal, or the festivals of initiation which celebrated the introduction into the community of the new age class, and these festivals also could celebrate the individual's happy destiny beyond death.

In the most ancient epochs of the great civilizations of Babylonia and Egypt, from the IVth millenium B.C. onwards (and certainly in earlier epochs also) the central element of religious life and of the concepts of salvation is the safeguarding, through ritual, of the great life cycle: every year the life of the land and of the community dwelling on it, impersonated by the king, must be ensured. So seasonal fertility is renewed by means of the king's sacred marriage with the Great Goddess, which we see was celebrated in Mesopotamia already in the IIIrd. millenium B.C., when the king, performing this rite, impersonated Dumuzi himself, the spirit of fertility. In another context, which we cannot immediately identify with this, it was said that Dumuzi, when a seasonal guest in Hades, substituted the goddess of life and by so doing freed her for ever from the Underworld. There is a similar Phoenician myth (and rite) about Adonis, who is called Tammuz (= Dumuzi) in Palestine. While the Great Goddess remains constant in her sovereign function as life-giver, every year her bridegroom, the spirit of fertility, after having ensured the fertility of the land, returns to the Underworld to await the time of his reappearance on earth. In this way is created a cycle of events which, with its seasonal crises, guarantees the life and perpetuity of the land and of its community. It is not however clear from the available documents to what extent a happy fate in the world beyond is guaranteed for the individual, [140] especially if we remember the melancholy fate reserved for man, incapable of attaining immortality, in the Babylonian myths of Adapa and Gilgamesh. But elsewhere this

---

[140] This seems to be guaranteed for the King, as is shown in an Assyrian text published by Ebeling, *Tod und Leben* (text No. 1).

aspect does not seem to have been neglected, as we see in what Egypt has to say about Osiris, the 'dead' God (who lives in the Underworld as the king of the dead) and about the life beyond (still in Hades) of the dead man, now grown similar to Osiris—a fate initially reserved —as it seems—for the king only.

These two aspects, the collective intention to ensure the yearly renewal of the land and therefore the salvation of its inhabitants, and the individual intention to ensure a particular happy fate in this life and in the life beyond, are united in the Greek Mysteries, particularly in those of Eleusis which celebrated the renewal of agrarian fertility and at the same time ensured the future bliss of the initiates in Hades, with Persephone, Queen of the Underworld. Certain Dionysiac rites resembled these, at least in some respects.

But in the 6th-5th centuries—as we have already observed— there occurred in Greece, and perhaps elsewhere also, especially in India, a religious revolution of great significance: the fertility cycle which, with its ritual and mystic celebrations ensured life through death, became the object of harsh criticism by daring thinkers, [141] and was now considered in its negative aspect: the cycle of new births was now seen as a cycle of new deaths, which bind the individual, or rather his soul (of divine origin) to an ever renewed captivity in a mortal body. Hence arose—together with other trends of pre-Socratic thought—Orphic and Pythagoraean speculation destined to be perpetuated, through Plato but more markedly in others, until it was absorbed in the Gnosticism of late antiquity, which was directly opposed to the body and to matter in general, attributing them to a creator understood to be an inferior and tyrannical god from whose sphere the soul, a divine spark, must flee in order to return to the divine sphere. In India men struggled in the same way against the grievous 'cycle of re-births'. Buddhism is the supreme example of this tendency which, in order to establish in an absolute form the connection between desire and pain, between this life and death, and the primary necessity of liberation, by breaking away from these, forbids all earthly desire and even, with Buddhism, all dangerous interest in another life and in immortality (which however it does not deny programmatically). [142] Later on, however, possibly to strengthen this position, it

---

[141] Cf. Heraclitus' grave condemnation of the rites of Dionysus.

[142] Cf. the well known example of the man who, wounded by an arrow, must think of saving his life before he enquires by whom and with what kind of weapon he has been struck.

even denies the pre-supposition for it, the 'permanent' soul. So the *Nirvana* is identified with the Absolute of pure liberation, understood as the final amnihilation of that *'karma'* which is the cause of empirical existence and of pain. [143] But the philosophy of the *Upanishads* and the whole teaching of the *Vedanta*, and modern Hindu thought also, teach that salvation is to be found in identification with the *atman*, the first and universal principle of life.

The 6th century, however, saw the reaffirmation of a faith that had long been established in Palestine. It was original in as much as, being monotheistic, it rejected the deification of nature and of her vital forces, as well as the extreme spirituality that repudiates these vital forces. This is the faith in Yahweh, which condemns the fertility cults of Baal and Tammuz, with their claim to the manipulation and control of the forces of life by magic power. Unlike the extreme spirituality of the re-incarnationist doctrines, it sees death as the consequence of sin. This was to be one of the elements contained in the new Christian doctrine of salvation, in which the Christological outlook is added to the monotheism of Israel. In this faith the deity is no longer dependent on an eternal alternation of life and death, as in the fertility cults and the Mysteries. On the contrary, it asserts that the Son of God suffered death in order to conquer both sin and death for ever. Sin, and the first sin is given prominence, in the Christian outlook, in the very frame of the theme of salvation, the Christian theme *par excellence*, implicit in the very meaning of the word 'Gospel'.

The Islamic faith is to some extent a continuation of the faith of Israel, for Islam also clings to the promise given by God to Abraham; the God of Islam is 'mild and merciful', and Islamic mysticism went far beyond the simple, but firm and fundamental, notion of salvation preached by Mohamet.

The concept of salvation in Mazdeanism, or Zoroastrianism, is dualistic (on this concept see on p. 155 ff.), but quite different from the Greek or Gnostic concept, which saw matter as opposed to the idea, or the spirit, in fact so sharply opposed as to be, for the 'Gnostics', incompatible. Here also the purpose is to safeguard creation and life; evil is an aggressive force existing outside creation, which breaks into it to destroy it. Eschatology, centred in the figures of the 'saviours' (*saošyant*), foresees that at the end of a single cycle (not destined

---

[143] 'Existence', in this context, must always be understood as an experience of suffering and of constriction. See p. 158 et sqq.

to be repeated) evil will be defeated and banished from the world; from this point of view the concept is not very different from the Biblical, Messianic eschatological concept. What distinguishes it from this is—*inter alia*—the ontological-cosmological character implicit in its dualism, which conditions the ethical-historical aspect of the struggle between god and evil peculiar to this concept.

35. *Iran and the history of religions*

The Iranian religion has always had a fundamental importance in historical-religious studies.

The ancient world had already mythicized Zoroaster as a teacher of religion and wisdom, making him the Master of Pythagoras and the forerunner of Plato, identifying him with Jewish and non-Jewish characters in the Bible or presenting him as Christ's prophet, thus weaving a tangled web in which the erudite scholars of the 16th and 17th centuries, and the Illuminists of the 18th century, were to seek confirmations of their respective interpretations of sacred history and of the growth of religion. This is demonstrated in Thomas Hyde's book, *Veterum Persarum et Parthorum et Medorum Historia* (1st ed., 1700, 2nd ed. 1760) in which, in spite of the confusion of materials and the arbitrariness of his criteria, an attempt is made to compare or rather to re-associate, diverse religious traditions, an attempt which accentuates the central significance of the problems inherent in the religious history of Iran.

Anquetil-Duperron's discovery of the sacred scriptures of the Parsees, the *Avesta* (so full of confused rituals and repetitions of formulas) and the presentation of the new texts in 1771, seem to have had a disturbing effect on the old concept of a Zoroaster who was a very ancient Master of philosophy, or indeed, as the Illuminists asserted, of natural religion; but they laid the foundations of a more authentic knowledge of Zoroastrian religious literature. This gave rise to new problems, while old problems were reformulated, including those resulting from comparative studies, to some of which we have already referred in the preceding paragraph. Other and different aspects of Zoroastrian religious speculation, more or less well known, raise questions of interest to the historians of religions. Among these questions are monotheism, a term which has sometimes, rightly or wrongly, been applied to Zoroastrian dualist theology, (as well as dualism, a phenomenon which always appeared at home in pre-islamic Iran) and, finally, the wisdom of the Magi and of their alleged leader, Zoroaster.

As regards Zoroastrian monotheism, apart from the theories of earlier scholars, repeated and amply discussed by Hyde, some more modern scholars (Spiegel, De Harlez, Pettazzoni) thought it had Hebraic origins. Certain passages in the *Gatha*, in which Ahura Mazda is spoken of in terms and expressions somewhat similar to those found in the Psalms, or in which the difficulties encountered by Zoroaster in his mission are lamented, make this hypothesis attractive, if not convincing. In fact, even today, the unique position of the god Ahura Mazda in the *Gatha* texts, in other parts of the *Avesta* and in the royal inscriptions of the first Achemenid Kings (a position which, at least in the *Gatha*, may be correctly called monotheistic) presents some unsolved problems which in any case depend on a general interpretation of the Iranian religious traditions which is still *sub judice*.

In fact, the problem of the relation between the Zoroastrian religion and the Iranian world is complex. One may wonder whether, and within what limits, the Mazdean religion of the Great God (and its characteristic dualism), wholly directed against those powers which sought to corrupt all life and Mazda's creation, can be separated from Zoroaster himself, or at any rate from the tradition deriving from him: this does not seem possible. One may also ask whether Mazdeanism in its more general sense, is identical with the Iranian religion. This seems to be an undoubted fact, at least in less ancient periods, in opposition to the tendency of Benveniste and the Scandinavian school to admit several Iranian 'religions'. Are the Achemenid inscriptions, which are certainly Mazdaean, also Zoroastrian? This seemed evident to E. Meyer, but not to other scholars. One questions whether Zoroaster reformed a naturistic and polytheistic 'paganism' (as Pettazzoni and others believed) or (as Dumézil asserts) was the author of a subsequent 'second grade' reform. One wonders also whether the religious class of the Magi was bound from the beginning to Zoroaster (as Messina believed) or did the Magi belong in their own right to the Iranian, and particularly the Mazdaean religion, as is generally, and with good reason, believed? Did they form a sacrificial priestly class or rather an élite, at the centre of a series of concentric circles composing the complex Iranian religious world (as Molé asserts)?

Is Zoroastrianism a theology, an ethical system and a way of living, with a ritual intended to safeguard and promote life, as the *Avesta* suggests, or was it primarily a 'Magic', in the sense of a technique and an occult knowledge of the energies of the cosmos and of man (as G. Gnoli asserts)?

One may also ask what is the connection between certain typical Mazdean customs and the customs of peripheral Iranian, or even Aniranian, peoples. Nyberg asserted that he saw in Zoroaster a shaman figure, an ecstatic personage, in the context, well attested for central Asian peoples, of the use of fumigations of hashish, in order to obtain visions of the super-human world. As for Dualism, apart from its obvious connection with a radicalization of the struggles between life and non-life, one sees that it is possible to study it in the context of a dualistic mythology diffused over an area covering great tracts of Central and Northern Asia, which can explain traces of the existance of a minor Iranian mythology, repudiated by official Zoroastrianism.

Other problems concern the relations between Iran and the West. Much has been written about eventual connections (dating from the Babylonian exile onwards) between Iran and the Hebrew religion, concerning some 'Messianic' prophecies, concepts of the final resurrection and, in general, eschatology, the soul, angelology and demonology. All these are questions in which, however, one must take care that the discussion is never reduced to theoretical notions of absolute (that is, abstract) chronological priority. It must also take into account the connections, diffusion, circumstances and, which is very important, the peculiarities of the respective concepts, and their place in history and in the evolutionary process of the various religions, in short, their *Sitz im Leben* in order not to run the risk of identifying things which are only partly comparable.

As regards Greece, the possibilities of contact may be found chiefly in the Late Achemenid era (that is, in the century preceding Alexander) and, naturally, in the Hellenistic Age. For some time past there have been discussions about eventual (but difficult to prove or formulate) relations between pre-Socratic philosophies and Iran; but the most lively debate concerns Plato who seems in his later works (see the *Laws*) to re-echo not only Chaldaean astrology but also Iranian dualism (if he really wrote *Alcibiades* he was familiar with the figure of Zoroaster, though much transformed).

In the Hellenistic and Roman-Hellenistic Ages the cultural exchanges were more intense and the borrowings more frequent and involved. A whole literature based more or less on 'Zoroastrian' ideas seems to reflect the presence, to the west of Iran, of the *Magusaioi*, the Hellenized Magi of the Zoroastrian *diaspora*; ancient Persian sages, Zoroaster and others, are said to be the authors of pre-eminently syncretistic doctrines which suggest interesting problems for the religious history of the ancient world. These are presented in a masterly way, with careful documentation by Bidez and Cumont (*Les Mages hellénisés*, 1938). Thus a new literature was created, its fundamental themes being of a hymnic or oracular nature (the trend is political, pro-Oriental and anti-Roman) with theories about nature (botanical and lapidary treatises), astrology, the occult sciences and alchemy; Zoroaster is referred to in Patristic literature and by the Gnostics, and the Messianic prophecies of Hystapes are quoted. [144]

There are many western elements in the Iranian world naturally first appearing with Alexander, when all the Orient, as far as the Indus, became subject to Greek influences, and later in the Parthian Age when the Iranian religion itself seemed to adopt a Grecian form, and this Western influence continued till the time of the Sassanian Kings; late Zoroastrian theological treatises also reveal traces of Greek influence. In the next paragraph we shall speak of R. Reitzenstein's Iranian comparisons in connection with the history of Gnosticism and Christianity.

36. *The 'Religionsgeschichtliche Schule'*

The question of the relations between Christianity and the non-Biblical religious world has, as is well known, opened up a vast field for religious-historical studies.

This complex of problems was studied with special interest by a new school called the *Religionsgeschichtliche Schule*. This name does not imply that it enjoys a monopoly of the comparative-historical method, but has its precise significance in a new development in the study of religion in late antiquity—shortly after the beginning of the century.

The presuppositions of the 'religious-historical school' differ from other well known interpretations of the history of Christianity and we mention them merely to point out an example of methodological discussion.

They differ from the Hegelian methodology of the scholars of

---

[144] G. Messina, *I Magi a Betlemme e una predizione di Zoroastro*, Rome, 1933, pp. 74 et sqq.

the Tübingen school who, with F. C. Baur, applied to the history of Christianity that pattern of thesis—antithesis—synthesis which Wellhausen would have tried out in the study of the Old Testament. They differ also from the presuppositions of Adolf von Harnack, and from the position he assumed in the question of the relations between Christianity and Gnosticism, which was fundamental also to the investigations of the *Religionsgeschichtliche Schule.* Harnack assumed a characteristic attitude with regard to Marcion whose doctrine appeared to him an example of a univocal interpretation of Christianity, carried to a point beyond Christianity itself. Harnack considered that by rejecting the Old Testament Marcion had broken the fundamental polarity character of the Great Church. His own theory was that Christianity preserved a fundamental continuity with Judaism, but was enriched, like late Judaism itself, with various elements from different sources, and so was able to extend itself syncretically over diverse, sometimes even mutally opposed positions, in a kind of *complexio oppositorum*, which he sees, for example, in its attitude to involvement in the world and flight from it (this latter being on the contrary a univocal characteristic of Marcionism) or in a controlled Hellenization, whereas Gnosticism corresponded, at the other extreme, to an 'acute Hellenization of Christianity'. But it must not be overlooked that, as for the Christianity of Jesus, or the 'essence of Christianity', Harnack's interpretation is influenced by a central option which deliberately represses not only doctrinal but also mystical elements, resulting in an exclusively ethical interpretation of the evangelical message of the divine Fatherhood, in the context of a trend towards a 'liberal theology'. [145]

---

[145] Harnack's interpretation of Marcion as being extraneous to the Gnostic movement is today generally refuted (A. Adam, R. M. Grant, K. Rudolph, H. Jonas, U. Bianchi); cf. the Author's *Marcion: théologien biblique ou docteur gnostique?* in *Studia Evangelica*, V ed.; F. L. Cross (*Texte und Untersuchungen*, vol. 103) pp. 234-241 and *Vigiliae Christianae*, 21 (1967) pp. 141-149. Moreover, although Marcion may in one way 'simplify' (but arbitrarily, as regards not only the position of the Church but also as regards the figure of Jesus) by refusing to acknowledge the God of the Old Testament, in another way he complicates matters by introducing two Gods, the God of the O.T. and the God of Jesus, thus producing a host of complications on theological and ethical planes, which lead him to Gnostic positions. As regards Harnack's interpretation of the figure of Jesus, although in one way it enables us to perceive essential aspects of evangelical spirituality, sometimes obscured by certain theologians of a philosophical origin (as we see in gnosticism, 2nd-3rd centuries A.D.), in another way it ignores certain not less essential aspects of Jesus, for example those of the mystery of the 'Son of Man' or of the particular relationship between Jesus and the God he calls 'his' Father.

The interpretations of the *religionsgeschichtliche Schule* are not equally systematic. These scholars concentrated not so much on a general interpretation of the Christian phenomenon as on a study of the individual links, or historical 'derivations' of Christian or Gnostic doctrines and practices from other religious *milieux*. A characteristic concept of this school is the concept of *Erklärung*, by virtue of which they consider as historically 'explained' every element of religious belief or practice for which precedents have been found, or conjectured, in other religious forms.

The religious-historical methodology, instead, cannot ignore the fact that links and resemblances must be studied in connection with the chronology of the texts, (the *religionsgeschichtliche Schule* was not always strict about this) as well as the fact that what is historically comparable may not be reduced to individual or particular aspects of belief or worship but must include concrete historical complexes and processes. In particular, the *religionsgeschichtliche Schule* was over eager to discern the frequent, even typical, occurrence of syncretism in the religions of late antiquity. This is, however, a very specific type of phenomenon and should not be quoted too frequently, especially when the circumstances and motives of such supposed minglings of elements of various origins are not presented, and when there has been inadequate investigation into the question of how a religious element of belief or worship, supposedly 'derived' from another religious *milieu*, functions in the religious complex in which it has found expression.

The *religionsgeschichtliche Schule* paid special attention to the delucidation of the essence and origins of Gnosticism, which seems to have played a particularly important role in the religious history of the ancient world, because of its connections with pagan Eastern (particularly Iranian and Mesopotamian) and Mediterranean (Syrian and Egyptian) religions and with Judaism and Christianity. So a 'heresiological' view of Gnosticism (that is, its interpretation as a heresy of Christianity, the most ancient of all heresies, fomented by the Greek pagan mentality) was replaced by a 'religious-historical' view, the result of an extended comparative study. After a first essay of minor documentary significance, by W. Anz (1898) were published the *Hauptprobleme der Gnosis*, by W. Bousset (1907), one of the most typical treatises on this subject, studied in all its aspects by the comparative method, but substantially devoid of conclusions on a factual historical plane. The Iranian influences, with dualism, which is however of a different nature from that of Gnostic dualism, and Greek influences (for the doctrine of the *pneuma*) do not suffice to provide Bousset with a unitary concept of the genesis of Gnosticism, which is in any case not easy to discover on the plane of the purely analytical comparison of individual elements. It is to be found primarily either through an intuition of the 'principle of construction', in the manner of H. Jonas, who sets the Gnostic phenomenon in a new and specific *Weltanschauung* of the late antique world, or by the patient analysis of affinities and possible derivations (based on precise historical processes, even when these are aberrant), from pre-existent traditions. True, these are identified individually by various scholars in different religions, Judaism (E. Peterson, R. M. Grant, G. Quispel), Christianity (A. von Harnack, G. Pétrement), Platonism (A. J. Festugière), and, more generically, Greek mysticism (H. Leisegang) and the Iranian religions (G. Widengren).

A definite decision in this sense was made by P. Reitzenstein, the most active member of the *religionsgeschichtliche Schule*, who in a series of studies tried to interpret the fundamental doctrine of Gnosticism, and essential parts of the Christian dogma, in relation to the doctrine of the *Anthropos*, a celestial figure, both Saviour and saved, to whom he attributed an Iranian origin. This hypothesis met with strong opposition because of the insufficient attention he paid to the chronological problem (the Gnostic *Anthropos* in the double role assigned to him by Reitzenstein, being present in documents like that of the Naassenes which were attested only at a later date) and because of the absence, in Iran, of a typology of the Primordial Man that could properly be compared with that of the Gnostic *Anthropos* —whereas a Manichaean text of 'Zoroaster', on which Reitzenstein set great store, was quite extraneous to the Zoroastrian tradition, and appears to have represented a mature form of Manichaean Gnosticism. [146]

After Reitzenstein the *religionsgeschichtliche Schule* broke up, and only in recent years have some of its tenets been taken up again by G. Widengren, particularly those regarding the question of Iran's contribution to Gnostic themes. [147]

---

[146] The question of a pre-Christian Gnosticism is still *sub judice*, but in any case it is no longer set in relation to the Reitzenstein theories, which lack the Iranian presupposition.

[147] Other students of the same School and engrossed in similar problems, were Norden, A. Dieterich, H. H. Schaeder (at first, not later on) and R. Bultmann.

37. Italian Modernism and the history of religions

The *religionsgeschichtliche Schule*, together with Biblical philology,[148] the French history of religions and R. Otto's theories on the 'holy', had a certain influence over Italian Modernism in the first decades of this century. Nevertheless it remains paradoxically true that Modernists, who played such an important part in arousing Italian interest, favourable or unfavourable, in the history of religions, have not been pre-eminent in the history of this study. This is explained by the fact that although they made full use of the data of historical religious research, they integrated these in a sphere of interest and enquiry which was fundamentally philosophical in character and (in the sense in which Modernists used this term) 'apologetic'.

For their point of view it is worth while reading the observations made in 1912 by Pettazzoni, in the Preface to his first book on the history of religions (*La religione primitiva in Sardegna*), about the Modernists' approach to this branch of study. In fact, they seem to have been willing to confuse scientific and religious interests in an ambivalent methodology which could meet neither the needs of purely historical research nor those of theological tradition. Nor could they satisfy current 'lay' speculation, whether positivist (to which Pettazzoni owed much of his training) or of Italian 'storicismo assoluto' (Croce's *fin de non recevoir* to Buonaiuti is well known). Where Modernism ended in pure 'rationalism' and positivism, with A. Loisy's 'religion of humanity', there had been not so much an agreement as the complete absorption of the former in the latter. Italian Modernism never got to this point: it could define its own apologetics as the 'attempt to escape from agnosticism, as a doctrine of knowledge, by transcending it—just as agnosticism had been an attempt to transcend materialistic positivism'.[149]

Italian Modernism moreover did not completely accept the dogmas of R. Otto's philosophy of religion, with which it had nevertheless some points of contact: Buonaiuti translated the Marburg theologian's *'Idea of the Holy'*, but mentioned in the Preface his own reservations, as a Modernist of Catholic extraction, regarding Otto's characteristically Lutheran presuppositions. The final outcome of Buonaiuti's philosophy of religion was, as is well known, a Mediterranean religiosity which denotes a further development of his thought in the direction of what one might call religious historism.

---

[148] See S. Minocchi.
[149] *Il programma dei modernisti*, reprinted Turin, 1911, p. 95.

As regards the actual religious-historical position of of the Modernists, and in particular of E. Buonaiuti and their contribution to positive research, one must refer here to their preoccupation with the question of heresies, this also being conditioned by problems of a theological nature and of the interpretation of the history of Christianity and of the Church. We must mention Buonaiuti's works on *gnosis* and on Manicheism, as well as his history of African Christianity. As regards the works on *gnosis*, [150] one cannot deny that, in accordance with some questionable conclusions of E. de Faye, they underestimate the dualist position, as taught by the Gnostic Doctors, which places the Gnostics in a line which diverged not only from the dominant line in the history of the Church and of orthodoxy, but also from the central presuppositions of Christianity, which are in fact extraneous to Dualism. Harnack, as we have seen, admitted this, although he too was inclined to value highly the evangelical character of the doctrine of Marcion. Analogous observations concerning the heretical dualist movements of the Middle Ages may be applied to the views of Italian Mediaevalists like R. Morghen, who were not unaffected by certain aspects of the Modernist movement, as we shall see in the next paragraph.

38. *An example of comparative investigation: Dualism*

Gnostic Dualism and, more generically, a form of Dualism characterized by a concept according to which the very constitution of our world and of man derives from two clearly distinct, in fact contrasting, entities, a Supreme Being and an inferior Demiurge, his rival and imitator, offer an excellent example of the way in which certain religious concepts persist and spread in time and space, in spite of changing cultural situations.

From a certain point of view Dualism, as we have defined it (the notion of a dichotomy, or rather of an opposition between the principles, whether co-eternal or not, which are responsible for the existence of whatever is found in this world) is already present among various primitive peoples, and even outside that Central Asian area which presents particular problems because of the presence of the great historical dualistic religions, Mazdaeism and Manichaeism. Very clear dualist concepts which in certain respects resemble Iranian symmetrical

---

[150] Cf. for example his interpretation of Basilides and Isidore (*Frammenti gnostici*, Rome, 1923, p. 67), concerning which see author's paper in the *Studi Pincherle* (in *Studi e materiali di storia delle religioni*, 38) 1967, p. 79 et sq., nn. 1 and 5.

Dualism (two beings, promoters respectively of life and death, both authors of a creation, one beneficent, the other maleficent) are found among the Iroquois Indians in North East America. Others which imply an original dualism between two unequal but irreconcilable beings are found also among the very primitive peoples of central-northern California, where a typical figure of a 'trickster Demiurge', the Coyote, an ambiguous figure both from the ethical point of view and as regards his creative (or rather 'transforming' or demiurgic) activity sometimes appears in direct opposition to a Supreme creative Being, whose creation he mars by introducing death and other features of present human experience, which make him from some points of view not altogether unlike that Demiurge of certain Gnostic cosmogonics and anthropogonics. Figures of this type are found along the whole central-northern belt of Asia, where the definitely destructive features and the ambiguous demiurgic characteristics (of a fatal rivalry, more or less successful, with the Supreme Being) are seen in characteristic mythological personages among the Yacuts, Buryats and Turco-Tatars (cf. the figure of Erlik among the Tatars, and, respectively, the Raven of the Palaeo-Siberians). Even the Ahriman of certain minor Iranian mythology has characteristics very different from the purely sinister and destructive qualities typical of him in Zoroastrian literature, for here he assumes the unexpected role of God's counsellor in matters relating to the creation. In the complicated Manichaean cosmogony even the functions of God and those of Anti-God, of the elements of 'light' and matter, of divine and demoniac beings are mingled in a web—sometimes expressed in a very crude mythological form—of extreme complexity. Moreover, surprising anthropomorphisms and realistic beliefs are found in classical Gnostic systems, including the philosophical system of Valentinus.

But there is another analogous comparative question, relating to other dualist doctrines and sects of the Near East, in particular to the Mandaeans. Certain forms of 'Sabean' astrolatry of Harran seem to constitute the link between Mandaeism on the one hand and an extreme advanced form of the Babylonian religion on the other. The Mandaean astral gods assumed a negative character although they still ruled the world, as forces of the *heimarmene* ('destiny') identified with the dread 'seven' demons already known to the Babylonians of the classical age.

Still in the same region, strong ethnological elements are present in the dualistic doctrines of the ancient sect of the Yazidis, the 'devil-worshippers', the devil being a form of Demiurge rival now reconciled with the Supreme Being. Yazidi mythology seems to repeat (but in another context) the ancient theme of a Demiurge in the form of a bird poised above the waters, typical of some Central Asian ethnological myths, in which he functions as the collaborator of the Supreme Being, for whom, diving to the bottom of the primaeval sea, he procures that handful of mud from which the Supreme Being created the earth. This theme, of the fishing up of mud by a water bird, is found also in North America, but without dualistic connotations, which therefore seem to have been accessory, that is, later additions, to the Asiatic myths. Nevertheless, the dualistic theme is frequently found even in America.

The theme of the Demiurge as rival is typical of a certain folklore and of a whole series of apocryphal narratives found in Eastern Europe, from Russia to the Balkans. Here the question again arises: are these the last remnants of Gnostic concepts inherited from the mediaeval dualist heresy of the Bogomiles and widely diffused in these lands, [151] or was there in fact a primitive substratum still existing in these regions, orientated in a dualistic direction? [152] In fact, the theme resembles so many myths and legends of Central Asia (the above mentioned myths of Erlik among the Tatars of the Altai mountains, and others found among the Buryats of Baikal, etc.). It is true that in these cases also there is a possibility, indeed a probability, of the existence of profound Manichaean as well as Zoroastrian influences (or even of Russian folklore, also of Bogomile origin) but it is also

---

[151] The Messalians and the Paulicians also could exert an influence.

[152] To explain this affinity scholars usually refer to the diffusion in Europe of Bogomile legends, which contained elements of Biblical culture as well as popular, folkloristic and ethnological elements. But the very existence of this Bogomilism, so composed, raises a genetic, and therefore a historical problem which cannot be studied apart from a vast series of comparative-historical problems concerned with the history of religions. The comparative panorama is still more extended, involving already certain features of Greek religious speculation (the myths of Prometheus, the Demiurge rival and 'trickster') and not only in the texts of Hesiod and Aeschylus but also in certain minor mythologies, in which the Titan has characteristic features not unlike those of the ethnological and folkloristic dualist conceptions we have already mentioned. In some of the mentioned doctrines or myths there is the idea that man was moulded, as regards his physical attributes and inferior psychic qualities, by a Demiurge—rival of the Supreme Being as in the well known myth of Prometheus creating man, in whom Athena, acting for Zeus, then sets a soul. This theme corresponds to those of the Gnostic narratives of the creation of man— we mention this without any intention of 'reducing' Gnosticism, and only to emphasize certain fundamental dualist connections. It is clear that concepts of this type influence notions about man and about ethics.

true that dualist concepts af various types are found throughout Central-Northern Asia, as far as the Pacific and beyond, as in the dualistic North American myths we have already referred to.

This whole question therefore is a most interesting testing ground for comparative historical enquiry, presenting problems concerning the relations between ethnological cultures and 'higher' cultures, and also questions of historical continuity and typological analogies between 'higher' religions across time and space. Moreover, religious phenomena that appeared in the West, such as Catharism in its various forms, raise not only the question of a historical derivation from the East, through connections not always traced but which the careful Mediaevalists make rightly an object of historical inquiry, but also the question of the undeniable persistence of a dualistic 'logic' which renders more comprehensible the Catharist theological and cosmogonical teaching when compared with the above mentioned dualistic religions and concepts; and this is the 'typological' aspect of that comparison which mediaevalists would be unwise to ignore. [153]

39. *An Eastern example of a universalist religion: Buddhism*

We have already referred to Buddhism and to the way in which it originated in Upanishad speculation, sometimes directed by lay leaders and showing some originality when contrasted with the priestly theorizing in the texts called *Brahmana*. In these, sacrifice is elevated to a cosmic mystique, in a creative symbology which makes the sacrifice itself—and, even more, the formulas which give it validity—the creative act *par excellence* by means of which the world perpetuates and renews itself. In fact, speculation about the sacrifice grows more and more subtle until it becomes separated from the material offering itself and is resolved into the pure magic of the effective knowledge of the meaning of the sacrifice. At the same time, and in relation to this same theme, always centred in the renewal of life and the attainment of immortality, there arose a speculation about the First Principles, the *Brahman*, the transcendent power of the sacrifical act and the essence of the world, and the *Atman*, by means of which the *ego* of the wise man, through his own penetrating vision and mystical exaltation, became identified with the universal *Atman*, the essence of being, which is identical with the *Brahman*, transcending the gods

---

[153] For a more extended study of Dualism see p. 41 et sqq.

and mythology and the source of the personal revelation itself, Brahma as the Supreme deity, in which the First Principle is manifest.

In this speculation, if the efficacy of the sacrifice and in general of the whole action which is essentially sacrificial creates the world, it also creates, in some way, that web of what we might call 'second grade' reality that binds man to a cycle which, making him resort to action, runs the risk of separating him from a possible reunion with the *Atman*, beyond the world of illusion (*Maya*), in which both gods and men are constrained to act. Hence there is a sudden reversal of the whole situation: action, and the desire for action, with their fruit, (*Karma*), are indeed the source of life and prosperity, but on an inferior plane, which really implies the impossibility of deliverance (*mokṣa*) in the direction of the real substance of being, the *Atman*. In fact, the *karma*, by continually increasing, is the cause of that 'cycle of births' which is a fatal, dread and inexorable cycle of new deaths, and of lasting separation, through this endless alternation, from the hope of a deliverance from time, destiny and death, disguised as life and action. Much of the post-Upanishad speculation, as seen in the Mahabharata for example, was intended to find a way of reconciling the needs of the Absolute with the needs of life in this world, and to give a meaning and legitimacy to action, when disinterested, which will then become lawful, and no longer the cause of evil.

Now we come to thee teaching of Siddhartha Gautama Sakyamuni, called the Buddha, or the 'enlightened one'. The origin of rebirths is desire, which is the cause of suffering. Therefore no more thoughtless wordly vanity, and not even asceticism which is permeated with desire, the desire for existence—but a total annihilation of desire through knowledge of its origins and consequences. Therefore there is no *ego* or permanent soul in any of these reincarnations, nor (in some instances of developed Buddhist speculation) substance of any permanence, but the total unmasking of the *Maya* which expresses itself in all these things. Hence a complete deliverance, in which (and not in being absorbed into an Absolute understood as the principle of the soul) Nirvana consists for Buddhism.

It has long been questioned whether this form of Buddhism, which seems to be the original form in as much as it expresses the essence of almost all the Buddhist schools and religions, [154] is to be considered a religion in itself. It is pointed out that it lacks the soul, God, the

---

[154] But not in that important form: Amidism.

world beyond, the notion of 'being'. Yet it seems impossible to exclude Buddhism, even in its original form or inspiration, from the category of religious experiences, in which in fact it enjoys a preeminent position. The Buddhist doctrine, or rather Buddha's first intuitive knowledge, is religious (in the 'analogous' sense proper to this adjective) because it is a doctrine of liberation, and because it refers to something which is in its own way an Absolute, Nirvana, totally different from this world of desire and illusion. This is in spite of the paradoxical way in which it denies substance to Nirvana, but admits it as a negative (but from its own point of view totally positive) point of reference. Liberation in Nirvana, reduced to the pure state of liberation, that is, of the cessation of *Karma*, is in fact something ab-solute.

It is easy to understand how such a doctrine revolutionized India, partly conquering it, and was then almost totally rejected, except in peripheral regions like Ceylon, Burma and Nepal. The rejection was unusual for India, which is accustomed to the religious assimilation of all, even of foreign, importations.

Buddhism, on the other hand, did not reject assimilations and syncretisms, even from religions of a clearly inferior cultural level, in Japan, Indo-China and Thibet. But India rejected Buddhism because it contradicted the very basis of Indian thought: it was the only 'heresy' which this thought could not accept: the contradiction—arisen in India—to the principle of Indian mysticism: the return to the First Principle, the final substance of being.

From another point of view also India's rejection of Buddhism is characteristic. With all her multiform speculation about 'being', expressed in the most varied religious forms and on all levels (worship, literature, popular customs, folklore) Indian faith is and will always belong to the type of ethnical religion, with a highly sophisticated tradition. It is an ethnical religion which, with its fondness for theosophical thought, seems capable of absorbing, in its own way, all the religious beliefs with which it comes into contact. But it is still an ethnical religion that does not take kindly to iconoclasm, especially that extreme form of iconoclasm which cuts away the ground from under all its gods, those of folklore as well as those of supreme and gnostically rarefied speculation. Buddhism, however, in dissolving all this, while admitting the possibility of the existence of various levels of progress on the way to liberation, presents itself as a universalist religion. This adjective, in the case of Buddhism (very different in this from, say, Christianity: see below) means as a religion which asserts its capacity to embrace all rites and cults; but it also means, and primarily, as a religion which appeals directly to the individual, at least in all that regards what matters most, liberation, and, with this prospect in view, totally rejects all caste distinctions, which constitute, or constituted, the true Hindu orthodox doctrine or practice, in which there was no possibility of compromise because they depended on the vision of the cosmos as a differentiated whole and a differentiated order, according to the most authentic Indian tradition, that is, as a great life cycle, which is renewed, according to merit and good works, through the process of metempsychosis.

Pettazzoni has pointed out that Buddhism, in its historical dynamism, was somewhat similar to Christianity in the West. Both were rejected by the religion and the people of their own land, of which the respective founders were nevertheless very eminent personages, and both were widely diffused, with a universalist trend, because of their appeal to the individual, for they preached a doctrine, or rather a way, of salvation.

Yet, Pettazzoni observes, these two religions are very dissimilar. Christianity is anti-syncretical whereas Buddhism comes to terms with gods and rites of different cults. The reason for the dissimilarity is of course evident: it depends on their respective starting points, their respective centres of interest, and on the questions to which both wished to give an answer. Christianity teaches the universal and saving Fatherhood of God revealed through his Son, whereas Buddhism teaches the necessity of un-masking the sources of suffering. The former preaches one God, instead of the 'unknown god' worshipped by the pagans, and the latter preaches that all desire for existence, known by so many names, is incompatible with the Absolute. No other gods but the one God for Christians, and many, in fact, all gods for Buddhism, because it teaches no absolute Primal Entity.

Buddhism then is a religion which may be said to be in direct opposition to the basic beliefs of the religion from which it stemmed; it does not express itself, however, in a worldly atheism, but, on the contrary, in a form of unworldliness which, being absolute, absorbs into itself the world of gods and the Absolute itself, and therefore, because it is unconditional and anti-mundane, is paradoxically religious.[155] Its religiosity, however, remains in the sphere of Indian

---

[155] It is much nearer than Gnosticism to a Nihilism of an existentialist type, but also contrary to gnosticism in as much as it is directed towards the extinction of existence, not towards liberation from this world.

speculation which, starting from the experience of existence and suffering, seeks ways of deliverance from these; a proceduree, a 'way' and a 'religion' opposed to the Christian faith which sees, even in this world of suffering, the coming of a heavenly messenger, a bearer of salvation. In this we seen an opposition which is possibly not a mere contradiction but, perhaps better than any other confrontation, expresses the concept that the religious world is a world of 'analogies' (see on pp. 5 et seqq., 201 et seqq.)—not a world in which one and the same question is simply answered by the different religions by 'yes' or 'no'.

CHAPTER FOUR

MODERN PROBLEMS OF METHODOLOGY AND INTERPRETATION

1. *Dynamism of religions and sociology of religion*

Various critics have pointed out that the study of religions cannot be restricted to a research which concerns only historical forms and developments, especially those relating to remote origins and periods, but must instead consider the present day life of religions, their dynamism, their problems, agreements and disagreements, in relation to all the aspects, religious and non-religious, of the modern world, including those of Western civilization, of technical progress, industrial organization, 'secularization' and atheism. [1]

This is sound criticism, and the history of religions, when truly historiographical, cannot disassociate itself from any of these problems, and still less from the dynamism of religions, since the historical method itself is interested in seeing the facts and historical processes as dynamic factors, in action. On the contrary, we may reproach certain phenomenologists, psychologists and sociologists, whom we have already for various reasons criticized in these pages, for seeing religions, like any other phenomena, as it were, fossilized in forms and classifications outside the main stream of history. One must, therefore, study the history of religions and religion as they are today, or at least as they are in modern times, in the complex framework of the modern world. One must however, be clear about this: it is not only the modern world which is complex and raises problems like those already indicated; moreover, interest in today's events does not in any way deprive of their decisive importance problems of genesis and developments in past, or even in remote, times.

By believing the contrary and acting accordingly, one runs the risk of forgetting the very extent of the field of phenomena one intends to study. In fact, a sociological and psychological analysis of modern forms of Buddhism and Christianity would be valueless if one were to be ignorant of, or to neglect, what both these religions have been in

---

[1] See the numerous examples of various problems given in J. Folliet, *Naissance et mort des religions*, in Brillant and Aigrain, *Histoire des religions*, Vol. V, pp. 305-337.

the past, and what localized their origins, without prejudice of their universalism (see on pp. 177-178 n. 28, at end).

This must be vigorously asserted, in opposition to all those scholars who, in one way or another, think they can dispense with true historiographical research, or replace it by their own efforts of 'interpretation', or propose to deal with a merely 'modern' range of questions. It is true, for example, that, both in the ethnological field and in the sphere of the great religions of today, we are often aware of forms of modernization [2] which are, in one sense or another, forms of Christianization, a consequence of Western cultural influence no less than of specifically religious influences, due to Christian Missions and the diffusion of the knowledge of Christianity. But we are faced with historical phenomena which cannot be studied without the help of historians. It would be of little avail to give an account of the present situation of a non-European faith or 'milieu', for example African,[3] Japanese[4] or

---

[2] Cf. *The Impact of Modern Culture on Traditional Religions*, vol. 1 of the *Proceedings of the XIth Int. Congress of the Int. Assoc. for the History of Religions* (Claremont, California, 1965), Leiden, 1968 (see also vol. 3).

[3] We refer, for example, to 'nativistic-prophetic' movements among various African, American and Oceanian peoples, which cannot be understood apart from their respective historical context; they are born of a reaction, positive or negative, to Christianity, or to other cultural elements introduced by European civilization. These movements resemble each other only generically because they start from a) a pure and simple reaction of rejection, as in the 'dance of spirits' movements or that of *peyotism* among the North American Indians, who desired only the return of their ancestors and of their own civilization, represented as a Golden Age, b) a reaction of purely materialistic appropriation, as in the Oceanian *Cargo Cults*, in which a mythical ship is expected, which will bring to the natives, not only their ancestors but all the advantages of white civilization with a reversal of the roles of the races; and c) the complex typology of the Messianic nativistic movements of Africa (of which the most famous are those of Harris, in some countries in the Gulf of Guinea, and of Simon Kimbangu in the Congo), which are an African version of a Christianity variously adapted, or sometimes, more simply, an ecclesiastical-denominational proliferation, but always with ethnic-racial features, as in many 'Ethiopian' churches of South Africa. Other movements are connected with the preaching of Negro 'Messiahs'. It would be too arbitrary to group these churches, even generically, under the same denomination as the American and Oceanian groups already mentioned, even if all share the theme of 'reaction'.

[4] The extremely complex nature of the new Japanese religions that have sprung up since the war complicate the question of Japanese religious history and of the determining influence on this of contact with the western world. Classical Shintoism also, in its most solemn, that is 'State' form, raises some interesting questions for religious historical methodology to investigate, as also for missiological theory and practice (like the famous 'question of rites' in earlier centuries).

Before the war it was possible to debate whether ceremonies relating to the Japanese Emperor constituted 'religious' acts, and the answer, on the basis of an official Japanese declaration, could be negative. Naturally, one must know in what

Indian, [5] if one failed to understand the historical significance of the various components or various reactors at work in that situation. Otherwise, one would run the risk of concocting a totally false and featureless history of the religions of Africa, Japan or India.

Moreover, and without venturing into sociological questions, it is true that the history of religions is not only the history of religious believers. This is the grave limitation of that dialogical (and ecumenical) 'personalization of comparative religious studies' of which W. C. Smith speaks (see above, p. 25 n. 13), and reveals the arbitrary nature of his assertion (which however, is not without some element of truth, above all in relation to certain insipid academic conclusions of the old Positivist history of religions) that the student makes good progress when he realizes he has to do 'not with religious systems basically, but with religious persons or, at least, with something interior to persons'. [6] This is all the more arbitrary, when the author distinguishes between the 'externals' of a religion (symbols, institutions, doctrines, practices) and religion itself, which is more concerned with what these 'externals' signify for the believer. This distinction is not without a certain significance for the historian, but its individualistic and 'intimistic' presuppositions render it equivocal. There is a history of religions and of religious social bodies and relative structures, but not one merely of individual believers. [7]

The sociology of religion, as we know, is able to provide an interesting and stimulating typology of religions and of their dynamism (religions just beginning, religions in decay or on the point of death,

---

sense either party spoke of 'religion'; it is true that, as a result of the Christianization, or rather the Westernization, of the terminology to which the Japanese authorities referred, one may conclude that serious misunderstanding did not arise, the crucial point at issue being above all the state of conscience of those Japanese Christians who took part in the acts of homage in question (an analogous case, but not quite similar, is that of the homage paid to Confucius in Republican China).

[5] Personages like Ramakrishna, Tagore and Gandhi would be incomprehensible if they were not seen in a precise historical context which, from one point of view, is no less European and Christian than Hindu. This does not mean that, from the point of view of the history of religions, they may be called Christians (cf. J. Folliet's observations in *op. cit.*, p. 324).

[6] Eliade-Kitagawa (ed.), *The History of Religions, Essays in Methodology*, cit., p. 35.

[7] Similar, and disputable even on the religious historical plane, because too generic, is the distinction, almost the contrast, which the same Author points out in *The Meaning and End of religion* (1964) between 'religion' (this time considered only as 'external' forms and defined as 'accumulated tradition') and 'faith'. (See the following paragraph). Moreover W. C. Smith admits that his historical interest is more in religiosity in itself than in the various religions (*The History of Religions, cit.*, p. 55).

the typology of sectarianism, heresy, schism and diffusion, and of so many other categories of great interest). But what matters most is that these typologies should be understood and studied from the historian's point of view. They must be understood on the basis of punctilious and specific study of the various phenomena, and the various historical processes which have placed the religions in question in those situations which sociological typology must study in order to be able to classify them. Otherwise these categories may be abstract and worthless, except for publicity purposes and to satisfy an uninstructed curiosity. [8] For example, it is futile to ask whether religion is 'progressive' or 'conservative', whether it is moving backwards or forwards, on the basis of religious statistics in Europe and Japan, two cultural-historical *milieux* in which religion, or religions, have a very different meaning, and differ greatly also in their expression of the dynamism of history.

The same observations are valid as regards that kind of interpretation of cultural phenomena which today is called 'cultural anthropology', in whatever form it assumes, for example in the 'patterns of culture' made famous in Ruth Benedict's book of that title, or in those functional researches which produced modern cultural anthropology. It is often said that B. Malinowski, one of the founders of 'functionalism', had no special interest in the history (and even less in the comparative investigation) of the communities he studied in their

---

[8] Thus, it is useless to enquire whether a religion gains or loses in consequence of being institutionalized, unless one considers what type of religion and what type of institution is in question. It is likewise useless to enquire whether the support of established authority and wealth is an aid to religion if, for example, one does not distinguish between a) a religion of a transcendent soteriological type, awaiting the 'Kingdom of God', in which case mundane concerns are harmful because they contradict its historical-typological and theological principles, especially when they exceed certain limits considered necessary for its structure. (These necessary structures are to be varying evaluated according to the times and the functions shared by that religion also in the social system, as, for example, in mediaeval European Christianity), and b) a national or city-state religion of a polytheistic type, which is obviously stronger for being merged with social organization as, for example, in a sanctuary-city of ancient Mesopotamia, or in the ancient Egyptian empire. In the same way, it is too facile to theorize generically about an opposition between spontaneity and institution, or between 'faih' and 'religion', as W. C. Smith does, or between the intimate awareness of the divine and specific beliefs, or between the instance of a popular and innovating movement and that of a conservative institution; these are 'oppositions' dear to various schools of thought, from Illuminism to Modernism and to a certain reformed Marxism (seen e.g. V. Lanternari, *La religione e la sua essenza; un problema storico*, in Nuovi Argomenti 49-50 (1961) p. 58 et sqq.). Lanternari gives more concrete—not without, even here, some generic, disputable presuppositions—results in his research into the *Movimenti di libertà dei popoli oppressi*, where the problem is specifically that of nativistic movements).

present day equilibrium, scientifically measurable and formulable. The attribution to Malinowski of this theoretical position is not quite exact, but, by and large, this was his attitude. It is clear that the study of an internal dynamism of cultural societies, even of a primitive kind, cannot dispense with a study of the chrono-geographical and comparative-historical situation. This is even more true of those generalizations, 'idealizations' and classifications, frequently resorted to by cultural anthropologists, which lead to 'types' of modern civilizations (civilization of the Renaissance, of Islam, etc.) or of primitive cultures, as seen for example, in the above mentioned work by Benedict. This means of course that these cultures must not be made the object of an abstract or purely arbitrary treatment, as usually happened with evolutionistic theories or even in certain over-simplified and generalized cultural-historical reconstructions of cultural 'cycles' and 'strata'. The same danger is present however, in those globalistic or 'holistic', essentially intuitive, reconstructions produced by functionalism and the cultural anthropology and what preceded it (for example, the interpretative method of Frobenius and, in later times and within certain limits, of A. E. Jensen).

2. *The 'para-religions'*

Religious sociologists and historians frequently speak of para-religions, that is of phenomena which, although not religious in the same sense as the traditional religions, seem nevertheless to have religious features or connotations and to fulfil a psychological or sociological function analogous to that of religion.

We have already alluded to the 'religion of humanity' in the sense in which A. Comte uses the term, and to the 'religion' or 'myth' of progress, etc. Religions or para-religions are mentioned also in connection with totalitarian political-social movements, which have their own 'mystique', like the Communism of Lenin and Stalin, as well as in connection with ambitious or capricious movements in the same field, like the political movements of an adventurous or romantic nature, such as Hitlerism, and the theories of Alfred Rosenberg (who sought to combine neo-paganism with German Christianity). In Italy too, though on quite a different plane, there was the Fascist 'mystique'.

It is true that a prudent sociologist like J. Folliet (op. cit., pp. 323 et sqq.) speaks not so much of a religion as of a 'religious aspect', a 'secondary religiosity', and of 'derivations of the religious feeling' or, for certain naturalistic trends, of a 'para-religious phenomenon'. Nevertheless, if these descriptions have any sociological and psychological, or even philosophical or theological, meaning (in relation to certain forms of radical secularism, of the 'death of God' movement etc. or in relation to the question as to whether there really are any true atheists) one must be more cautions in granting them (from the point of view of a historian of religions) a meaning analogous to that of 'religion' or 'religious'. In fact, in this field of studies, as we learnt in the dispute about Durkheim, one must distinguish between phenomena which are substitutes for the religious sense in the context of human sentiment and social cohesion, and forms which, although 'analogous' and not univocal, legitimately represent religion and religiosity. The historian of religions would be more willing to acknowledge an epistemologically specific religious character of the above mentioned phenomena if they were seen to be in an objective relationship, in actual history and not only in general psychology, with genuine religious forms (as for example happens in the case of a transition of an 18th century philosopher from a Christian to a 'deist' faith, or in that of a 20th century Modernist, whose God is—or at least is said to be—in a more or less constant continuity of line with the god he formerly accepted and believed in). Otherwise one runs the risk of including in a religious phenomenology (which, in order to be legitimate, must be historically verified in its concrete connotations) what might at most be a religious 'print'.

One must, moreover, make a distinction here. A 'panic' sentiment of the 'divine' and of the 'whole', of a Romantic nature (as the 'religion' of such writers and musicians often was) is one thing; quite different is the case of a total dedication to a Messianic ideal and to a final purpose, even if mundane (but no longer entirely mundane if it is final and total and understood mystically as having saving power); quite different again is a nationalistic-literary utilization of pagan mythologies of the ancient and mediaeval world. Yet another thing is a Masonic pietism, which may contain a survival of Gnostic thought and of occultist traditions, combined with the deist and humanitarian religion which is allied to some specific developments of thought. Quite different also is a 'spiritism' in which one should again distinguish between occultist and Gnostic traditions (or revivals) on the one hand and para-scientific experimentalism on the other. Diverse also is the case, discussed by Folliet, of Gandhi, with his objective links with Indian 'paganism', that is, with a religion of a markedly ethnical type, a case which would better be described as a form of personal religion (with strong Christian and Western influences). Similar observations apply to a more decided theosophical creed of the Vedantic type, that is, traditionally Hindu, exemplified in Ramakrishna and Tagore, who are part of the religious history of an India which, at the same time, accepts and repudiates Christian universalism and spirituality.[9] A similar position is that of the Founders of 'Babism' and 'Bahaism', in the context of Ismailian tradition and Western and Christian influence.

Significant problems are also raised by movements of a Gnostic type which, parasitic on the great religions, are not religions in the same sense as these, as is evident in certain Gnostic scientialist attitudes (very different however from modern scientialism) but even more in the concept of divine consubstantiality of the gnostic, and in his love of magic (alchemy, astrology, etc.) sometimes of a Faustian type.

Of great interest also are forms of 'inverse' worship, parodical but with undertones of magic (like the Black Masses and the *Sabbat*) in which the re-emergence of old rituals recalling aspects and figures of ancient fertility cults must not lead one to assume the continuity of old forms of pagan and popular religiosity, before one has adequately investigated the question of how many of these beliefs depend on the very nature of 'inverse' worship, which is necessarily as obscene, vitalistic and daemoniac as the official cult is spiritual, pure and pious.

On a more sophisticated plane, and with different cultural associations, similar observations may be applied also to 'Satanism'.

Finally, interesting problems are raised by ritualistic revivals in totalitarian anti-religious *milieux*, as in the 'wedding palace' of Leningrad, referred to by De Martino, or in the requests for new 'red' rituals in communist countries or *milieux* (initiations and weddings—phenomena which, if on the one hand, like the cult of the goddess Reason, they represent a reaction against religion and worship, in certain more significant cases, like those we have referred to, of the 'wedding palace' and of 'initiation to the Party' and to social maturity, etc. they express the desire for a ritualistic structure.

3. *R. Otto and the Marburg School. The 'holy'. The Religionswissenschaft*

In chapter I we have already referred to methodological problems suggested by certain trends in research which may be summed up in

---

[9] The Hinduism of Radakrishnan is more lay and polemical.

the terms: 'phenomenology of religion' and 'Comparative Religion'.

We have noted that these researches do not always and precisely correspond to the methodology of the history of religions. They have at times an intuitionistic and postulatory character (admitting the testimony of the various religions, especially that of the great living creeds, [10] as an immediate and self-authenticated revelation of a generic 'divine'). They seek a 'mutual understanding' among religions, which shall be not only an acknowledgment of the specific and significant nature of religions and religion in the course of human history, but also an endeavour to establish a spiritual unity of purpose for the inter-creeds dialogue, and for the auto-testimonies of creeds, a purpose which does not, *in itself*, pertain to the history of religions—as we have said before. It is logical that students with this goal in view should be willing to admit, more easily than religious historians of the historical-philological tradition, the historical-religious legitimacy of certain studies conducted in Asiatic countries which are more concerned with testimonies of present day religious systems and experiences than with research conducted according to a historical methodology primarily interested in the philological study of 'sources'.

The presuppositions of a 'phenomenology of religion', understood in this sense, may be found in the work of some important German scholars of the last fifty years, J. W. Hauer, R. Otto, H. Frick, F. Heiler and, more recently, G. Mensching and E. Benz. The chief centre of these studies was the University of Marburg (a city which, in the Castle of the Margrave of Hesse, the scene of the famous Colloquy on the Eucharist between Luther and Zwingli, houses a small but significant museum of the history of religions, founded by R. Otto). In fact, in Marburg in 1960 the Xth Int. Congress of the History of Religions saw the beginning of a divergence of views concerning the nature of this branch of learning, a divergence occasioned by the appearance of an 'Oriental trend' in religious-historical studies, a trend which had already emerged in an earlier Int. Congress held in Tokyo in 1958. On that occasion the influence of the Oriental *milieu* had been decisive for the choice of subjects for discussion, chiefly Asiatic-Oriental, and for the methodology of various speakers, which was more systematic and expository than truly historical and philological.

Among the German scholars we have mentioned, Hauer is the author of a book on 'Religions, their growth, meaning and truth'

---

[10] Hinduism, Buddhism, Christianity, Islam.

(1923), in which he devotes most of his research to religion among primitive peoples, as being a 'feeling', an 'experience', with strong intuitionistic and irrationalistic tendencies. In his latest works also he proposes to investigate the origins of religion without the help of a historical method (which, he says, would limit his research, at most, to the origins of the races now living) but using a 'psychological-anthropological method', and in relation to animal and infantile psychology (an ontogenetic-phylogenetic correspondence). But this 'natural history' of religion—Hauer adds— does not 'explain' its last cause. Moreover, to the religious man the Primal Cause is precisely that unknown creative power which is 'quite different', 'transcendent' 'unearthly'. Religion, the science of religions, and philosophy all come here into consideration and the problem of the relationship between reality and the awareness of the numinous, that is, the question of the truth of religion (the *Wahrheitsfrage*) now arises. Hauer points out that the question as to whether the unknown and unworldly creative power is in fact the First Cause must be answered by the testimony of the *homo religiosus*, a testimony which transcends science and philosophy. [11]

It is clear that in these statements Hauer is influenced by some of the best known theses of Rudolf Otto, the famous theologian of the University of Marburg, well known for his theory on the 'holy'. The best known of his books, *Das Heilige*, was first published in 1917 and appeared in an English translation, *'The Idea of the Holy'*, in Oxford in 1928. [12]

---

[11] Cf. Hauer's report to the International Congress of the History of religions in Marburg (*X Int. Kongr. f. Rel. Geschichte*, 1960, Marburg, 1961, pp. 189-191). One point on which Hauer insists, even in opposition to the historical-cultural school, is the variety of experiences and 'functions', and of the consequent religious representations, among primitive peoples. The same point of view (with reference also to the study of evolution and phylogenesis) is expressed by the Italian palethnologist A. C. Blanc (*Il sacro presso i primitivi*, Rome, 1945) who admits, in the somatic as well as in the ideological field, an original polymorphism; 'wherever today we observe relatively simple and pure forms of belief, this would be due to processes of partial segregation, of a 'ideolysis' concerning the fundamental psychic attitudes of Man, which in other ideological fields, as in the most ancient history of art, are easily recognisable. Even in the history of spirit, as in that of living beings, the distinct or 'pure' forms would therefore to be considered as arrival points, not starting points' (op. cit., p. 180). This leads Blanc, an evolutionist, to criticize, as a problem wrongly presented by classical evolutionism (he also disagrees with historical-cultural ethnologists) the tendency to 'seek a primary form of religion which is, at the same time, its minimal definition' (ibid., p. 181).

[12] Cf. also *Das Gefühl des Überweltlichen* (*Sensus numinis*), Munich, 1932, more analytical from the religious-historical point of view.

Otto considers that the basis of religion is the sense of the 'holy', a feeling which contains ambivalent elements, not in the somewhat materialistic sense of the sociological school (purity and 'impurity' of the holy, sometimes beneficent, at other times harmful) but in a more spiritual sense. He means that, whereas on the one hand the 'holy' or 'numinous' (awareness of the mysterious presence of a divine power) is 'tremendous' and sacred, arousing feelings like those expressed by the Greek *thambos*, the English 'awe' (or even the *'effroi'* of Pascal's famous exclamation before the vast silent spaces of the heavens), it is also *fascinans* and irresistible; it is always mysterious and 'totally different' (*ganz anderes*).

It is perceived by means of a special faculty, distinct from but comparable to the aesthetic sense (category of the 'sublime').

It is clear that this vivid and effective description of the 'holy' as an *'a priori* category' [13] implies a point of view which is at the same time intuitionistic (since it is largely a description of a feeling that is experienced, that has an object, the 'holy', which is *arrheton*, secret, and must not be defined or conceptualized) and irrationalistic (in the sense, Otto explains, that the awareness of the holy transcends all conceptual categories). But it is also a psychologistic point of view.

It is chiefly because of this aspect that Otto's interpretation suggests reservations from the point of view of the history of religions, as also of the phenomenology and psychology of religion. In no religion, and in no phase of religious history or evolution, does the 'holy' or the 'divine' exist by itself, *simpliciter* (even when it is 'diffused' in a rather indiscriminate primordial complexity of beliefs which are formally diverse and distinct); but God exists, the gods or spirits, etc. exist. And here one can see an analogy between two objections which may be raised against Otto's theory, and against the earlier theory of 'mystery' advanced by Fries, whose influence is to be seen in Otto's work: [14] one of these objections is philosophical or theological and the other is religious-historical. Both might complain that the analysis of the content of religions, of the 'holy', is limited to negative conceptual notions such as those of immortality, freedom, the 'absolute':

---

[13] This does not mean 'innate': *'A priori'* knowledge is not what every reasonable man *possesses* (in which case it would be 'innate'), but what everyone *'may have'*. *A priori* superior knowledge are awakened through the stimulus of other, more gifted, men: *Das Heilige*, 30th edit., p. 204. But generally speaking, every form of religious sentiment and cult is for Otto an 'institution' (*op. cit.*, p. 146).

[14] As is also for the theory of Schleiermacher, for whom moreover the intuition of the divine is a presentiment, not true knowledge of the same, as it is for Otto.

according to Otto, we are made intuitively aware of the reality of these notions on the transcendental plane through our experiences of their opposites on this earth. From a religious-historical point of view, which is what matters here, one way even doubt whether these notions always correspond to the content of religion, of all religions and of all religious forms and experiences, and therefore whether they are really and absolutely 'negative', that is, without positive content. [15] One wonders how far (even in Otto's description of the 'holy' as 'totally different') he was influenced, after his Lutheran training, by his first-hand experience of study in India, and the reference to the Indian (Upanishadic) *anyad-eva* (the 'totally different'). [16] Therefore, when it is asserted [17] that it is the awareness of the supernatural and of mystery that makes possible a belief in spirits, demons and gods, one must ask whether this feeling is the same as that *Gefühl*, an apperception of something overpowering and spell-binding (*tremendum et fascinans*) which seems to have conditioned so much of Otto's analysis of the religious feeling; and one must ask (although this seems unlikely) whether this feeling may be, purely for purposes of study, isolated from the real objects of religious belief, which differ greatly among themselves. This must be said even if the category of 'mystery' seems to express effectively an aspect common to all religious experience. [18]

Otto's interpretations aroused much criticism in Germany, for example, from W. Baetke, the Emeritus Professor of Nordic philology at Leipzig, [19] who asserts the communal and institutional character of religion. He says that the history of religions is not primarily concerned with religious men and their 'experience' but with religions and with the communities which diffuse them, the religious experience of the individual being fundamentally conditioned by the religion of the community to which he belongs. Baetke also criticizes Otto's

---

[15] Cf. for example, a religion and religiosity like that of ancient Rome, which was so 'juridical' and 'earthly', although firmly anchored in the mystery of the gods and the attempts, controlled but always precarious, to have peace with them.

[16] Cf. A. Jundt, who writes in the Preface to the French edition of Otto's book (Paris, 1949, p. 14): 'The study of the religions of India, confirms in a particularly important matter the conclusions of the religious philosophy of Fries. The feeling of mystery or of *anyad-eva* is the fundamental religious sentiment...'.

[17] An example of the application of Otto's principle is found in the Introduction by G. Mensching (successor to C. Clemen in the University of Bonn) to the volume written in collaboration *Die grossen nicht-Christlichen Religionen unserer Zeit* (1958).

[18] See the following page.

[19] See the following note.

psychologistic and subjectivist treatment.[20] Naturally the former of these two criticisms does not—in our opinion—imply his adoption of the hypotheses of Durkheim's school, or the negation of the role of the individual in religious history, or the obliteration of the historical and interpretative value of the distinction between 'ethnical' and 'founded' religions, and of the phenomenon of the 'Founders' or prophets. What Baetke asserts is that 'the history of religions does not find in the initial stage a religious *Urerlebnis* (a primordial experience), a numinous 'emotion', or the 'onrush' of a 'primordial numinous' feeling, but instead everywhere and above all finds institutional religions fully developed, and men who belong to this or that historical religion',[21] and so all the feelings and experiences to which Otto refers always presuppose historical (that is, concrete and institutional) religion, and the 'holy', as it is concretely expressed in a religious tradition, is a phenomenon which precedes the religious man who becomes aware of it.[22] Here also, moreover, and in homage to the practical aspects of historical-religious investigation, we note that a feeling already protected, as it were, by a religious tradition, lasts as long as it is appropriated and realised, made permanent and progressive, by the individuals who are its representatives, in the context of a community, although sometimes they play an innovatory and revolutionary role in relation to this.

In other words, it is not so much a question of the relationship between the individual and society in religion (a question that must be studied from a historical point of view and not from the angle of a generic and abstract sociology) as a question of a historical treatment of the history of religions and of religious individuals, a treatment which must take into account concepts of development, historical processes, continuity, innovation, tradition and revolution, all these phenomena being capable of investigation only by a study of the course and material of history.

In conclusion, the argument may be reduced to an epistemological problem. What Otto proposes is more a 'philosophy of religion' than

---

[20] Cf. K. Rudolph, *Die Religionsgeschichte an der Leipziger Universität und die Entwicklung der Religionswissenschaft* in *Sitzungsberichte der sächsischen Akademie der Wissenschaften zu Leipzig*, Philol.-hist. class, Vol. 107, No. 1, Berlin, 1962, p. 165.

[21] *Das Heilige im Germanischen*, p. 28, quoted by Rudolph, *op. cit.*, p. 166. It is true that Otto does not neglect the consideration of the 'institution' (see above, p. 172 n. 13.

[22] Cf. Rudolph, *loc. cit.*

a history or 'science of religions'; but even as a philosophy of religion Otto's theories must take into consideration the dangers inherent in generalization.

The prominence given by Otto to one aspect of religion or religiosity is more legitimate, for philosophy as well as for the history of religions: we refer to the feeling of 'mystery', which in fact characterizes everything which relates to the world of the superhuman, and of religion. This 'mystery', however, must not too lightly be associated with Christian or Indian values, for in many religions it concerns also beings and phenomena very unlike the 'sublime' of which Otto speaks. For example, there is the variegated world of spirits, often anything but 'edifying'. Yet, even belief in these spirits is part of religious history and there is no reason to admit with Otto—on the basis of a historical-inductive enquiry, the possibility that beliefs and fears, however primitive but not religious (or merely pre-religious) became transformed into religious states of mind when they expressed an awareness of the 'holy' corresponding to the description given by the Marburg theologian.

A similar tendency towards a *Religionsphilosophie* is seen in the 'science of religions', as understood by Friedrich Heiler, until a few years ago Professor of 'Comparative History of Religions and the Philosophy of Religion' in the University of Marburg.[23] According to Heiler, the purpose of *Religionswissenschaft* is to study religion in itself, its essence, genesis, formation and importance in the history of the spirit and the history of culture. It forms the basis for a philosophy of religion to which are related the comparative history of religions, the phenomenology and sociology of religion, and should be crowned by a metaphysics of religion.[24] Whatever may be thought of this system, which implies—as far as the 'science of religions' is concerned—views somewhat similar to those of R. Otto, one must bear in mind that Heiler was also a distinguished historian of religions, as is proved by his publications[25] and by his acknowledged eminence in the field of German studies of this very science.

---

[23] H. Frick, the author of a *Vergleichende Religionswissenschaft* (1928) was once Professor of Systematic Theology and 'General History of Religions' in the same university.

[24] Cf. Heiler, *Erscheinungsformen und Wesen der Religion*, Stuttgart, 1961, in the series *Die Religionen der Menschheit*, of which this is the introductory volume.

[25] A famous book on prayer in the history of religions, and the manual written in collaboration with K. Goldammer, G. Lanczkowski, Annemarie Schimmel and other scholars, called *Die Religionen der Menschheit*, Stockholm, 1959, with the book mentioned in the preceding note.

But his interest in the study of religions goes beyond the field of this branch of study, for he was one of the most enthusiastic promoters of a cooperation of religions, similar to a sort of inter-confessional ecumenism, in fact an inter-religious ecumenism, which one cannot here pause to analyse or discuss but which is very characteristic of his personality as a historian of religions. In this also he shows the influence of R. Otto, to whom he referred, in his opening speech at the above mentioned Int. Congress of the History of Religions held at Marburg in 1960, as a 'prophet' of the '*Begegnung* of world religions' and as the founder of a *Religiöser Menschheitsbund*, which aimed at inter-religious exchanges and human promotion. In a study on *The History of Religions as a Preparation for the Co-operation of Religions*, included in the volume *History of Religions*, edited by M. Eliade and T. M. Kitagawa (Chicago, 1959) Heiler states that one of the most important tasks of the science of religions is to bring into the light the unity of all religions, [26] a unity, however, that must be relative, and graded according to the religions considered in the varying degrees of their affinity, not a unity formed of syncretism or conversion.

The danger here is of course that of transforming the study of religions into an inter-religions enterprise, as is seen in a statement like the following: "Thus scientific insight into this unity calls for a practical realization in friendly exchange and in common ethical and social endeavour which the British call 'fellowship' and 'co-operation". [27] Here the research student, to whom Heiler assigns the task of investigating what he calls the 'unity' of religions (a concept which may have its own significance also in the history and phenomenology of religions) has become the subject of this unity; there is that identification between the subject and the object of the history of religions that is characteristic of the whole of Otto's school and also of most of the phenomenologists influenced by it.

An interest of this kind, clearly theological and ecumenical (although of a very specific kind of theology and ecumenism) emerges also from the researches of another Marburg Professor, Ernst Benz, who in fact suggests a 'new theology of the history of religions', for the purpose of an understanding which, however, he does not think will be easy, as is proved by the difficulty even of translating words and concepts; this warning should not be disregarded, as it represents

---

[26] See p. 155.
[27] *Ibid.*

a real necessity, like that of historical methodology. This methodology, because of its strict philological principles, is one of the most pertinent contributions that the history of religions, without trespassing in other fields of enquiry, can make to the noble attempt to promote mutual knowledge between men, cultures and religions. Another contribution, but one which must be considered with extreme caution and subjected to a strict investigation, is that of providing an account of the complex religious history of mankind, with all its complications and, as far as they can be traced, all its dynamic impulses, together with its historical typology, all reconstructed on the basis of the historical-comparative method. But this is something quite different from ecumenism and the theology of religions. [28]

---

[28] For which see pp. 25, 183. Heiler accepts, within certain limits, Toynbee's criticism of Biblical religions as being tendencially exclusive and intolerant: but the discussion on 'exclusiveness' necessarily raises the problem 'religion and religions', which occupies the philosophical and theological speculation of K. Jaspers (in the above mentioned volume *Die grossen nicht-Christlichen Religionen unserer Zeit*); although Jaspers points out the defects of intolerance and a fanatical exclusiveness, he also points out the vacuity and the abstract character of a concept like that of a truth being common and unitary to all religions. 'Whoever liked to believe in that abstraction as in a truth common to all religions, that is, in the universal elements about which all were agreed, was forced to conclude that he believed in nothing' (*op. cit.*).

This is useful testimony from a philosopher, not only to the necessity of studying the history of religions, in order to know religion in its concreteness, but also to the necessity that a philosophy and theology of religions should take into account the results of such studies. Jaspers gives his well known solution to the problem, negative from the theological point of view even if encouraging on the dialogical plane: 'The unity that is lacking as universal validity of the content of faith, is possible as a notion of the need for human participation. In fact, our historical multiplicity must have its roots deep in that soil from which we all spring' (*ibid.*): a position somewhat similar to that expressed by Pettazzoni, when he spoke of the 'mystery which, when revealed, divides us and, when it is endured, unites us' (*Oriente e Occidente*, in *Rendiconti Adun. Sol. Accad. dei Lincei*, VI, 2, 1959). Without entering into an argument which only in one aspect concerns the history of religions, we consider that this branch of learning may help to criticize Jaspers' theoretical alternative choice between 'exclusiveness' and parithetic possibility of religions. We suggest these different types of consideration, all relating to religious-historical research: 1) the discernment of the substance of a question which a religious gospel or tradition answers, or which it raises (this is particularly evident in the case of Buddhism) even in the context of a general concern for religion; 2) the discernment of a system, or of a historical dynamic, in which religions are not all on the same plane of a world history, or even of a vast regional history; 3) the universalizing and universalistic capacities of a religious gospel, verifiable also by studying its influence on the plane of cultures and of the acquisition of values which are common on a world wide basis (e.g., charity), as well as by studying its influence on other religious traditions (for example, aspects of a Christianization or at least of a Westernization of great Asiatic religions or primitive *milieux*). Naturally,

4. *The phenomenology of religion*

In this category, which owes its success in the field of religious studies to P. D. Chantepie de la Saussaye, we include today a group of studies which, in their interpretative principles and epistemological presuppositions, owe much to the phenomenology of Husserl, but is not without profound traces of the influence of Otto and his school. The principal representatives are the Dutch scholars Gerardus Van der Leeuw, formerly Professor of the History of Religions at Groningen (d. 1950) and C. Jouco Bleeker, Professor Emeritus of the same branch of study in the University of Amsterdam, and the German Joachim Wach, who settled in America, well known also as a religious sociologist. [29]

The chief work by Van der Leeuw, [30] the *Phänomenologie der Religion* (which was expanded in the French version, *La religion dans son essence et ses manifestations—Phénoménologie de la religion*) [31] is more than a study of the theory of the science of religions: it is a vast typology of religion and it does honour to its author's skill and learning; its analytical bibliographies add to its efficacy. The examination of any of the sections into which the work is subdivided such as, for example, that on sacrifice, suggests all the objections which a historical treatment of the same subject might raise. In fact there is no attempt to establish a relative chronology, or a historical-cultural localization of the facts he quotes: and Van der Leeuw deliberately chose this manner of exposition and interpretation, declaring at the end of his book (in a phrase for which Pettazzoni reproached him): 'phenomenology knows nothing of a historical 'development' of religion (here he refers to Wach, op. cit. (1924), p. 82) and *a fortiori* nothing of an 'origin' of religion'.

Now, one cannot oblige a scholar who uses a non-historical method of study to turn to historical research (and, if he were to do so, he would fail, as was seen in the case of the evolutionists, and also in

---

assertions of this kind, relating to the historical dynamic of religions, in the context of the great history of human civilizations and of the universalizing process which largely characterizes it, are distinct from the philosophical and theological problem of 'religion and religions' which do not concern us here.

[29] *Das Verstehen* (1926-33); *Religionswissenschaft* (1924). For the phenomenology of religion see Eva Hirschmann: *Phänomenologie der Religion. Eine historisch-systematische Untersuchung von 'Religionsphänomenologie' und 'religionsphänomenologischer Methode' in der Religionswissenschaft* (1940).

[30] To whose studies on 'primitive man and religion' (see above p. 83) we have already referred.

[31] Paris, 1948.

the manner in which R. Otto imagines the history and pre-history of religion). Nevertheless, one has yet to see whether it is possible to dispense with historical research (understood more as the localization of the facts in question than as an attempt at chronology or a discovery of origins) when one is describing and trying to 'understand' a phenomenon, since 'understanding' is the main object and boast of phenomenology. One must therefore ask whether a term like 'sacrifice' really covers facts of the same ('univocal') significance, that is, whether it expresses substantially *one* fact and *one* structure. Van der Leeuw is brought up against this problem when he speaks about the various aspects of 'sacrifice' in the history of religions; but his reply is positive, and he speaks of the 'fundamental unity' of the sacrifice itself. The alternative reply, favoured by a methodology more pertinent to the history of religions and more rooted in actuality, would instead be, in our opinion, that the term 'sacrifice' covers 'analogous' (i.e. not 'univocal' nor 'equivocal') concepts and facts, in the sense of a concrete and historical, not purely conceptual, analogy; this obviously necessitates a historical-cultural analysis of the relative sources.

Nevertheless, we consider that the effort of 'understanding' made in a phenomenology as well documented with facts as that of Van der Leeuw is undoubtedly useful to historical-religious research, even if the theoretical presuppositions of this 'understanding', put forward by philosophical phenomenology (Husserl) leave some fundamental perplexities.

This will be more obvious when we consider the words with which Van der Leeuw concludes his exposition of the phenomenological method, ending with the sentence we have already quoted concerning historical problems. He says: 'The phenomenology of religion must then, before all else, deal in names, sacrifice, prayer, a saviour, myth, etc. In this way it designates the phenomena. Secondly, it must incorporate these in life itself, methodically experiencing and living them. [32]) Thirdly, it must stand aside, and practicing *epochè*, try to consider what is set before it. Fourthly, it must try to elucidate what it has seen and fifthly (reassuming all preceding acts) it must try to understand what was set before it. Finally, it must examine chaotic 'reality', the signs that have not yet been interpreted, and testify to what it has understood...'. [33])

---

[32] It is the concept of *Erlebnis* (experience).
[33] *La religion, cit.*, p. 670.

Concerning his link with the speculation of R. Otto, there is a great difference, in as much as Van der Leeuw is inspired by the philosophy of phenomenology: according to this, if 'lived' experience is a 'phenomenon' and if the answer man gives to 'revelation' is a phenomenon, revelation itself is something quite different. The phenomenology of religion, adds Van der Leeuw, is not the philosophy of religion, even if it leads to questions of a philosophical and metaphysical nature which it is not itself authorized to raise. But he points out that the philosophy of religion cannot dispense with the phenomenology of religion, in order to avoid dangers of an ethnocentric nature. From the point of view of the history of religions, one must agree with him on this (cf. above, pp. 19-23).

A further step towards a historical treatment of the study of religious phenomena may be found in the work of the other Dutch scholar we have already mentioned: C. J. Bleeker. [34] Given a common human religiosity, which he calls a *religio perennis*, founded on the fact that all men are capable of the same thoughts and emotions (which make mutual understanding possible) he emphasizes the need to study culture and religion in their various forms, due to historic 'options'; so the history of religions should attempt 'not so much to describe the common spiritual good of humanity, but to clarify what is typical, unique, exceptional in the religions of the world.' [35] Bleeker's position (op. cit., p. 8) is not very clear on the following question: if the history of religions has the task 'to understand the faith of believers' (according to W. B. Kristensen's definition) that is, of penetrating the secrets of the essence, meaning and significance of religious phenomena, a task difficult in itself, how shall we discriminate between an understanding which is the result of a historical-religious enquiry and an understanding which is the result of intuition (or testimony)? In this two-fold eventuality what significance will be attached to the *Erleben* of phenomenology?

That this question is no mere abstraction is proved by the Bleeker's assertion that 'religion is born of man's encounter with the Holy' [36] and that religion would be denatured if it reduced 'to such purely human factors as social and psychological forces'. Here the just demand to exclude a postulatory or programmatic 'reductionism' which would

---

[34] The author of various studies on the 'phenomenological method'.
[35] *Proceedings of the XIth Int. Congress of the Int. Assoc. for the History of Religions*, 1, Leiden, 1968, p. 10.
[36] *Op. cit.*, p. 8.

fail to take into consideration the peculiar characteristics of religious facts, reducing them methodologically and methodically (i.e. programmatically) to social and psychic phenomena, is combined with an equally postulatory affirmation of the superhuman origin of religion, which it is the proper function of philosophy and theology to examine and discuss, and which cannot constitute an *a priori* of historical-religious research. [37])

5. *The 'history of religions' and 'comparative religion' in the U.S.A.*

Certain currents of historical-religious studies, related to the phenomenology of religion, have had a profound influence in the United States. Certainly there have always been, as now, scholars trained in historical-philological methodology, especially as regards ancient religions (A. D. Nock, d. 1963, Professor of History of Religion at Harvard, one of the most knowledgeable students of the religions of the Hellenistic Age, E. R. Goodenough, R. M. Grant and others); but American 'Comparative Religion' is above all interested in the great living religions, sometimes with the aim of promoting mutual understanding between different religious traditions, in a spirit which in some ways recalls that famous 'Parliament of religions' which met in Chicago in 1893 and was the first example of an attempt to find in the context of an international meeting mutual understanding between different faiths, even those most dissimilar and least accustomed to mutual contact, a meeting promoted by the universalist humanitarianism of that time.

American studies in the history of religions were much encouraged by the acquisition of European scholars, first of all Joachim Wach, whom we have already mentioned, and Mircea Eliade who, while occupying the Chair of History of Religions at the University of Chicago, promotes a series of initiatives, among which the most notable is the publication of the review, 'History of Religions' [38]) (which pays much attention to the great living religions of Asia) and of some volumes written in collaboration, dedicated to the present day

---

[37] Cf. above, pp. 20 et sqq. and below, pp. 188 et seq., 190 et seq., 199 et seq.

[38] In which Eliade rightly defends the role of the history of religions in contemporary culture and in the understanding of the modern world (including literature and art). The historian of religions must understand and make understood those religious contents which ethnocentric prejudice, incompetence or carelessness might otherwise irretrievably lose.

problems of this branch of learning, seen through the eyes of the American academic world. [39]

These studies contain some criticisms of the traditional European history of religions, criticisms which however it would be difficult to support *in toto*, because they do not always take into account the essential links between historical methodology and the history of European culture. Consider, for example, J. M. Kitagawa's remark that 'from the time of the Enlightenment *Religionswissenschaft* has been operating with Western categories in the study of all religions of the world...'. [40] This is certainly true if one remembers a certain obtuseness, in the interpretation of facts of the religious history of all humanity (and not only of Eastern regions) in some fundamental trends of modern Western thought; there may be a foundation of truth in the remark that even the students 'concerned with Eastern religions have asked, unconsciously if not consciously, 'Western' questions, and have expected Easterners to structure their religions in a way which was meaningful to Westerners'; [41] it is also true that Western scholars have been preoccupied with 'conceptualization', in order to include the Oriental religions in their systems of *'Religionswissenschaft'*. Nevertheless, the fact remains, and is admitted by the author himself, that in their turn Oriental scholars have been noted for their insistence on an 'immediate apprehension of the totality or essence of Ultimate Reality'. Now, no one is prevented from conducting a study of religion with the means he prefers, intuitive or inductive, internally (from testimony and experience) or by means of an 'objective' analysis. But the fact remains that the history of religions, once the hypotheses of a scientalism which are extraneous to true positive-inductive research have been eliminated, must start its research with a documentation, understood above all in its philological meaning, and localized in time and space, even with all necessary consideration of traditions and their persistence.

This methodology is of Greek origin and was born in Europe. Therefore one cannot accept Kitagawa's assertion that 'the difficulty

---

[39] M. Eliade and J. M. Kitagawa (ed.), *The History of Religions, Essays in Methodology*, Chicago, 1959, pp. 22 et seq., and *The History of Religions, Essays on the Problem of Understanding*, edited by the same, Chicago, 1967, vol. 1 of a series of works devoted primarily to philosophical-hermeneutic studies and not to the history of religions.

[40] *The History of Religions in America*, in *The History of Religions*, Chicago 1959, pp. 22.

[41] *Ibid.*

is that the assumptions and methodology of *Religionswissenschaft* are also products of Western historical culture'. We say this with all necessary reservations concerning the *philosophical* assumptions, however diverse and frequently contradictory, which have accompanied in Europe (as well as in Northern America) the development of the history of religions considered as a science.

All this makes it hard to accept Kitagawa's statement that 'American scholars in the field [history of religions] are in a strategic position to mediate between European and Asiatic schools of thought'. [42]

The American history of religions too, as Kitagawa points out, is conditioned historically, because in some ways it depends upon that 'comparative theology' which was an object of primary interest not only for theologians (especially in certain American inter-confessional *milieux*) but also for those thinkers who in 18th century America inherited Illuminist and scientistic theories.

As regards American 'Comparative Religion', it corresponds to an interest and a methodology which are not precisely the same as those of the history of religions, as we have had occasion to observe in connection with W. Cantwell Smith (see pp. 25 n. 13; 165) and the same must be said of that *'Theological History of Religions'* [43] in which Kitagawa sees some affinities with the trend which, according to D. T. Suzuki, sets out to study Buddhism 'trying to resort to its own dialectics' (p. 24). This proposal is certainly fruitful, but it cannot legitimately avoid answering problems of a philological and historical order, which are moreover not only requirements of the history of religions but also problems of the Indianist or Sinologist, etc. (as well as of—at least—Christian and Hebraic theologians). Nor can the historical-religious problem be brushed aside with the excuse that the origin of religion (why not then the origin of religions also?) is a metaphysical and not a historical question, even if the study of origins meets with the objective difficulties arising from the material available, especially if prehistoric, or with the difficulty that, beyond a certain limit, it is impossible to explore the intentions of the Founders of religions. This is a question which, in different ways, interests the religious historian, the philosopher and the theologian (see Chap. I).

---

[42] *Op. cit.*, p. 25.

[43] Which, however, Kitagawa distinguishes from the history of religions, *op. cit.*, p. 24 (cf. Eliade, *ibid.*, p. 89, n. 6). The expression 'theological history of religions' is in any case incorrect. It is instead legitimate to speak of a Theology of Religions, as a branch of theology, that is, as theological reflections on the fact of the existence of other religions.

6. Mircea Eliade and the 'Morphology of the holy'. Contrasting opinions on the 'holy' and on history

From several years American historians of religion are able to count among their number Mircea Eliade, well known for his researches on a series of aspects of religion, which range from the morphology of the 'holy' (*Traité d'histoire des religions*, 1949 to the *Mythe de l'éternel retour, Images et symboles, Naissances Mystiques* (on the subject of death and initiation) and to *Das Heilige und das Profane*, etc. a series of titles which reveal the interests of this author, one of the most eminent and most widely read modern historians of religions. The opposition between sacred and profane (which he treats in the same way as Roger Caillois, *L'homme et le sacré*), the concept of hierophany ('something which reveals the holy', 'a modality of the holy', necessarily historical but also, sometimes, capable of ecumenical expansion, like the cosmic tree, the object of numerous variations which however all help to make its value understood as a symbol, that is, a means of revealing the holy), myth and the age of myth (as the foundation of all that is historical and profane and the guarantee of a periodic restoration of the world to its original state of purity and integrity, as it was when creation came forth out of chaos), initiation as a *regressus in uterum* ('return to the womb') and as re-integration and rebirth, through a ritual death, are all themes treated in his books, and referred to by us here and there in the course of this volume.

Of particular interest in this context is Eliade's defence of a history of religions which is not afraid to study great comparative themes, wihtout reducing itself to a philology and without submitting to theories elaborated in other fields, sociological, ethnological, anthropological and philosophical: a history of religions which can make modern culture aware of the importance, the specific meaning and unique contribution of religion and religions. This position is fundamental to Eliade's thought, from the beginning: '... a religious phenomenon will not reveal itself as such unless it is apprehended in its own quality—i.e. unless it is studied on a religious plane. To attempt to filter this phenomenon through physiology, psychology, sociology, economics, linguistics, art, etc. means to betray it: it means missing its unique and irreducible characteristic, its sacredness'. [44]

---

[44] *Traité d'histoire des religions*, p. 11. Moreover, the author states that there are no 'pure' religious phenomena, that is, phenomena exclusively and uniquely religious, because man does not live outside the sphere of language and community life.

This is a very clear indictment of 'reductionism'. The phenomena of religion, even the crudest, must be 'taken seriously': even the most primitive and exacerbated hierophanies, today surpassed and replaced polemically also by other hierophanies furnished with new potentialities and values, reveal the sacred, so that 'the immediate reality of these objects or actions 'bursts' or 'explodes' under the irruptive force of a more profound reality'. [45]

Eliade's interpretations have had a wide influence in the history of religions and in other fields of study, even among phenomenologists, philosophers of religion and theologians. They have met with objections on the part of historians of religion, especially of scholars trained in the comparative-historical method. Among these the most eminent was R. Pettazzoni, who criticized Eliade's theory, or philosophy, of religion in notes which were to be the last he wrote (1959) before his death. [46] Nevertheless, the Rumanian scholar's interpretations, although contested, provide in the field of methodology itself a most useful term of reference.

What Pettazzoni objects to in Eliade's position is fundamentally the theory of 'archetypes' which concerns (significantly coupled together) both the manner of interpreting religious constants and the object of these. In other words, according to Eliade, religious symbols (that is, in a broad sense the hierophanies and in a stricter sense the 'signs' which 'reveal' the sacred in its unfathomable profundities) are certainly part of history, but they also transcend it, as is shown by the frequency of their ecumenical role and by their profound significance: moreover the myths, which narrate the events of the origins of the world, and the rites which are a re-enactment, in historical time, of the fullness and sacredness of the time of origins (*illud tempus*), show that the 'holy' transcends history also in the sense that it precedes it and serves as its foundation and, in the myth of the 'eternal return', it resolves it and absorbs it into itself, not merely in the sense of a return to a primordial chaos, but in the sense of the return, by means of the augural rite which is a rite of foundation or re-foundation, to that moment in which the world was created, complete and integral, out of initial chaos. There is therefore—in our opinion— as it were, a certain ambivalence in Eliade's thought about the origins: these are initial chaos and initial creation, an ambivalence, however, which is structured diachronically precisely in the sense of inaugura-

---

[45] M. Eliade and J. M. Kitagawa (ed.), *op. cit.*, page 103 (about 'symbols').
[46] Cf. *Studi e materiali di storia delle religioni*, 31 (1960), pp. 31-55.

tion (the creation issues forth intact and perfect from chaos).

The negligence of this last particular aspect of the 'ambivalence', as we shall see, invalidates some of the objections raised against Eliade's work by supporters of historicism.[47] It is true that Eliade himself, when asserting the paradoxical character of the 'holy', of which the *coincidentia oppositorum* is a typical feature (a deity that is at the same time creative and destructive, etc.) because, as he says, it indicates the absolute transcendence of the holy over all worldly contingencies, has in fact rendered less valid the distinction, even if 'seriated' or diachronic, between the chaotic origins and the beginnings of creation. Thus, for example, a correct interpretation of an 'orgy' as symbolical of 'a return to the amorphous and confused, the recovery of a state in which all attributes are abolished and contraries coincide',[48] is obviously incomplete if no attempt is made to identify the various successive moments in which chaos and re-integration are distinct and follow each other, because the cosmos, not chaos, is the final purpose of these rites. The same observation is valid for Eliade's interpretation of the immersion rites as a *regressus in uterum*, a return to pre-natal life, and as a 'beginning'. But we shall say more of this later.

Pettazzoni's criticisms of Eliade are two-fold; first of all they concern more directly the history of religions: the so-called 'archetypes' are in reality historically conditioned and therefore not outside time. Jung himself, speaking of archetypes, admits that they took shape in time, however remote and indefinable. Pettazzoni, instead, thinks it is possible to trace in history the birth of these fundamental ideas, for example, that of the 'eternal return' which must have had some connection with an agricultural civilization, aware of the recurring rhythm of life and death. Eliade does not think this connection is certain. But, apart from this discussion, it still remains—in our opinion—that Eliade's concept of religion, in contrast with history, as the re-integration of original perfection (i.e. the restoration of the mythical age) is somewhat forced. One does not in fact see why religion, as such, should be absolutely antipathetic to history, since it is the foundation of life and therefore positively concerned with it.

---

[47] It will result clearly from what we say that we do not seek to identify in any way the comparative-historical method with 'historicism' (in the technical-philosophical sense of the term, especially the absolute historicism [*storicismo assoluto*] of B. Croce).

[48] *Traité*, p. 358. For example the end-of-the-year rites in communities of primitive farmers, or in folklore; cf. also the Roman *Saturnalia*.

Moreover, if one considers together the two aspects of Eliade's interpretation: a) opposition and transcendence of the holy in relation to the profane and revelation of the holy in hierophany and symbolism, b) opposition and transcendence of the primordial, as opposed to the historical present, which is insignificant and 'fallen' compared with the primordial—it still appears that the 'holy' in its fully generic nature is presented in a somewhat postulatory way and therefore is susceptible of being overthrown, which is exactly what the historian critics of Eliade suggest. In fact, on the one hand Pettazzoni affirms, speaking from the point of view of hermeneutics, that it is not the mythical primordial world which gives meaning to the present, historical world (which, according to Eliade, is inaugurated and regenerated as much as the mythical age is renewed and restored); it is rather the present day world which describes the original world as different from the present, as being opposed to it, and therefore chaotic and disordered, if the present, that is our world today, is understood as functioning and therefore as ordered. This is the myth of the world of the origins being the 'upside-down world'. [49] Hence, Pettazzoni opposes the philosophy of Eliade with another, a contrary philosophy, which gives importance to history, to the 'worldly', to this life and this world, but in the light of the perennial efficacy of the 'religious value'. [50]

We must now pay more attention to distinguishing and putting in an ordered series the two aspects of primordial time, the aspect of formless chaos and that of primordial time as the age of intact and perfect creation: this is naturally a distinction which, when it is possible to make it, must be according to the conclusions of the history of religions. If, on the one hand, the two aspects of primordial time (the chaotic and the perfect, or that of the god who gives life and that of the god who destroys it, frequently combined in the same figure or symbol) are compatible with a speculation of the Indian type, they are not compatible, for example, with the history of the world as seen in the cosmogony and history of mankind which we find in the Old Testament and in Christianity, which have a 'linear' and Messianic concept of human and cosmic history. This restores a

---

[49] See above, p. 81. Note that Pettazzoni is here speaking from a hermeneutic and philosophical angle, because on the other hand he asserts the 'existential truth' of myth which, when believed in, rules the conduct and the life of the group which owns it (see above, pp. 93 and 112).

[50] Cf. the *Ultimi appunti* (posthumous) in *Studi e materiali di Storia delle religioni*, 31 (1960), p. 46, and the works quoted below, p. 199 et seq.

human, earthly, historical and active dimension of religion, or at least of some religions, like those based on the Bible (but also Zoroastrianism and various others, not only among the 'great religions').

It is true that Eliade admits that the Biblical religions occupy a place apart, and are an exception to the rhythmic theme of the 'eternal return'. Nevertheless he believes that he can discover in these too the archetypal themes (for example, the notion of baptism as a rebirth in water, a natal or pre-natal element: [51] a language, he acknowledges in *Naissances mystiques*, adopted only later by Christian writers, while the rite itself has its proper origins in the very beginnings of Christianity). Notwithstanding this limitation of his thesis by Eliade, we must remark—apart from other specific considerations of this example —that historical typology casts a doubt over one of the most alluring but dangerous hypotheses put forward by Eliade: that is that the symbols, hierophanies and archetypes may have a kind of life of their own and in themselves, a fulness of meaning which runs through all history, even transcending the awareness their respective believers have of these archetypes. This critic we express without denying the amazing diffusion, permanence, polyvalence and semantic, psychological and 'functional' profundity of religious symbols. So we shall have achieved two results: we shall have vindicated the rights of history, which can concede much, but not all, to these 'symbols' which, in Eliade's opinion, exercize such sovereign sway over history; and we shall have identified a postulatory aspect which governs Eliade's notion of the symbol, of hierophanies and archetypes, and which is

---

[51] His attitude is more cautious and more historically articulate in *Naissances mystiques*, Paris, 1959, p. 243: if baptism which also is an initiatory act, 'became a sacrament for the first Christians, this was precisely because it had been instituted by Christ'. Later on, with the diffusion of Christianity, Christian writers were to refer also to the 'universal religious language' of archaic symbols, to initiatory themes and to Greek philosophy, without, however, denying the historical truth of Christ, as was instead the case with certain Christian heresies and Gnosticism (*op. cit.*, p. 247 et seq.). In *Le mythe de l'éternel retour*, 2nd ed., Paris, 1949, p. 237, Eliade wrote that the faith of Abraham and the Christian faith form a new category and, in contrast with a faith in archetypes and repetitions, have a creative freedom. Nevertheless he subjects Christianity to his usual method of interpretation by (*op. cit.*, p. 240) persisting in seeing 'history' as 'fall', implying the 'definitive abandonment of the paradise of archetypes and repetition'. In this attitude he does not take into account the theme of the Incarnation, or of the *felix culpa*, or even of the command 'Be fruitful, multiply, fill the earth and conquer it' of Genesis 1, 28. On all this subject matter see, for certain currents of ancient and modern thought, U. Bianchi, *Péché originel et péché 'antécédent'* in *Revue de l'histoire des religions*, Vol. 170, 2 (1966) pp. 117-126.

quite extraneous to positive research, in as much as it appeals instead to a presupposition of a philosophical nature, analogous to Otto's presupposition of the 'holy' which he says is immediately revealed as eternal, free, and absolute, by man's awareness of the contrary attributes of this world in which we live.

Whatever value this theory may have in philosophy, it can certainly not be used as a key to historical-religious interpretation. Equally postulatory, and inadmissible from the historical-religious point of view, are those positions which overthrow that of Eliade but yet in a certain way adopt it, for they identify the religious feeling with the flight from history, the flight from the existential crisis, with escape into the periodic or final timelessness from the anguish caused by the crises of living in this world (or *Dasein*), with a recovery of the 'presence', by finding a temporary refuge in myth and rite, when faced with the danger and distress caused by feeling responsible for one's own destiny.

This is the position of Ernesto De Martino and of V. Lanternari, and is in part adopted by R. Pettazzoni. [52] It is significant that De Martino's attitude with regard to the exception represented by the Biblical religions is the same as Eliade's. He admits that there are exceptions, less alien from modern thought, intent on historicity, but finally reducible to a characteristic feature which De Martino finds in all religion: the flight from the worldly towards the transcendent, with the purpose of obtaining an external guarantee of life, which is identified with life in this world (mundane life). Now, it is indubitable that Christianity and, to a lesser extent, or better, in its own way, the Hebrew religion also imply a tension between what is worldly and what is religious ('flesh' and 'spirit' in the Pauline sense, not in the Gnostic sense, 'this' world and the world 'to come' in the Messianic and eschatological sense proper to Judaism and to Christianity and here too not in the Gnostic sense) but it does not follow that from the point of view of history and of the historical typology of religions Eliade's analysis and the corresponding, 'overthrown' thesis of De Martino on this matter are well founded. For the same reason there is no foundation for the theories of those 'death of God' theologians who also, like Altizer, [53] considered, and from quite another point of view, that they could twist Eliade's theory, by radical-

---

[52] *Appunti, cit.* Concerning the limitations of Pettazzoni's acceptance of this interpretative theory see above, p. 187 and below, pp. 199 et seq.
[53] T. J. J. Altizer, *Mircea Eliade and the Dialectic of the Sacred*, Philadelphia, s.a.

izing it, to a conclusion that was quite extraneous, or in fact contrary to its meaning in Eliade's thought, that is, to immanent Now—it matters little whether this is the 'worldly' of De Martino's absolute historicism (*storicismo assoluto*) and Marxism, or the 'worldly' of the immanentist incarnationism of the 'death of God' theologians.

In other words: one must contest the adequacy of the basis for a concept of the 'holy', such as is implicit in Eliade's research: one must raise an objection, not only of a general methodological type but one based also on specific reasons of a positive-documentary nature, once this concept is seen to be historically conditioned or in any case specifically conditioned, by a particular view of the 'holy', a view typical of Indian speculation, found already, although not exclusively, in the late Vedic books and later on in the whole Upanishadic and Vedantic tradition, and in any case more typical of this than of other traditions, especially the Hebraic and the Christian.

Having said this, we consider that there is in Eliade's interpretation much that is valid for the historical comprehension of religion and of religious phenomena, and that it will gain much from being freed from all the philosophical and postulatory (or 'revelatory' [54]) elements which characterize it (even if such an operation may seem or is in fact to some extent, a vivisection of a speculation which has a strongly unitary and lively character). In fact, Eliade's insistence on taking religious phenomena 'seriously' and on opposing all attempts at a reduction which would *a priori* prevent this comprehension, can only be beneficial, once it ceases to found itself on an a postulatory *a priori*. The student who wishes to treat religious phenomena in a scientific way must not speedily resort to sociological or psychological 'explanations' of religion, but must, without excluding *a priori* and methodologically any conclusions even in this sense—make a profound study of religious thought and practice (all that is capable of scientific exposition and investigation) in all their profundities, ramifications and wealth of significance. This research must, of course, make use of documents but not be a slave of a 'documentarism', especially if this is careless or prejudiced. From this point of view, Eliade's research is a model of devotion to the problem of the history of religions, and his phenomenology, or morphology, of the 'holy' is a valuable contribution of fresh blood for the vague spectral figure to which the

---

[54] In the sense in which Eliade uses this term (see above).

frequently necroscopic anatomy of 'religious scientists' have reduced religion itself.

We find a special significance in a concept to which Eliade has recourse in order to describe his own concept of religion: that of a 'breakthrough' (*rupture du niveau*), produced by religious belief and practice: a concept which corresponds to a positive and scientific analysis of religious phenomena much better than the vaguely postulatory concepts of 'hierophany', 'symbol', 'onrush' or 'revelation of the holy', and better also than that 'concern with ultimate reality' which is inappropriate for various types of religious experience which are not so much concerned with the primary and sacred origins of life as are, and *in toto*, the very doctrines of the great religions.

Eliade must also be commended for his vigorous defence not only of the 'science of religion' but also of the history of religions, understood as a study which must evoke human testimonies which it is the duty of science to make known, and to illustrate in all their significance and their specific characteristics (that is, not merely as religion but also as *a religion*, even if remote from the experience of our own *milieu*), and, in a word, to 'understand' them.

7. Examples of 'reductionist' theories

(A) '*Psychologism*' — As we have already mentioned, the postulatory tendency to 'reduce' *a priori* religious facts to facts of another nature may be seen in two forms: psychological and sociological. To deny the validity of this process of reduction *a priori* does not of course mean, as we have pointed out, to deny the legitimacy of the psychology of religion and of the sociology of religion, or to limit the explanatory possibilities of religious historical research concerning its own particular problems, which must also deal with questions of the genesis of religious phenomena.

One of the best known 'reductionist' methods is found in the psycho-analysis of S. Freud, whereas the presence of such a method in that of C. G. Jung is not so clearly proved.

The Freudian theory has been so often contested by ethnologists that there is no need to dwell on it here.

But one must add that a justifiable criticism of Freudism as an explanatory theory of religion does not imply that it is without value in the sphere of the psychology of religion, as long as one does not generalize in a non-historical way and does not forget that the psychology of religion may be treated also from different angles.

Moreover, Freudism, although notably reductionist as regards the wealth and the specific character of questions involving religion, is also, and arbitrarily, selective in its use of documentary material. *Totem and taboo*, Freud's well known book (and also *The Future of an Illusion*, and his book on monotheism) are themselves the proof of this. Jung's theory is different in tone, and has aroused the interest of various students of the history of religions, particularly because of his study of 'collective archetypes', which—in Jung's opinion—command mythology. For Jung these archetypes are not innate but acquired ideas, historically acquired (but of an indefinable historicity) and handed down by means of a sort of 'profound' collective memory (whereas Freud insists rather on the individual unconsciousness, occasioned by trauma in the subject's personal history, but always in harmony with typical experiences—the best known being that of the 'Oedipus complex'—which Freud endows with universal validity).

So Jung's collective archetypes, even if included in individual histories of cultures and religions, afford material for a vast comparative study, on the basis of figures like the 'divine maiden' which, as K. Kerényi maintains in a book written in collaboration with Jung, is found in a remote Indonesian mythology as well as in the Eleusinian myth and rite. But the discoverer of the singularity of this Indonesian mythology, A. E. Jensen, does not agree with the archetypal theory, for he is convinced that the mythological theme in question was historically connected with a particular civilization of primitive farmers (see above, pp. 99 et sqq.).

Whatever use may be made by religious historians of Jung's theory of 'depth psychology' (a theory sometimes resorted to in the case of a certain phenomenological presentation, to which therefore may be applied the observations already made about that interpretative trend) the fact remains that in Jung's theories, with regard to the problem of the essence, or origin, of religion, a fundamental ambiguity is present. We wonder to what extent Jung's theory 'reduces' religion to psychology, and to what extent it relates psychology to religion. Most philosophers and theologians identify Jung's position with the former of these two alternatives and conclude that he 'reduces' religion to psychology. What interests us, however, in this matter is that Jung's 'psychologism' implies a selection and an interpretation of his material which are very remote from the methodological exigencies of history.

(B) *Marxist sociologism* — As far as sociological 'reductionism'

MODERN PROBLEMS OF METHODOLOGY AND INTERPRETATION 193

is concerned, we need not here deal with the French sociological school, with E. Durkheim, or the theoretical systems of the positivists from Comte to Spencer, because we have already spoken of these. We shall instead take a brief look at Marxist studies of religion, considering not so much the theories of Marx and, above all, of Engels, (which, like those of Feuerbach which inspired them, do not belong to the history of the history of religions but to that of the philosophy of religion, and of a philosophy of religion understood as a corollary of the theory of historical and dialectical materialism) as certain more recent theories which present themselves as positive research. It is nevertheless true that even in these cases Engels' theory remains the theoretical foundation, from which, once it has been combined with the contributions proceeding from this or that positive research, are *deduced* the results of this research, and the interpretations to which these give rise.

This is particularly evident in the ethnological studies conducted in the Soviet Union. In these studies the treatment and the terminology used by Morgan in relation to society and family relationships [55] (studies which were essential in their own period but today are certainly in every sense inadequate) are still determinant. In a similar way, as regards the history of religions in Soviet studies, the insistence on concepts long ago discarded, when not totally arbitrary, is very notable. These concepts, together with the theoretical presuppositions to which we have already referred, have a negative influence over research and give it a strange character of cultural archaism [56] (although one cannot deny the usefulness or the freshness of approach in certain spheres of interest to which these researches have contributed most largely, in particular in what regards the Siberian and Central-Asian peoples and their religions and folklore). Thus one commonly finds, even in relatively more advanced scholars like S. A. Tokarev, conceptual identifications which are, to say the least, strange, like that of sacred objects and fetishes, [57] or that between sacred *formulae* and magic *formulae*. Equally arbitrary is the use of the term and con-

---

[55] Cf. U. Bianchi, *Storia dell'etnologia*, 2nd edition, Rome, 1971 (the chapter on the ethnographical studies in the U.S.S.R., pp. 227-239).

[56] Cf. E. De Martino's severe observations in the Introduction to the volume *La religione nell' U.R.S.S.*, Milan, 1961, pp. VIII-XI, and observations of V. Lanternari in *Nuovi Argomenti* 49-50 (1961) p. 54 et sqq. and 59 et sqq.

[57] S. A. Tokarev, *Les problèmes de l'étude des premières formes de la religion d'après la science soviétique*, Moscow, 1964 (report to the VIIth Int. Congress of Anthrop. and Ethnol. Sciences), p. 3.

cept of totemism, often connected with Morgan's theories of the origins of society and marriage. This is all the more surprising because, in some researches in which Soviet ethnologists are involved in a more personal and original manner, one sees opportune vindications of the historical and localized character of terminologies. For example we see a correct vindication of the specific character of Shamanism as a typical phenomenon of Central and North-Asian ethnography, comparable only partly with other phenomena of other geographical localities, which militant ethnologists perhaps too readily describe as 'shamanic'.

One must note also that this incorrect insistence on 'totemism' (as on other terms like those already mentioned) seems to be typical not only of the Soviet *milieu* but also fo the writings of Marxist theoreticians of Western Europe. As we shall see it is chiefly in Italy that we find scholars, although more or less inclined towards Marxism in their fundamental attitudes, who do not accept the 'official' analysis of the nature and origins of religion, although they are contradicted and declared extraneous to authentic Marxism.

As regards religion in itself, this is, for Sovietic Marxism, the object of an official theory and practice, of a policy which complicates still more, and in a two-fold way, a truly scientific discussion of these problems. It is well known that the theory of Marx, and still more that of Engels, on religion is profoundly influenced by Feuerbach. For him religion is the result of a phenomenon of projection and compensation of earthly experiences and aspirations in a fantastic transcendental. The founders of Marxism synthesized this theory with their theory of society and of its final emancipation, according to their belief that the 'human essence is not an abstraction inherent in the isolated individual'. Feuerbach had said: 'The divine Being serves to compensate the lack of a divine character in nature and in man... The real essence which is lacking in man is replaced by an ideal Being... The negation of the world beyond necessarily produces the affirmation of this present world'.[58] Note the paradoxical affinity between the first of these three postulatory affirmations and Otto's theses: see above p. 172f.). Hence the official Soviet definition: 'Religion is one of the forms of the social consciousness; it is the distorted, fantastic reflection in men's consciousness of the natural and social forces to which men are subjected. Religion is faith in the existence of supernatural

---

[58] Cf. H. Desroche, *Marxisme et religions*, Paris, 1962, p. 8 and p. 6, note 1.

forces, gods, spirits, souls and such like...'. [59] Thus, whereas primitive religion, in the epoch preceding the formation of classes, is thought to depend on the ignorance of the savage faced with the overwhelming forces of nature, in the successive periods, when classes were formed, religion was said to be founded on the transposition into a transcendent sphere of forms of actual dependence characteristic of societies built on class divisions, and on the transposition into the transcendent sphere of the need for liberation and of feelings of frustration, caused by alienation inherent in the very organization of society.

Hence the theory of religion as a superstructure, as an obstacle ('opium of the people') and as destined to disappear with social emancipation and the establishment of Communism as the final eschatological resolution of class tensions: the final phase of a cycle which had begun with an earlier primitive Communism, before the coming of class divisions.

In this presentation of religion (we restrict ourselves to those aspects only which concern historical methodology) the insistence on the concept that religion is primarily an ideology, rather than a form of social behaviour or an institution, or a means of understanding one's own existence, is very noteworthy. This insistence reveals the epoch in which Marxism was born and flourished, the epoch of Comte and Tylor, totally dedicated, on scientist and Illuminist premises, to the search for the 'ideas' or notions that could have given rise to religion (and to magic) in men's *minds*; magic as a 'false science', (that is, as the mistaken application of the principle of causality) was soon to be formulated by Frazer, and Tylor maintained that belief, or better the idea of soul, and, originally, the 'image' of 'souls', appearing in dreams or 'visions' to men's minds, was the source of religion, with the subsequent transformation of the 'souls' into 'spirits' and deities (the Animist theory; see above, pp. 83 ff.). As is well known, all non-materialistic conceptions are described *en bloc*, in Soviet culture and in general in political Marxism, as 'idealistic', but in the definition of this 'idealism' certain theorizations analogous to those of Positivist ethnologists like Tylor exert their influence. Moreover, it has been frequently pointed out that Animism, in so far as it expresses a genuine tendency of primitive religious thought, has facilitated the formation of the concept of a 'pure' spirit, separate from matter, but

---

[59] See the 'Great Sovietic Encyclopaedia'. Cf. also I. A. Kryvelev, *On the nature of the concept of religion*, Moscow, 1964 (VIIth Int. Congress of Anthrop. and Ethnol. Sciences).

also that of a concept of 'pure' matter, independent of spirit, and has likewise facilitated the possibility of ideological accentuations and absolutizations in the 'spiritualistic' ('idealistic') or in the materialistic sense. So the Marxist contrast: materialism-idealism, and its relevant dialectic, are seen to be historically conditioned by over simplified interpretative principles, similar to those which Tylor was to use later on. This is not surprising when one thinks of the positivistic-evolutionistic origins of the theory of Marx and Engels about the history of mankind, a theory which assigns the first appearance of 'idealistic' concepts, before the formation of social classes, to the 'superstition' of savage man, according to a criterion of typically evolutionistic character, proper to Comte and Tylor (cf. Ugo Bianchi, *Storia dell' etnologia*, 2nd ed., p. 98 et seq. [n.]).

The Marxist theory of religion, and its interpretation of the history of religions (which is all that concerns us here) have been the objects of severe criticism, even from scholars in sympathy with its cultural presuppositions. V. Lanternari, asserting that religion indicates a salvation which is outside history and outside this world, and leaving aside 'the metaphysical problem of the *intrinsic* value of the religious phenomenon', sees in religion a positive historical value which demands a 'historical-cultural interpretation of the religious life of peoples', and invites the Marxist critic historian to abandon his prejudicially and generically negative position, conditioned, in his opinion, by the historical situation in which Marxism arose. Marxism should instead 'opportunely consider' what function, 'culturally positive or negative, promoting renewal or conservation or a dynamic equilibrium, has been performed by each and every form of religious manifestation in the framework of the civilization in which it has been operating'.[60] Naturally, the programmatic 'reductionist' philosophy of the 'mundane' is pre-supposed in Lanternari's words, and the exclusion of the contrary presupposition, that is, of a prejudicial positive answer to the problem of the metaphysical value of religion, is not enough to lead us back to the plane of pure historical methodology (see above, pp. 20 et sqq. and 189 et sqq.). The proof of this is seen in the fact that on the historical plane (which, as we said, is the only one which concerns us here), Lanternari identifies the 'positive' element of religion with popular religious movements (which he has studied as an ethnologist) and the 'negative' element with the 'institutional' phase

---

[60] *Nuovi Argomenti*, 49-50 (1961), pp. 53 et sqq. and 57.

of a religion (two phases which moreover, he points out, tend to generate each other). But—in our opinion—this alleged contrast between these alleged two phases too is conditioned by historical and cultural facts and therefore invalid when understood generically. In fact, the 'institution' was 'positive' in various religious civilizations, whether ethnical (one thinks of the rise of the first Mesopotamian city-states, centred in a shrine or in a priesthood) or 'founded' (one thinks of Islam in the golden epoch of its history, and of so many moments in the ecclesiastical history of Christianity, which were not 'negative' from the historical-cultural point of view), [61] as well as in their beginnings.

Lanternari also reproaches classical Marxism (and we must add, as before, official Soviet Marxism) and all who adopt it in Western Europe also, like C. Hainchelin, [62] for the schematic nature of the theory of structure and superstructure and the gratuity of the theory of 'primordial atheism' and of 'primordial Communism', and points out the presence of 'that sort of Millenarianism or Utopianism which animates the whole [Communist] movement in its popular [and, we add, not only popular] interpretation'. In this he finds a mythical and religious element, and the expectation of 'deliverance from evils of every kind and origin'. [63] And in fact, if among these evils we place death, as a human fact in the full sense of the term, and not merely in its biological and social aspects, the actual problem of the genesis and forms of a great deal of religious experience is still more clearly seen to be much more complex than Marxist reductionism is willing to admit.

E. De Martino [64] occupies a prominent position in the studies undertaken, at least in part, with materialistic and dialectic presuppositions (if not precisely Marxist presuppositions) in the Western world. He constructs a synthesis of historicistic speculation, of psychologistic ana-

---

[61] See above, p. 166 n. 8. Moreover, the use of the terms 'positive' and 'negative' is rather questionable as regards historical studies, without the necessary details about the object and scope of the judgment.

[62] This position is sustained also, in Italy, by A. Donini, in his book *Lineamenti di storia delle religioni*, although he adds some personal judgment of the value of certain moments of religious history. But it is above all on the question of the suitability of his training in those matters which are always specialized and do not admit of casual treatment that Donini's book is open to severe criticism, all the more so as this scholar comes from an Italian *milieu* of studies which is particularly rich in the pre-requisites of historical methodology (as he himself had shown in other precedent writings).

[63] See above, in the paragraph on 'para-religions'.

[64] Already in *Morte e pianto rituale nel mondo antico*, Turin, 1958. Also in *La terra del rimorso* and *Sud e magia*.

lysis and of an immanentist and materialistic theory of the 'mundane', with his theory of religion being a means of overcoming the crisis of *Dasein*, or of presence, the anguish of history. In this way he thinks that religion has a de-historifying function. This is a theory which repeats and utilizes one of the most fundamental theses of Eliade (a scholar with a very different orientation), but uses it inversely (see above, p. 189 et seq.). Eliade's point of reference is the intact sacredness of the time of the world's origins, and he maintains that by re-evoking and re-enacting this the world assumes a meaning and is re-created.

But for De Martino, on the contrary, the point of reference is the 'mundane', identified with history and with creative activity, while the pauses, the de-historified intervals, are a function of this mundane —they ensure its recovery or its deliverance.

Naturally, this way of interpreting religion implies an ideological 'option' like that of De Martino concerning the designation of the 'mundane' as the point of reference of the 'sacred', an option which is by no means the same as the concept that the historian is not called upon to express an opinion about the transcendent origins of religion, which he studies as a 'fact' in the context of human history, and must investigate according to a positive inductive method.

In other words, De Martino's option not only is not pertinent to the history of religions, but conditions it with extraneous presuppositions. Moreover, this option, and the theory which expresses it, although presented as historicistic, are in reality strongly conditioned by a psychologistic position which is extremely generic and un-historical. In fact, the pattern 'anguish—crisis—deliverance' is for this option and theory universally valid and underlies *all* manifestations of religion. Even if De Martino (as, before him, Eliade) recognizes in this pattern a position peculiar to Christianity, which introduced the concept of a *purposeful* history, that is, of an acquisition of *new* values, his final judgment on every form of religion remains the same: hence De Martino's insistence on themes (studied by him mainly in the sphere of folklore and its 'survivals'),[65] in which he can best point out that 'technique of deliverance' which he himself indicates as the nature of religion. The history of religion, however, in its multiple and varied forms, still remains outside his scope, without being given sufficient attention, or, still less, explanation.

---

[65] These subjects concern the 'ritual lament', 'tarantolism' and magic.

8. *The comparative method and the category 'religion' in R. Pettazzoni. Observations on the theme of the universality of religion*

We have on several occasions referred to Pettazzoni's contributions to the historical-comparative method, as opposed to phenomenology of religion studied from a non-historical position. But Pettazzoni is far from denying the value of the phenomenology of religion, in fact he acknowledges its essential importance in religious studies for the purpose of discerning the essence of religion itself. 'Religious phenomenology has the merit of having based its methodology on the fundamental concept of the specific value of religion in the life of the spirit. Comparative study is necessary in order for phenomenologists to deduce from the similarity of the *structures* the fundamental meaning of religious phenomena, that is their own proper religious meaning'. [66] Therefore Pettazzoni's speculation excludes the typical position of the absolute historicism (*storicismo assoluto*) of B. Croce, which is willing to resolve religion in ethics or philosophy, just as it excludes the 'reductionism' of E. De Martino, to whom we have already referred, in whom there undoubtedly persists, in his constant pattern: anguish—deliverance, a fundamental psychologism.

According to Pettazzoni, what is lacking in phenomenology is the idea of development, which 'is instead at the heart of historicistic speculation, whereas historicism remains extraneous to that requirement which is fundamental for phenomenology, the recognition of religion as in itself an autonomous value. This concept of religion as a unique experience produces for phenomenology the need of a specific method for the study of religion, a method not derived from any other branch of learning, whether linguistics or philology or anthropology. Therefore, this methodological requirement also is extraneous to historicism. There is then a clear choice between a phenomenology without historical vigour and a history without an adequate religious sensibility', [67] an alternative which Pettazzoni resolves in a complementary manner. 'In systematic terms, it is a question of transcending the unilateral positions of phenomenology and historicism by integrating them mutually, and by so doing reinforcing religious phenomenology with the historicistic concept of development, and reinforcing historicistic historiography with the phenomenological insistence on the autonomous value of religion; in this way one will resolve

---

[66] *Il metodo comparativo* in *Numen*, VI, 1 (1959) p. 8.
[67] *Il metodo comparativo, cit.*, p. 10.

phenomenology in history and, at the same time, recognize religious history as a qualified historical science'. [68]

Less involved in philosophical terminology, suggested by the term 'historicism', is an analogous formulation by Pettazzoni in a treatise explicitly dedicated to the relation between 'phenomenological structure and historical development': [69] 'Phenomenology and history complement each other. Phenomenology cannot do without ethnology, philology and other historical disciplines. Phenomenology, on the other hand, gives the historical disciplines that sense of the religious which they are not able to capture. So conceived, religious phenomenology is the religious understanding (*Verständnis*) of history; it is the history in its religious dimension. Religious phenomenology and history are not two sciences but two complementary aspects of the integral science of religion, and the science of religion as such has a well-defined character given to it by its unique and proper subject matter'.

In our opinion, if one ignores its reference to a specific philosophy the final formulation of the preceding conclusion may be better phrased: phenomenology, more than a science in itself, it fully at ease when it is incorporated in history, a history which must take into account not only the concepts of diffusion, convergence, etc. but also of historical typology; it is the meaning of the definition of that *analogon*, or 'structure' which, present in individual religious phenomena, is religion itself. [70] As for the irreducible nature of religion as an activity of the spirit, it may not be pre-supposed *a priori*, just as it may not be denied *a priori* but will express itself, methodologically, in the need, which we have found legitimate also in Eliade's theories, to investigate religious facts in all their aspects and in all their ramifications, without arbitrary, *a priori* reductive selection. It will also be expressed, theoretically, in the need, before defining religion phenomenologically, to consider religions in their complex variety and in their world wide concrete and historical development.

This concept of religion as a 'concrete (i.e. historical) universal', [71] studied by history, rather than as a generic 'universal' resulting from a theoretical option, seems to us to satisfy more adequately the requirements of the history of religions.

---

[68] *Op. cit.*, p. 14.

[69] *The Supreme Being: Phenomenological Structure and Historical Development*, in Eliade and Kitagawa, *History of Religions*, Chicago, 1959, p. 66.

[70] For these concepts see Chap. I, pp. 5-12 and *infra*, pp. 207 ff.

[71] For the meaning of this expression, differing from its meaning in Hegelian (or Marxist) terminology, see our *Storia dell'etnologia*, 2nd edition, *op. cit.*, pp. 250 ff.

CONCLUSION

THE DEFINITION OF RELIGION
On the methodology of historical-comparative research

Comparative history or cultural anthropology?

In this discussions on historical-religious studies, a major importance is given to the problem of the definition of religion and the problem of method: two matters that really identify with each other. As a matter of fact in these studies it is not a question of a theoretical and abstract definition of religion but of a definition that results from a method of positive survey and is able to cover a vast and quite different series of facts, that belong to different cultures; facts, whose partial 'religious' homogeneity is empirically agreed with already from the start, without any previous and surely adequate definition of their object. Furthermore to obtain a concrete definition of religion, i.e. a definition resulting from a more complete analysis of the facts that seem adapted to substantiate it, two methods are at disposal. A first one is the phenomenological method that, though it admits the necessity of proceeding in a positive manner, presupposes a previous granting to religion of a general autonomy of an atemporal category, and thus of an univocal basic meaning. A second one is the historical method which, seeing religion and its elements as historically qualified, considers as essential the very problematic of genesis and development, and it is in the frame of this context that a general concept of religion is to be tested, as well as the concept of a categorial autonomy (or to say it with Pettazzoni, [1] of an 'autonomous value') of same.

What do 'religion' and 'religious' mean? And not only 'religion' and 'religious', but even all those concepts and terms that have been at turn exchanged with the former, or in some way used during analogous speculations? I refer here to such terms as 'the sacred', or 'ultimate concern', or 'the sense of absolute', or 'breaking of level', or similar, which all more or less express modalities of religion that take their effective result from a positive research, but are all conditioned in their value, whenever they aim at defining 'religious', were it only for a description of it.

---

[1] 'Il metodo comparativo', in *Numen* VI, 1 (1959), p. 14.

And this goes also for that concept of 'sacred' which people intend as coextensive with the very concept of 'religious' itself, wherefrom 'sacred' would be the most true and intimate essence. Now, let us consider Otto's quoting certain religions or religious forms wherein the sense of sacred is more evident in comparison with other where it is felt less, [2] while other scholars have contested the general applicability of Otto's categories. [3] This leads us to accept that the 'sacred' itself, at least in the meaning that Otto gives to the word, must be studied, phenomenologically and historically, against a more general 'religious' background (whatever the meaning of 'religious' could be: see below).

Same remark goes for such concepts as 'ultimate concern', which could be referred to other human experiences too, but on the other hand matches instead perfectly in certain definite religions, for which the expression has been formed, and also in certain well-defined religious tempers.

But especially those definitions that call themselves 'functional', and are at the same time frequently 'reductive', i.e. destined to 'explain' and 'solve' religion (its origin and its persisting) in motivations of a sociological and psychological order, reveal themselves to be absolutely inadequate for a useful definition of religion in our studies. And this we affirm without referring to any opposite philosophical presupposition, as could be of religion as an *a priori* form of the spirit, gifted *de iure* with a universality and an ever-lasting presence during history and through all the historical possibilities. [4] A 'functional' definition of religious is for instance the one given in Italy by E. De Martino, with his theory of a 'de-historifying' function of religion, as a technique for the resolution of frightening existential anxieties, of the 'crisis of presence'. [5] But here Melford E. Spiro, a social anthropologist, observes (although not in relation with De Martino's theory): 'Social solidarity, anxiety reduction, confidence in unpredictable situations, and the like, are functions which may be served by any or all cultural phenomena—Communism and Catholicism, monotheism and monogamy, images and imperialism', [6] so that 'as long as reli-

---

[2] Cf. R. Otto, *Das Heilige*, 29. 30. ed., München s.a., p. 116 (ch. 14).

[3] K. Rudolph, *Die Religionsgeschichte an der Leipzige rUniversität und die Entwicklung der Religionswissenschaft*, Berlin 1962 (Sitz. Ber. Sächs. Akad., Philol.-histor. Klasse. Bd. 107, H. 1), p. 55 ff., 164 ff.

[4] See below.

[5] U. Bianchi, *Problemi di storia delle religioni*, Rome 1958, pp. 127-130 (= *Probleme der Religionsgeschichte*, Göttingen 1964, pp. 86-88). See also above, pp. 189 et seq., 197-199.

[6] In M. Banton (ed.), *Anthropological approaches to the study of religion*, London 1966, p. 90.

gion is not substantially defined (the Author means: in relation to its own object), it is impossible to trace its borders'. And further he observes: 'Similarly, if communism, or baseball, or the stockmarket are of ultimate concern to some society, or to one of its constituent social groups, they are, by definition, sacred. But beliefs concerning communism, baseball, or the stockmarket are not, by definition, religious beliefs, because they have no reference to superhuman beings'. [7] And herewith Spiro introduces his 'substantive' definition of religion, whose necessary key-element is 'faith in the existence of superhuman beings'. [8]

We do not keep ourselves up with this definition, which is certainly very pertinent, and in any case much more legitimate than others, partly similar, that have been expressed during the past century (especially Tylor's: 'faith in spiritual beings'). Be it enough for us to stress one incoherency of Spiro: while he rightly refuses to use the attribute of 'religious' for phenomena whose categorial pertaining clearly differs from religion, such as for *communism* or, more clearly, for *baseball*, he fails to use the same caution with the term 'sacred'. This he uses instead—be it only in a hypothetical or paradoxical way—in a rather 'analogous' meaning, or even in a substantially equivocal meaning of something that it intouchable, important, out of common, something that carries away, that is not to be discussed, something that implies an 'ultimate concern': an expression which, in Spiro, looses the real meaning that Tillich had given to it when first using it.

Of course, other and less banal examples could be given of an improper and equivocal use, or at any case of a most problematic use of the term 'religion': for ex. in talking of a 'religion of the fatherland', 'of liberty', 'of humanity', of 'sacred values', etc. (which has nothing to do with the effective existence of religions of a 'national style', with cults of the 'polis', etc., although in some cases a *certain* continuity could be supposed, though always in the context of a *metabasis eis allo genos*).

And thus we are brought back to a difficulty wherefrom it seems difficult to escape: 'It is obvious', says Spiro, 'that while a definition cannot take the place of inquiry, in the absence of definitions there can be no inquiry—for it is the definition, either ostensive [9] or

---

[7] *Op. cit.*, p. 96.
[8] Cf. *op. cit.*, p. 91, 94, 96, and 98.
[9] 'Unless he knows, ostensively, what religion is...'; *op. cit.*, p. 90. 'To define a word ostensively is to point to the object which that word designates' (p. 87).

nominal, [10] which designates the phenomenon to be investigated'. [11] And Spiro continues observing how right Evans-Pritchard is when be requires that each generalization be founded on particular previous conclusions. Evans-Pritchard affirms that in the frame of a research-work 'one must not ask "what is religion?", but what are the main features of, let us say, the religion of one Melanesian people'; and afterwards, comparing the results of the researches on various peoples of this part of the world, we will get at generalizations about a Melanesian religion *in toto*. [12] But, apart from the obvious statement that such a type of research is already in practice in Ethnology—(we mean the method aiming at defining the cultural areas, as a method that keeps in mind the historiographical requirements of individualizing ambients and historical concrete contexts, in order to widen the conclusions, step by step, on a comparative and inductive basis)—we must also observe that from his point of view Spiro marks his step in noting that, if the scholar does not know 'ostensively, [13] what religion is, how can our anthropologist in his Melanesian society know which, among a possible *n*, observations, constitute observations of religious phenomena, rather than of some other phenomenal class, kinship, for example, or politics?' And we feel that he is not absolutely wrong here, although this reasoning of his through categories or classes may in fact hurt against the organic complexity of the phenomena. As we have seen, an essential element of religion, that allows to ascribe a fact to one category and not to others, is instead—according to Spiro—the belief in super-human good and evil beings. Besides, he observes, nothing implies that a definition of religion, resulting from a comparative research, must necessarily reflect facts that are universally spread over the world: i.e. that religion 'must' be a universal phenomenon proper to any civilization and to any human society. [14] On the contrary, the study of its real diffusion would give to any research a sense of major historical concreteness. And element of comparison here is

---

[10] 'Nominal definitions are those in which a word, whose meaning is unknown or unclear, is defined in terms of some expression whose meaning is already known'. *Op. cit.*, p. 85. This is akin to verbal definition and internationally standardized conventional definition (which on the other hand could easily be crypto-ideological).

[11] *Op. cit.*, p. 90, cf. p. 89.

[12] *Op. cit.*, p. 90.

[13] Cf. supra, n. 9.

[14] *Op. cit.*, p. 88. As for the other aspects touched upon by Spiro, and his conclusions (which we are far from sharing) they lie outside our scope, and do not pertain to the field of the History of Religions. They owe to psychologistic reductionism.

to Spiro the usual one. the case of Buddhism of the Small Vehicle, of 'atheist' Buddhism,—though Spiro does not fail to note that in the very Small Vehicle itself there are elements of faith in superhuman beings; and Buddha himself would be one of these, that realize the definition of the religion he proposes (while the remaining would be 'philosophy').

But we believe that this marks the limits of validity of the definition and of the methodology suggested by Spiro. As a matter of fact, if on the one hand it is perfectly coherent, or rather it is a requisite of a historical-positive research not to presuppose any universality or any *a priori* necessity, or co-extention with history of whatever phenomenon —in this case religion—, on the other hand the application of a rigid definition risks to break those tissues, those solidarities, that exist *in re* and are determinant: for ex. historical and objective solidarity between Buddhism and Indian upanishadic speculation, precedent and contemporary to it. And this solidarity does not concern those beliefs that even in the Small Vehicle may correspond to Spiro's definition, but concerns the substance itself of Buddhist preaching, the loosening of worldly chains in a freemaking that is a form of absoluteness, which for this very reason is implied in an atmosphere which is religious, [15] and could not cease to be so not even if some elements of it—though at their turn being essential, such as a doctrine of the soul and of Divinity—would come to vary or even, in extreme cases, would come to lack. Rather, if the Small Vehicle radicalizes, in a certain way, certain aspects of the upanishadic speculation, that are essential aspects of it and which nobody would intend to eliminate from the religious horizon of the Indian speculation, one cannot see how this radicalization of a categorial religious motive could end in a phenomenon that be categorically extraneous to religion. And herewith we do not intend to affirm that 'it is impossible to walk out of religion', and that any result of speculations and religious beliefs should be a new form of religion: it would be enough to consider certain aspects of the Greek philosophy, or the Sensism of Illuminism period. But in these last cases what is decisive, even if they maintain the Supreme Being or introduce the goddess Reason, is the insertion of a new interest, of new values, of a new concept of the world, opposite to the ancient one; whereas in the case of Buddhism the continuity with respect to certain

---

[15] On the other hand, it would be methodologically inaccurate to imply that 'loosening of the world chains' and 'absolute' are *as such* and *sine addito* specifically 'religious' concepts.

basic formulations, formed by the doctrines of the *karma*, of the *moksha* and the *Nirvana*, is essential, no matter the importance of the innovatory element, that may be felt as heretical and perhaps even athestic by India itself, where Buddhism has been rejected, but which other countries have been ready to agree with and to render co-acceptable with the most various traditional religious expressions.

Moreover it would be strange for Buddhism to be valued in its quality of 'religion', properly and only in value of its rather secondary elements instead of its basic inspiration.

This brings us back to what we started with; the problems of a definition of religion may be solved only in a dialectical manner: dialectics which should unite the two requirements, over and above any theoretical impasse: the requirement to possess already a certain idea of religion when we are studying the 'religious' concepts and practices of humanity, and the need for us not to take our start from preconceived and theoretical definitions, but to construct rather a definition basing ourselves on an inductive and positive enquiry. What is important is to have an adequate idea of these 'dialectics': it should not be reduced to the admission of an operative definition of religion limited to a working hypothesis, a conventional definition, or only a heuristic one: i.e. a hypothesis or a definition that should base itself on the research on such phenomena that happen to have in common *whatever*—be it only exterior—common feature.

At this point it is clear that the problem of a definition of religion is not the problem of an *a priori* selection of the facts to which research should be extended, and of which others should be left aside instead (or only considered as a frame, context, or outline). Better to say, it is not a matter of a merely horizontal problem, but of one of penetration; what matters is to understand the real connection between the problem of definition and the problem of a method of research; to understand *how* to build a definition and, in the same time, how to acquire an adequate knowledge of the object.

Thus, this relation between the definition or concrete, progressive (in the real meaning of the word) research of the definition, and the progress (or, the 'methodos', which means etymologically the same) of the research, is essential. And this suggests the question of what this method must be: should it be a 'phenomenological' method, or rather a typological or morphological one, or should it be a historical method, or some combination of both.

It is probable that the method should not be restricted to a typology, morphology or phenomenology that presuppose a concept of religion as something already defined; and this for the reasons already mentioned above. In case, it should touch a typological method able to individualize various types of religion and which could describe, and catalogue, their affinities or differences, to reach a view of those partly unitary and partly different, that is, of those 'analogous' things, that are 'religions'. But in this case, not only do we obtain for result a series of motionless pictures, in a certain way void of life and concrete motivation, but we also have to face quite some difficulties to intend the connections, the relations of contiguity, the very reasons themselves and the meaning of connection between the ones and the others. And before anything else one should question the legitimacy of the choice of 'that' particular unitarian point of view, of 'that' distinctive of 'religion' (for ex. the 'sacred', or the belief in superhuman beings, or similar) that has allowed to catalogue together or to list these phenomena instead of others; now, this would bring back to the impasse of a definition that would at the same time be existent and yet to be done. If instead we should keep to the dialectic of the cognitive process destined to form a concrete, inductive definition of the religious facts,—to the process, the 'method', capable of knowing these very facts,—we must also make sure that these dialectic does not center only on the affinities purely resulting from a decomposing and recomposing operation of elements of belief and practice. I.e., we must cure that the acquisition, through experience, of phenomena that were foreign to the basic culture of the scholar, be, at the same time, the extention of the historiographic experience of the same scholar. And this, to say the truth, is no easy job, due also to the documentation on hand; nor, for the same reasons, are the typological inquiries we were talking of above, deprived of any kind of merit.

History of Religions is a science which, different from *Social Anthropology*, be it Evans-Pritchard's or Spiro's, is not only interested in the study of functions, structures and definitions, but also in the study of a category for which Anglo-Saxon science, after the inadequate tryings of people as Tylor and Morgan, has lost most of its interest: the historical category of genesis and development. The problems about genesis and development do not end with the study of philologically proven relations between one fact and another, between one document and another, or in the study of phenomena of cultural diffusion or of 'stimulus diffusion'. Without excluding from history creativity or individuality (and even *Einmaligkeit*), those problems may extend themselves to what we call a 'historical typology', that discovers an analogy of historical answers to an analogy of situations and 'expectations' or 'demands', and this in the frame of a *Weltgeschichte* that results from such processes which take place on the same planet among the same humanity.

To give an idea of this historical problematic that is bound to the questions of 'analogy' and of 'historical typology of religion', we refer to the well-known distinction between 'ethnical' religions and 'founded' religions. The former, such as the Etruscan religion or the Greek, or the Aztec or Egyptian ones, are part of a civilization and of a culture, wherewith they rise (*in their fact as well as in the knowledge the scholar gets of them*), and wherewith sooner or later they are bound to disappear (more or less relatively, as they do partly survive in the sensitivity or in the experience of the related peoples, even when they are explicitly refused by them). The 'founded' religions, on their part, owe their existence to the sufficiently emerging ('emerging' in the reality of things *and* in the knowledge that the scholar acquires of it) individuality of a founder, naturally within the context (at least at their start and first affirmation) of a culture and a history.

Another example of what we intend with 'historical typology of religions', for a typology of religious histories, is the frequently mentioned example of polytheism: that is, the study of the historical circumstances in which polytheism was born, in various civilizations (circumstances that may happen in many places, although apparently —often—due to the presence of demonstrable historical influences or stimuli). In fact, polytheisms usually appear with superior old civilizations (although some of them, such as the Japanese one, are still alive), in relation with the rising of cities, states, empires, with specific sanctuaries and priesthoods and with a parallel development of social, political and sacral institutions that are such as to match with the organization of a polytheistic cult.

Similar researches of a historical typology—that do not exclude nor presuppose hypotheses of diffusion, although they are necessarily interested to them—are possible for other forms of culture and religion also, such as for ex. the archaic ethnological cultures of hunters and collectors, with certain rather constant and typical forms of belief and religious practice (hunting rites, tribal initiation, etc.). And all this—we repeat—without exclusion of those problems of cultural diffusion that do remain an essential object of the historical-comparative research, in the sense of a historical-cultural enquiry.

To conclude with, we shall say that History of Religions faces a quantity of historical processes, of well settled contexts of belief and practice, of religious 'worlds' that are more or less compact, even if more or less intercommunicating. Those 'worlds' on the one hand seem to correspond to a common human behaviour, a behaviour which we call 'religious', and herewith prove a more or less evident 'analogy' among themselves; but on the other hand they prove to be so very dissimilar among them that a good part of history and phenomenology of religions must be dedicated to establish a classification and, possibly, a historical and typological ramification of them.

This frequently results in a problem of 'historical typology' in the above explained meaning and in problems of historical (and not only phenomenological) 'continuity and discontinuity', such as is the case with the above mentioned relations between upanishadic soteriology and Buddhism. In this case we have a 'continuity' that does not prevent that phenomenon of novelty, of creativity, of religious revolution, and thus of discontinuity, that is so evident in the 'founded' religions. But the 'analogy' we were talking of above, puts a vaster problem, as it seems to extend to all the forms of religion. Such an 'analogy', obviously, does not only mean a partial affinity and a partial divergence of 'content' between religions, or a divergence in the way these could 'combine' elements that are apparently or really common; but it means also a diversity in forms, in quality. I.e.: the 'religions' are not all religions in the same meaning of this term (and this renders a positive definition of the concept of religion in the frame of History of Religions and in Phenomenology of Religion rather difficult). In other words, the religions are no 'species' of a 'genus' that would precisely be religion. Which is to say that, contrary to what happens for the genera and the species, we cannot say that, in the different 'religions', a *genus* (a general kind) 'religion' is present *in its whole*, taken in a univocal meaning, that may be verified for each single religion (as for example 'animal' for all zoological species). Such attempts to identify a lowest common denominator of all the religions, an attempt to identify a basis for belief and for a behaviour common to all of them, must necessarily fail, as cases of animism and the theory of the *mana* teach us. And false are the connected attempts, that evolutionistic History of Religions has made, to identify *mana* or animism with the *nux*, the embryo or historical origin of religion.

But to state the 'analogous' character of the concept of religion will on the other hand mean to state the existence of a common 'family ambit', or 'common aspects', between various religious forms (that actually render religious people mutually more sensitive—which at times may also mean to put them in a more marked contrast); although this statement could not impose itself by mere intuition nor—even less—could it do so by an unreflected 'participation' of the scholar (and even the reference to concepts such as *Erlebnis* is liable to quite some reservation).

As far as the contents of religion or eventual common contents are concerned, once the misunderstanding of the 'least common denominator', or of the 'nucleus' common to all religions, is eliminated (that would not give proper account and reason to any religion, and would instead harm all of them as it would deprive them of their typical essence), these contents will be enquired principally on the basis of researches of historical continuity and discontinuity of a type similar to the ones mentioned above for Buddhism; or with researches on those continuity and discontinuity that we may find among religions that have parallelly developed in different but contiguous cultural milieus; or even on the basis of such a 'historical typology' that was mentioned above about the 'higher polytheistic cultures', or the archaic hunters' cultures. To be sure, other researches of a typological nature, aiming at discovering solidary types of belief and practice, i.e. 'structures' (in the sense of a phenomenology of religion), prove to be very useful for a positive enquiry on religion and religions; but this only in case they prove not to remain indifferent to the historical problematic and as long as they undergo a philological checking of any eventual data and conclusions they get to.

Herewith a history of religions that includes also the right instances of phenomenology of religion fills a space that would otherwise be empty (and destined to be filled in an improper way) between a phenomenology of religion intuitive and too open to generalization, with a surrounding of implications that are not all scientifically valid (and at times manifesting some remainder of evolutionism), and a philology or a historiography that, dedicated to the study of single cultural milieus, would be reluctant at any comparison, and at any more vast horizon and any historical typology.

Finally, in this case, the judge of rights will be the fact itself. If, in their historical-comparative studies, the historians of religions will spur the philologians to new notions; or if they will show the existence of relations unknown before, between things or phenomena; or if they will give evidence of aspects neglected before, or of values and significations never explored before or even denied; finally, if they only suggest problems that nobody had thought of before, then they will (and surely they have often done so) have proven the scientific legitimacy of their discipline. Nor could one object that they have reached such acquirements only through their single philological capacities and for the field to which these refer; because these problems and acquirements often possess a far wider extension than that of any discipline related to a single people or a single cultural milieu.

This goes also for the problem of categorial 'autonomy of religion', an autonomy which is affirmed *a priori* in Phenomenology of Religion, but may be better explained, as a problem, by History of Religions, that —due to its purely historical-positive nature—should not fall into suspicion of philosophical or theological (or anti-theological) presuppositions. Besides, History of Religions is obliged by its very nature of philologically meticulous and historically probe research to run through and enlighten all the aspects, the turns and the meanings of the object in question, and this without biases or inclinations, except that of an open interest (a 'sympathy', in the sense of a scientifically proven human interest) that renders a 'comprehension' more easy, though distinct from a 'judgement of value'. In one word, we mean a research that is documented but no slave to disattentive documentarism, and which is not slave to equally improper 'reductionistic' formulations, sociological and psychological ones, that use to select facts and aspects for the sake of aprioristic, arbitrary theories. Thus to History of Religions 'categorial autonomy' of religion will signify primarily a problem, not an *a priori* concept which would be foreign to the positive-inductive nature of this science, nor, perhaps, a conclusion reached once and for all and valid for every successive research. But some kind of open research, as the one we hinted at above, will in any case warrant that no essential element be forgotten or empoverished through a conscious selection or option made *a priori*; i.e. that everything will have been valued. And this is the only methodological warrant that may be required from a historian. If this will have been done, then religion will certainly appear to us as an experience *sui generis*, and a wider historical knowledge of its forms will but render us more expert in discovering the variety, complexity and deepness of its references, be it in those religions that are more close to the basic culture of the historian, be it then in the more 'exotic' ones (related to time and space). And, last but not least, this knowledge will avoid losing (or failing to get) precious information about facts and human experience that it would be unjust and harmful for us to ignore, in such an epoch as ours, an epoch of the world's cultural unification and of a reciprocal knowledge of individuals and civilizations.

This 'Conclusion' was written by the A. on the occasion of the Rome symposion in the 10th anniversary of the death of R. Pettazzoni. We believe it useful to re-print the discussion which followed the original paper (this was re-written for publication).

Discussion

BOLGIANI. — I would like to ask my colleague Ugo Bianchi to clarify a few points. First of all, in his paper he used the terms 'analogy' and 'analogous' in a religious sense, and more especially, 'analogous' and 'analogy' in a comparative religio-historical context. I would like to have some clarification from him on what he means by these expressions 'analogy' and 'analogous' applied to the fields of religious history and methodology: they could in fact have a very significant critical importance.

My second point. I have the impression, if it is not mistaken, that Bianchi used such expressions as 'typology' and 'phenomenology' rather indiscriminately, when it seems to me that in the current state of 'religious sciences' we cannot purely and simply equate them. To set the bounds of the problem correctly it strikes me that we ought to distinguish between 'typology', 'morphology' and even 'phenomenology' of religions. To reduce religious phenomenology simply to a 'typology' of religions does not seem to me to be entirely right: indeed I feel that it entails the risk of confusion and misunderstanding. This clarification appears to me also to be useful in view of the forthcoming discussion on Professor Bleeker's paper.

My third point. Talking about the problem of the relationship between, on the one hand, 'higher cultures' and 'literate civilisations', and on the other, 'so-called inferior cultures' or 'illiterate ones', Bianchi spoke, with particular reference to the differing historico-cultural dynamics of both groups, of 'superior' cultures in the sense of 'ulterior'. A clearer statement on the term 'ulterior' applied to a culture hitherto called 'superior' (and in fact to a 'hot civilisation' as opposed to a 'cold' one, to use a term now fashionable) could perhaps assist in some way an anthropological analysis of the problem, and ultimately the historico-religious methodology involved: so I would like to ask Bianchi to give us some further details on this matter.

My fourth point. Here I am dealing not with individual aspects of Bianchi's paper, but with the paper in general, and particularly with the question (which in its time was also one of the problems dear to Pettazzoni) of the 'autonomous' value of religion, which could also be defined as the 'specific' character of religion. Does it have any meaning for Bianchi to speak of an 'essence' of religion? Does this 'autonomy' of religion we hear of bring us down to what some have fundamentally called the 'religious *a priori*', or are we in fact dealing with a value which is only 'autonomous' inasmuch as we can give it an appropriate and sufficient historical description? Or again, is it a case of a historiographic category which is more conventional than anything else? This clarification strikes me as especially important if we want to base, as Bianchi clearly does, our history of religion on comparative methods: by this I mean true *history*, and thus subject to historiography in its real sense, and not 'history' in the particular sense the term has acquired, for instance, in the *Traité d'histoire des religions* by Mircea Eliade.[1] In this work, as is well known, there is absolutely nothing 'historical', in the historico-historiographical sense; and what is more significant—and seems to have escaped many readers, whether supporters or opponents of Eliade—is the somehow 'unassailable' position which Eliade takes up towards history. Let me give an example: when in his *Traité d'histoire des religions*, on the subject of the ambivalence of the sun, Eliade quotes the Vedic variant of the sun god Sāvītrī, and points out that the nature of his mission without doubt reflects the attributes belonging to the sun god in primitive societies, he is careful and prudent enough to indicate that he is not talking about 'historical relationships' but of typological symmetry. And he adds: that before the history, evolution, diffusion and transformations of hierophany there comes a basic structure of hierophany; and he maintains that it serves no fundamental purpose trying to establish *to what extent* the structure of a hierophany was grasped, and that it is enough to distinguish between that which had some meaning, and that which can have none. Using this sort of criteria we can even end up by declaring that historical illustration is secondary and irrelevant, since

---

[1] [It is true that Eliade's *Traité* began with an *avant-propos* explaining the meaning of the title and ended with the announcement of a further more properly historical exposition about religious phenomena. Such is now being prepared by Eliade, according to reliable information. U. B.].

given a hierophany of known structure, we can already state what is and will be significant about it, as opposed to what will not be. This type of morphology makes history (inasmuch as the legacy of the past) entirely superfluous and opens on to the study of the religious 'futurology'. But setting aside here the case of Eliade (which here is nothing more than an instance of a particular use of religious 'a priori') I believe that it is necessary for those very people like Bianchi who want to remain within the area of the history, albeit comparative, of religions, to specify the meaning contained in the phrase 'autonomous value' of religion as an object of historico-religious study.

BIANCHI. — I am grateful to my friend Bolgiani for his remarks that confirm this paradoxical truth, namely that sometimes more attention and critical analysis is paid to a paper by scholars owing to a different methodological approach, than by others. In fact, Prof. Bolgiani did touch some items which I consider basic in my exposition.

As for the 'analogous' meaning of the concepts 'religion' and 'religious', I was referring to the meaning of the term 'analogy' in the logics (i.e., what is not 'univocal' nor 'aequivocal'; analogous are those phenomena which are not merely species of a genus but have somewhat in common, though they essentially differ for part of their respective contents or from other points of view).

How can a historian of religions give the name of 'religions' to certain things which he studies and which do not originally belong to his experience as a man? How is it possible for us to call—or not to call (here is the problem)—Hīnayāna Buddhism, 'religious'? I see it as follows—and I believe a colleague of mine, Vittorio Lanternari, to be of the same opinion in this. Just like any normal person the historian of religions takes his start from his own experience, whenever he starts an enquiry over things that he did not know before. Whatever he will find in them, that he feels partially akin and somehow familiar with his own experience or knowledge of what in his culture is named 'religion' or 'religious', this he will go on calling 'religious', but this time with an 'analogous' meaning of the word. It is only this way of escaping the difficulty, by the use of the historical-comparative method, that will allow us to solve a definitional (not only terminological) *impasse* which puzzles other scientifical milieus as well,—for ex. Social Anthropology—and that has not been and could not be otherwise solved. In other words, the only way to avoid the historical and typological problems implied in the use of the term 'religion' is to enter into the dynamic vision of the historical thought, i.e. to face—with an always growing historiographical experience—the partial heterogeneity of the facts and of the historical processes which are the object of our study. Thus we remain conscious of the complexity and variety—which is precisely 'analogy'—of these historical facts and processes we are prepared to call 'religious'; only when we possess enough experience are we entitled to give a positive, historical and phenomenological, content to the term 'religious'.

And here I pass to the second item. Some historians of religions have a certain tendency to use terms such as 'typology', 'phenomenology' and 'morphology' with a promiscuous meaning. The only distinction that is frequently made is this: when we talk of typology here in Italy we think of certain obsolete polemics with historicism, that was ignoring 'History of Religions' for the reasons given above. When we mention phenomenology we especially think of scholars such as Wach, Van der Leeuw and Bleeker; when we mention morphology then our mind goes especially to Eliade.

I agree that there is no interest in reducing phenomenology to typology. But what I would like to say is that one should not require the historian of religions to enter into philosophical quarrels with Husserl; this is why the historian of religions should not be expected to discuss about phenomenology with technical terms and in harmony with Husserl's philosophy; and even Prof. Bleeker agrees with this in his papers on religious phenomenology. Nevertheless, within the frame of that particular phenomenology—not strictly intended in the technical Husserlian sense—it is a fact that when scholars talk of phenomenology, they mostly refer to so-called 'structures' or 'systems' wherein they make those phenomena fit and have a 'meaning'. But how could we delineate these 'structures' (or, as we prefer to put it, 'religious worlds'), were it not by means of positive and inductive, historical research? That is, by means of a research considering not only the internal, structural or functional equilibrium of those 'systems', but also the dynamic and the circumstances of their development and—as far as it is possible to detect—of their origins.

Now since, in my opinion, phenomenology, as we understand it here, is often hinting too empirically or too intuitively at 'meaning', 'structure', 'system' or 'whole', I prefer to speak of typology. But I do admit that there is a certain tendency to mix the terms, and use them indifferently.

As far as the third item is concerned: the concept of 'superior' and 'ulterior'. The higher cultures are 'superior', but obviously not in the sense of an evaluation of moral or civil or other merits, but rather in the sense of a development, of a cultural-historical complexity, of a certain type of historical process, which is superior for being more complex, for its being 'ulterior', with reference to other cultural achievements or types. And this without dropping into 'evolutionism'. Thus a 'higher culture', a 'superior' culture, is the cultural achievement of a society which, at a given moment, has 'taken its flight' and has started a chain reaction, a multiplication of cultural experiences by geometrical progression, that is proper to the cultural progress of the so-called superior cultures; it is obvious that in this meaning of the word 'higher' or 'superior', such a culture will be 'superior' and 'ulterior' to those other cultures that were not involved in this historical phenomenon, in this process, and are thus still 'anterior', and, in this sense—historically relative and not offensive, I hope—'inferior' or 'primitive. And this remains true even when a few rather recently formed 'inferior' cultures are concerned: here we apply to the concept of historical typology (see *Anthropos* 63/64, 1968/69, pp. 852-857).

Fourth item: The 'autonomous' value of religion. Here I split a little from Pettazzoni's opinion (above, p. 199 f.). I believe that the historian of religions should not base his work and his interpretations on the previous assumption of an 'autonomous' value of religion, intended as a general and constitutive category of the spirit, i.e. as a philosophical, gnoseological and ontological '*a priori*', at least not at the beginning of his research work. Nor should he apply to opposite assumptions, i.e. reductive (psychological or sociological) criteria of interpretation, or feel engaged—as a few historians of religions do nowadays, even in this Country—to equivocally philosophical-historical prophecies about a 'death' of religion. The only thing the should do is to study the facts with a positive-inductive method. It will only be at the end of his research, and due to the positive historical kind of work gone through, that he will be entitled to propose more or less ascertained conclusions over dynamisms and current evolutions, or historical-typological generalizations, or to propose historical judgements about the anthropological and historical-cultural radicality of religion and the meaning of the immense geographical diffusion of the same. This is as much as the historian will be able to contribute to the argument in question. As far as Eliade is concerned, it is obvious that he poses religion as an *a priori*, were it then an *a priori* that is suffering a crisis in our contemporary world. And I feel that he coincides in his interpretation of the trends of modern Western world with the analyses of absolute 'secularists', except that Eliade considers this crisis negatively, as an enormous 'loss of the center'.

But to me Eliade's position seems strongly phenomenologistic and even psychologistic, arbitrarily generical, i.e. not taking into due consideration that, factually as well as conceptually, 'religion' and 'religious' are not univocal terms, but do correspond to different, though partially related, realities; that is to different *genomena* and dynamisms, in the complex frame of human evolution and history. Not less general and arbitrary are the positions of those secularists with whom Eliade polemizes, but with whom he greatly agrees when he instaures an opposition between a 'religious' world of yesterday and a modern tendentially 'non-religious' world. Finally as to the 'archetype' and 'hierophany', I must refer, for the sake of brevity, to the chapter on Eliades' thought in my forthcoming book 'The History of Religions' (in the Supplements to *Numen* [that is here, pp. 184-191]).

DHAVAMONY. — I would like to raise only two points briefly. The word 'historical', and the meaning of 'historical comparative method'. What does Prof. Bianchi understand by 'history'? Does it mean a narrative history (histoire historisante), or a history such as is done by 'historiens-sociologues', who find organisms, patterns, models, types of events, and so on? Because by mixing these two meanings of 'historical' one also mixes, it seems to me, the two meanings of the word 'phenomenological': the mere historical structure of a phenomenon and the meaning behind this structure, which can be obtained only in the context of different patterns and generalities. The second question is that by making use of the historical-comparative method you arrive at the meaning of the religious fact in as far as it is historical and cultural, because a religious fact is also historical and cultural; at least it is an event taking place in a particular culture and period. But does it really —the historical-comparative method—does it really get the religious fact *as religious*? That is the point of Eliade's saying that the historical comparative method, in as far as it is a cultural, ethnological quest, arrives at a historical fact *qua* historical, *qua* cultural, *qua* ethnological, but not *qua* religious, *qua* sacred. How can your method bring this aspect of the sacred *qua* sacred?

BIANCHI. — My point in order to defend the historical-comparative method as *the* method of the History of Religions is the following.

By history I mean the study of genesis and development, that is the study of concrete and individual processes which took place in time and space. These are religious processes—that is they do concern the religious nature of the facts considered—, naturally in the context of an 'analogous' appreciation of the terms 'religion' and 'religious' (cf. supra). By this we escape at the same time the mere descriptive, narrative, 'philological' meaning of the concept of 'history', as well as the merely sociological meaning of same. As for Eliade's concept of the quality 'religion': as I have pointed out in my answer to the preceding question, what I wouldn't like to accept is his concept of religion and religious (or the 'sacred') as a conceptual *a priori*, as a category, carrying a general, universal and univocal meaning of 'religion'. This is questionable also in the field of a true phenomenology of religion and of a 'science of religion', as well as in a history of religions. In my opinion, in so far as these religious disciplines are concerned (not e.g. in the case of theology, which benefits from its conceptual own sources and categories) 'religion' and 'religious' are historically and phenomenologically 'analogous' concepts, to be elicited by a philological, inductive, positive research in the field of what happened in time and space.

DHAVAMONY. — Thank you for the clarification that you do not admit Eliade's sense of religious as a category. Then the objection is serious from the point of view of distinguishing of what is religious and what is not religious, the profane. Because the historical and the comparative method analyses a fact, which is also common to the profane aspect of such a fact. For instance, how do you distinguish a profane faith from a religious faith, or in certain ideas of ceremony, religious ceremony from a social ceremony? A royal ceremony, e.g. coronation.

BIANCHI. — I must repeat that a distinction feasible for the History of Religions, between what is religious and what is not religious, as in the instance of a coronation, cannot be based on a theoretical definition of 'religion' and 'religious' previous to the research work, which is historical and comparative-historical work. All depends here upon a consistent use of the 'analogy' criterium. There is a dialectic between the 'form' (which is historical-comparative, extending to all that appears in 'continuity', even if partial, with what was already known as 'religious') and the very content of the research itself. Of course, to evaluate the reality, the limits and the *ratio* of that continuity, in order to exclude pseudo-religious or para-religious phenomena, may prove frequently to be difficult, and calls for a special sensitivity to all aspects of the facts considered (which does not mean as much as intuitionism, again a form of the discarded phenomenologism). Thus, a historical and phenomenological definition of religion is always *in fieri*, in connexion with the extension of the experience of the scholar (which does not mean theoretical or programmatic relativism).

GNOLI. — Prof. Bianchi has talked about 'ethnical religions' and 'founded religions'. Now, I believe that this distinction, which I made use of myself, because it is handy, should be given its true value; is it a distinction of opportunity, or something more? I mean that, if the 'founded religions' are those for which we may in fact consider the personality of a historical founder, as with Islam, will the 'ethnical religions' not be simply those whose origins are dwelling in a reality which, in the actual condition of our knowledge, are not to be historically grasped? Otherwise, we would be compelled to make a typological distinction between what is 'ethnical' and what is 'founded', with every problem this distinction would raise. In other words, in this case we should, without any doubt, accept the phenomenological point of view, and we should necessarily apply, for the 'ethnical religions', to the idea of a spontaneous and inconscious production of aspects and fundamental contents of the religious experience. As far as the criticism is concerned that is addressed to a certain type of historicism, we must agree that it is impossible to establish an a priori category for 'religion' or for 'religious'. We may, in case, discuss over the opportunity to ascribe religious experience to the ethical category, as with Croce's historicism, but we cannot deny that it is impossible to presuppose a category by itself for religion. The only way to study religion is to frame it in the general frame of history, were it then of course with the help of all those instruments and materials that doubtlessly help to a better study of the religious facts, beyond those philosophical and ideological presuppositions they are located in.

BIANCHI. — As to the first point, whether the concepts of 'ethnical' and 'founded' religions are categories of cognition or of reality, in my opinion they are both. These are tied by a kind of dialectical connexion, in the ambit of the historical thought and in the course of historical research. In other words, in most cases those religions for which the name and the figure of an historical personality of founder cannot be grasped by historical research, are also those religions which are best understood as integrating parts of a socio-cultural whole, whose history and vicissitudes they share, while the dynamics of a founded religion, though not always proving supra-national, are very different. As to the second point: as I answered to Prof. Bolgiani (cf. supra), it is precisely my opinion that the historian of religions could not start with the assumption of an *a priori* category of religion and religious, both in the cognitive (a previous, theoretical definition of religion) and the phenomenological or ontological realms (religion as an atemporal essence). The religious-historical and scientific elaboration of the concept and, possibly, of an autonomous category of 'religion' and of 'religious' will be the consequence of the historical-comparative research, with the aid of the concepts of 'analogy' and of 'historical typology' I tried to elucidate in my paper. It is clear that not only the affirmation of an *a priori* category of religion is to be avoided *as starting point* for the historical research, but also the opposite methodological presupposition, i.e. reductionism (psychological, sociological or otherwise).

BIBLIOGRAPHY

COLLECTIONS OF SOURCES

The Sacred Books of the East, series edited by Max Müller, Oxford, 1879-1910.
Kleine Texte für Vorlesungen und Übungen, series begun by H. Lietzmann, now ed. by K. Aland, Berlin, 1908 et sqq.
Quellen der Religionsgeschichte, herausg. im Auftrage der Religionsg. Kommission bei der Gesellsch. der Wissensch. zu Göttingen, Göttingen-Leipzig, 1909 et sqq.
Fontes historiae religionum ex auctoribus Graecis et Latinis collecti, ed. C. Clemen, Bonn, 1920 et sqq.
Textbuch zur Religionsgeschichte, by E. Lehmann and H. Haas, 2nd ed. Leipzig, 1922.
Bilderatlas zur Religionsgeschichte, ed. by H. Haas, Leipzig-Erlangen, 1924-34.
Religionsgeschichtliches Lesebuch, ed. by A. Berthelot, 2nd ed., Tübingen, 1926-32.
Testi e documenti per la storia delle religioni, ed. by R. Pettazzoni, Bologna, 1929, et sqq.
Miti e Leggende by R. Pettazzoni (vol. II by V. Lanternari), Turin, 1948 et sqq.
Classici della religione, series ed. by R. Pettazzoni, Florence (Sansoni), 1951 et sqq.
Ancient Near Eastern Texts relating to the Old Testament, ed. by J. B. Pritchard, 2nd ed., Princeton, 1955.
Motif-Index of Folk-Literature, revised and enlarged edition by S. Thompson, 6 vols., Copenhagen, 1955-1958.
Classici delle religioni (several series), Turin, (U.T.E.T.).
From Primitives to Zen. A thematic Sourcebook on the History of Religions, by M. Eliade, London and New York, 1967.
Iconography of Religions, illustrated and annotated in about 200 numbers, ed. by Institute of Religious Iconography of the University of Groningen, Leiden, 1970 et sqq.
Studies in the History of Religions (*Supplements to Numen*), Leiden, 1954 et sqq.
Religion and Reason (ed. by J. Waardenburg), The Hague-Paris, 1971.

COLLECTIONS OF MONOGRAPHS

Annales du Musée Guimet, Paris, 1880 et sqq.
Bibliothèque de l'Ecole prat. des hautes études; Sciences religieuses, Paris, 1889 et sqq.
Religionsgeschichtliche Versuche und Vorarbeiten, ed. by A. Dieterich and R. Wünsch, Giessen-Leipzig, 1903 et sqq.
Storia delle religioni, ed. by R. Pettazzoni, Bologna, 1920 et sqq.
Mana. Introduction à l'histoire des religions, Paris, 1944 et sqq.
Storia e scienza delle religioni, ed. by G. Castellino, Turin, 1952 et sqq.
Die Religionen der Menschheit, Stuttgart, 1961 et sqq. (publ. also in French, Payot, Paris).

ENCYCLOPEDIAS AND DICTIONARIES

Encyclopedia of Religion and Ethics, ed. by J. Hastings, 1908-26.
A. Anwander, *Wörterbuch der Religion*, Würzburg, 1948.
A. Bertholet, *Wörterbuch der Religionen*, Stuttgart, 1952.
Die Religion in Geschichte und Gegenwart, 3rd ed. Tübingen, 1956 et sqq.
F. König, *Religionswissenschaftliches Wörterbuch*, Friburg in Br., 1956.
Enciclopedia delle religioni (A. M. di Nola, M. Gozzini et al.), Florence, 1970 et sqq.

BIBLIOGRAPHIES

C. Clemen, *Religionsgeschichtliche Bibliographie 1914-1923*, Leipzig-Berlin, 1917-25.
International Bibliography of the History of Religions, Leiden, 1954 et sqq.
K. Smith Diehl, *Religions, mythologies, folklore. An annotated bibliography*, New York, 1956.

MANUALS

Lehrbuch der Religionsgeschichte, founded by P. D. Chantepie de la Saussaye, 4th ed. by A. Bertholet and E. Lehmann, Tübingen, 1925.
J. Huby, *Christus, Manuel d'histoire des religions*, 4th ed. Paris, 1927 (new ed. 1944).
Die Religionen der Erde. Ihr Wesen und ihre Geschichte, ed. by C. Clemen, Munich, 1927 (2nd ed. 1949).
A. C. Bouquet, *Comparative Religion* (Penguin Books), 1941.
G. Mensching, *Handbuch der Religionswissenschaft*, Berlin, 1948.
——, *Allgemeine Religionsgeschichte*, 2nd ed., Heidelberg, 1949.
Histoire générale des religions, ed. by M. Gorce and R. Mortier, Paris, 1948-51.
A. Anwander, *Die Religionen der Menschheit*, Friburg in Br., 1949, (with a brief anthology of religious classics).
F. König, *Christus und die Religionen der Erde. Handbuch der Religionsgeschichte*, Freiburg in Br., 1951.
N. Turchi (ed.), *Le religioni del mondo*, 2nd ed., Rome, 1951.
Histoire des religions, ed. by M. Brillant and R. Aigrain, Paris, 1953-56.
N. Turchi, *Manuale di storia delle religioni* 3rd ed., Turin, 1954.
H. Ringgren-Å. V. Ström, *Die Religionen der Völker*, Stuttgart, 1959 (French trans. Paris, 1960).
F. Heiler et al., *Die Religionen der Menschheit*, Stuttgart, 1959.
C. J. Bleeker and G. Widengren (edd.), *Historia religionum. Handbook for the History of Religions*, Leiden, 1969-71.
H.-Ch. Puech (ed.), *Histoire des religions* (Encyclop. de la Pléiade), Paris, 1970 sqq.
G. Castellani (ed.), *Storia delle religioni (fondata da P. Tacchi-Venturi)*, VIth edition, Turin, 1970-71 (with illustrations).
J. P. Asmussen and J. Læssøe (with the coop. of C. Colpe), *Handbuch der Religionsgeschichte*, Göttingen, 1971-75.
G. Lanczkowski, *Geschichte der Religionen* (Fischer Lexikon), Frankfurt/Main, 1972.

ON THE HISTORY OF RESEARCH AND ON METHOD

W. Schmidt, *Der Ursprung der Gottesidee*, 12 vols. Münster, 1912 et sqq. (2nd ed. of vol. I, ibid., 1926).
L. H. Jordan, *Comparative Religion, its adjuncts and allies*, Oxford, 1916.
R. Pettazzoni, *Svolgimento e carattere della storia delle religioni*, Bari, 1924.
H. Pinard de la Boullaye, *L'étude comparée des religions*, 3rd ed., Paris, 1929-31.
W. Schmidt, *Handbuch der vergleichenden Religionsgeschichte*, Münster, 1930.
W. Keilbach, *Die Problematik der Religionen*, Paderborn, 1936.
G. Mensching, *Geschichte der Religionswissenschaft*, Bonn, 1948.
G. Graneris, *Introduzione generale alla scienza delle religioni*, Turin, 1952.
R. Pettazzoni, *Essays on the History of Religions*, Leiden, 1954.
U. Bianchi, *Problemi di storia delle religioni*, Rome, (Series *Universale Studium*, no. 56), 1958. Germ. transl.: *Probleme der Religionsgeschichte*, Göttingen, 1964; Swed. translation: *Religionshistoriska problem*, Stockholm, 1968.
The History of Religions, ed. by M. Eliade and J. M. Kitagawa, Chicago, 1959.
J. de Vries, *Forschungsgeschichte der Mythologie*, Munich, 1961.
U. Bianchi, *Après Marbourg: petit discours sur la méthode*, in 'Numen', VIII, I (1961), pp. 64-78.

K. Rudolph, *Die Religionsgeschichte an der Leipziger Universität und die Entwicklung der Religionswissenschaft, Sitz.-Ber. der sächs. Akad. der Wissenschaften zu Leipzig*, Phil.-hist. Klasse, vol. 107, no. I, Berlin, 1962.
T. Margul, *Sto lat nauki o religiach świata*, Warsaw, 1964.
A. Brelich, *Introduzione alla storia delle religioni*, Rome, 1966.
The History of Religions. Essays on the Problem of Understanding, vol. I, ed. by J. M. Kitagawa, Chicago, 1967.
A. Brelich, in the above mentioned *Histoire des religions*, Encycl. de la Pléiade.
U. Bianchi, C. J. Bleeker, A. Bausani (edd.), *Problems and Methods of the History of Religions* (Studies in the History of Religions, Supplements to Numen vol. XIX), Leiden, 1972.
Th. P. Van Baaren and H. J. W. Drijvers (edd.), *Religion, Culture and Methodology*, The Hague-Paris, 1973.
J. Waardenburg, *Classical Approaches to the Study of Religion*, 2 vols., The Hague-Paris, 1973-1974.
G. Lanczkowski (ed.), *Selbstverständnis und Wesen der Religionswissenschaft*, Darmstadt, 1974.
Proceedings of the Turku Study Conference on Methodology of the Science of Religion (1973), in preparation.

FORMS OF RELIGION

G. Van der Leeuw, *Phänomenologie der Religion*, Tübingen, 1933; 2nd ed. Tübingen, 1956; French ed., *La religion dans son essence et ses manifestations: Phénomenologie de la religion*, Paris, 1948.
N. Söderblom, *Das Werden des Gottesglaubens*, 2nd ed., Leipzig, 1926.
——, *The living God. Basal form of personal religion*, London, 1933.
E. O. James, *Comparative Religion*, London, 1938.
M. Eliade, *Traité d'histoire des religions*, vol. I, Paris, 1948, 2nd ed. 1953.
J. Wach, *Types of religious experience, Christian and non-Christian*, London, 1951.
U. Bianchi, *Problemi di storia delle religioni* (= *Probleme der Religionsgeschichte*), quoted above.
Symbolik der Religionen, Series ed. by F. Herrmann, Stuttgart, 1958 et sqq.
G. Mensching, *Die Religion. Erscheinungsformen, Strukturtypen und Lebensgesetze*, Stuttgart, 1959.
K. Goldammer, *Die Formenwelt des Religiösen. Grundriss der systematischen Religionswissenschaft* (Kröners Taschenausg. 264), Stuttgart, 1960.
G. Graneris, *La vita della religione nella storia delle religioni*, Turin, 1960.
F. Heiler, *Erscheinungsformen und Wesen der Religion*, Stuttgart, 1961.
H.-J. Schoeps, *Religionen. Wesen und Geschichte*, Gütersloh, 1964.
G. Widengren, *Religionsphänomenologie*, Berlin, 1969.
G. Lanckzkowski, *Begegnung und Wandel der Religionen*, Düsseldorf-Cologne, 1971.

PHILOSOPHY, PSYCHOLOGY AND SOCIOLOGY OF RELIGION
(in relation to the history of religions).

Among the best known works: M. Weber, *Gesammelte Aufsätze zur Religionssoziologie*, 1920-23; E. Przywara, *Religionsphilosophie*, 1927; A. Dempf, *Religionsphilosophie*, 1934; C. G. Jung, *Psychologie und Religion*, 1939; G. Mensching, *Soziologie der Religion*, 1968^2; J. Wach, *Religionssoziologie*, 1951; the works of the school of Le Bras, and, in Italy, of S. Acquaviva; T. F. O'Dea, *Sociology of Religion*.
The periodicals *Archives de sociologie des religions* and *Sociologia religiosa*.
M. I. Berkowitz and J. E. Johnson, *Social Scientific Studies of Religion. A Bibliography*, Pittsburgh, 1967. *Atti* del Convegno di filosofia della religione (Parma 1974), in preparation.

REVIEWS

Zeitschrift für Ethnologie, Berlin, later Braunschweig, 1869 et sqq.
Theologische Literaturzeitung, Leipzig-Berlin, 1876 et sqq.
Revue de l'histoire des religions, Paris, 1880 et sqq.
Zeitschrift für Missionskunde und Religionswissenschaft, 1885 et sqq.
Archiv. für Religionswissenschaft, Leipzig, 1898-1942.
Anthropos Ephemeris internationalis ethnologica et linguistica, Mödling-Vienna, later Posieux, and then St. Augustin (Germ.), 1906 et sqq. (with a bibliographical chronicle and a review of Reviews).
Revue des sciences philosophiques et théologiques, Le Saulchoir, 1907 et sqq. (with periodical bulletins of the history of religions and similar matters).
Harvard Theological Review, Cambridge, Mass., 1908 et sqq.
Recherches de science religieuse, Paris, 1910 et sqq. (with periodical bulletins of the history of religions and similar matters).
Studi e materiali di storia delle religioni, Bologna, later Rome, 1924 et sqq.
The Review of Religion, Columbia Univ. Press, 1936 et sqq.
Zeitschrift für Religions- und Geistesgeschichte, Marburg, Leiden, later Cologne, 1948 et sqq.
Numen, International Review for History of Religions, Leiden, 1954 et sqq.
Euhemer. Przegląd Religioznawczy, Warsaw, 1956 et sqq.
History of Religions, Chicago, 1961 et sqq.
Rivista di storia e letteratura religiosa, Turin, 1965 et sqq.
Temenos. Studies in Comparative Religion, presented by scholars in Denmark, Finland, Norway, and Sweden, Helsinki, 1965 et sqq.
Religion, Newcastle/Tyne, 1972 sqq.

ERRATA CORRIGE

p. 39	line 39	*read:* more
p. 96	8	disinterestedness
p. 130	18	Orphic
p. 168	19	instead of god *read:* God
p. 175	41	*read:* Stuttgart
p. 184	6	1949)
p. 217	16	drop the first half of the line.

INDEX OF MODERN AUTHORS

Accame, S.   128 n.
Adam, A.   151 n.
Aigrain, R.   163 n.
Albright, W. F. A.   132 n., 137
Alföldi, A.   124 n.
Alt, A.   137
Altizer, T. J. J.   189, 189 n.
Ankermann, B.   85
Anquetil-Duperron   147
Anz, W.   152
Auboyer, J.   133

Bachofen, J. J.   62, 70, 72-74
Baetke, W.   3 n., 173-174
Banton, M.   202 n.
Bastian, A.   69 n.
Baur, F. C.   151
Bausani, A.   117 n.
Bayet, J.   115 n.
Benedict, R.   166, 167
Benveniste, E.   148
Benz, E.   170, 176
Bertholet, A.   68 n.
Bianchi, U.   33 n., 34 n., 43 n., 70 n., 105 n., 114 n., 115 n., 119 n., 122 n., 130 n., 132 n., 151 n., 155 n., 188 n., 193 n., 196, 200 n., 202 n.
Bidez, J.   120, 120 n., 150
Blanc, A. C.   171 n.
Bleeker, C. J.   114 n., 119 n., 132 n., 178, 180-181, 212, 215
Bolgiani, Fr.   212, 214, 220
Bouché-Leclercq, A.   27
Bousset, W.   152, 153
Brandon, S. G. F.   25 n., 113 n.
Brelich, A.   38, 81, 103 n., 123
Brillant, M.   163 n.
Broglie, de   27, 27 n., 28
Brosses, Ch., de   61, 63 n. 71
Bultmann, R.   140, 153
Buonaiuti, E.   154, 155

Caillois, R.   184
Calame-Griaule, G.   82 n.
Cassirer, E.   67 n., 127
Castellani, G.   32
Castellino, G.   132
Champollion, J. Fr.   109

Chantepie de la Saussaye, P. D.   27, 68, 178
Clavier, H.   6 n., 11 n., 69
Clemen, C.   173
Cocchiara, G.   81
Colpe, C.   118 n.
Comte, A.   37 n., 66, 68 n., 71, 167, 193, 195
Cook, T.   87
Coppens, J.   140 n.
Cornford, F. M.   130
Creuzer, G. F.   67
Croce, B.   9, 23 n., 28 n., 154, 186 n., 199, 219
Cross, F. L.   151 n.
Cumont, Fr.   120, 120 n., 150

Decharme, P.   27
Deimel, A.   108
Delitzsch, Fr. C. G.   136
De Martino, E.   32, 169, 189, 190, 193 n., 197-198, 199, 202
Desroche, H.   194
Devoto, G.   65 n.
Dhavamony, M.   217, 218
Dhorme, E.   111
Dieterich, A.   84 n., 153 n.
Dieterlen, G.   82 n.
Dodds, E. R.   84 n., 129, 143
Dörmann, J.   73 n.
Donini, A.   197 n.
Duchesne-Guillemin, J.   123
Dumézil, G.   111 n., 117, 117 n., 121-123, 148
Durkheim, E.   20, 30, 62, 78-79, 168, 174, 193

Ebeling, E.   144 n.
Eisler, R.   130
Eliade, M.   18 n., 23 n., 25 n., 47, 57 n., 62, 67 n., 93, 107, 107 n., 112, 112 n., 165 n., 176, 181, 181 n., 182 n., 183 n., 184-191, 198, 200 n., 213, 215, 216, 217, 218
Elliot Smith, G.   108
Engels, Fr.   193, 194, 196
Engnell, I.   115
Evans-Pritchard, E. E.   204, 207

Faye, E., de 155
Festugière, A. J. 153
Feuerbach, L. A. 193, 194
Filliozat, J. 124
Folliet, J. 163 n., 165 n., 167, 168
Fontenelle, B. 64
Forrer, E. O. 110 n.
Foucart, G. 70, 108
Frankfort, H. 109 n., 113, 114 n., 116, 119, 127, 140
Frankfort, H. A. 127, 140
Frazer, J. G. 16, 46, 47, 62, 72, 75-76, 79, 82, 114, 115 n., 196
Freud, S. 191, 192
Frick, H. 170, 175 n.
Fries, J. Fr. 172
Frobenius, L. 92, 98, 99, 167
Furlani, G. 112 n., 113 n.
Fustel de Coulanges, N. D. 61

Gandhi 165 n., 168
Gaster, Th. 111 n., 113 n.
Gennep, A., van 70, 72, 73
Gnoli, Gh. 132 n., 149, 219
Goblet d'Alviella 8, 28, 67-70, 73
Goldammer, K. 175 n.
Goodenough, E. R. 181
Gordon, C. 110
Grant, R. M. 151 n., 153, 181
Griaule, M. 82 n., 106, 108 n., 131
Grotefend, G. Fr. 109
Gruppe, O. 130
Guénon, R. 25 n.
Gunkel, H. 136, 137
Gusinde, M. 89
Güterbock, H. 110 n.

Haekel, J. 77 n.
Hahn, E. 73 n.
Hainchelin, C. 197
Harlez, de 149
Harnack, A., von 151, 151 n., 153, 155
Harrison, J. 84 n.
Hartland, E. S. 86, 88
Hauer, J. W. 67 n., 86 n., 170-171
Hegel, G. W. Fr. 66, 136, 150, 200 n.
Heiler, Fr. 170, 175-176, 177 n.
Heine-Geldern, R., von 104, 109 n.
Hirschmann, E. 178 n.
Hooke, S. H. 112, 113 n.
Hubert, H. 79 n.
Hultkrantz, Å. 87 n.
Husserl, E. 20, 179, 215
Hyde, Th. 147, 148

Irwin, N. A. 127

Jacobsen, T. 127
Jaeger, W. 128, 129 n.
James, E. O. 38, 113 n.
James, W. 62
Jaspers, K. 142, 177 n.
Jensen, A. E. 38, 62, 66 n., 73 n., 92, 98-101, 104, 167, 192
Jeremias, A. 108
Jonas, H. 43 n., 151 n., 153
Jundt, A. 173 n.
Jung, C. G. 62, 100, 191, 192

Kant, I. 20, 23 n.
Kerényi, K. 62, 74, 133, 192
Kitagawa, J. 18 n., 25 n., 165 n., 176, 182-183, 185 n., 200 n.
Koppers, W. 89
Kramer, S. N. 128
Kristensen, W. B. 180
Kryvelev, I. A. 195 n.
Kugler, Fr. 108

Labanca, B. 28
Lafitau, J. F. 61
Lagrange, M. J. 62
Lanczkowski, G. 142 n., 175 n.
Lang, A. 37, 65 n., 66 n., 71, 87-88, 91 n., 92, 94
Lanternari, V. 166 n., 189, 193 n., 196, 197
Lebzelter, V. 89
Leenhardt, M. 83, 112 n.
Leeuw, G. van der 29, 62, 83, 96, 178-180, 215
Lehmann, E. 68 n.
Lehmann, Fr. R. 3 n., 87 n.
Leisegang, H. 153
Lenin 167
Lévi, S. 124
Lévi-Strauss, Cl. 62, 77, 78, 121
Lévy-Bruhl, L. 48, 62, 77, 79-83, 127
Liagre Böhl, M. Th., de 115 n.
Lobeck, Ch. A. 130
Loisy, A. 66 n., 68 n., 154
Lubbock, J. 37 n., 71, 76

Mac Lennan, J. F. 70
Malinowski, Br. 62, 93, 112, 127, 166, 167
Mannhardt, W. 72
Marconi, M. 74

Marcuse, H.   129
Marett, R. R.   62, *86-87*
Marx, K. (with Marxism)   20, 21, 166 n., 190, *192-197*, 200 n.
Maspéro, G.   27
Mauss, M.   20, 21, 77, 78 n.
Mensching, G.   170, 173 n.
Messina, G.   148, 150 n.
Meuli, K.   62, 84 n., 143
Meyer, E.   148
Minocchi, E.   154 n.
Molé, M.   148
Morgan, L. H.   62, 193, 194, 207
Morghen, R.   155
Moscati, S.   128, 128 n.
Mowinckel, S.   115, 116, 134
Müller, Fr. Max   27, *62-66*, 70, 71, 108, 117 n., 127
Müller, K. O.   67
Murdock, J.   73 n.
Murray, G. G. R.   87 n.

Nestle, W.   127
Nilsson, M. P.   26 n., 27 n., 62, 74
Nock, A. D.   26 n., 181
Norden, E.   153 n.
Nyberg, H. S.   149

Onians, R. B.   131
Orelli, C., von   68
Otten, H.   110 n.
Otto, R.   3 n., 21, 62, 67 n., 83, 86 n., 107, 154, 169, 170, *171-175*, 176, 179, 180, 189, 194, 202, 202 n.
Otto, W.   74

Pascal, B.   172
Pedersen, J.   111, 137
Perry, W. J.   108
Pestalozza, U.   28 n., 62, 73 n., 74
Petersen, E.   153
Pétrement, S.   153
Pettazzoni, R.   21, 28 n., 29, 30, 37, 38, 62, 69, 74, *89-90*, 93, 94, 95, 97, 112, 112 n., 127, 148, 154, 161, 177 n., **178**, 185, 186, 187, 187 n., 189, 189 n., *199-200*, 201, 216
Piccaluga, G.   123 n.
Preuss, K. Th.   92
Puech, H. Ch.   28 n., 130 n.

Quispel, G.   153

Radakrishnan   169 n.

Radin, P.   91
Ramakrishna   165 n., 169
Reinach, S.   76
Reitzenstein, R.   150, 153, 153 n.
Renan, E.   69 n.
Réville, Al.   27
Robertson Smith, W.   62, 76, 136
Rohde, E.   62, 84
Rönnow, K.   125
Rose, H. J.   114
Rosenberg, A.   167
Rudolph, K.   3 n., 29 n., 151 n., 174 nn., 202 n.

Schaeder, H. H.   153 n.
Scharbau   39 n.
Schebesta, P.   48, 49
Schimmel, A.   175 n.
Schleiermacher, F. E. D.   172 n.
Schmidt, W.   37, 62, 73 n., *88-89*, 90, 92, 94, 102 n., 107 n.
Schmitz, C. A.   101 n.
Schuon, Fr.   25 n.
Schwartz, B.   22 n.
Shih, J.   8 n.
Simon, M.   29
Smith W. Cantwell   18 n., 23 n., 25 n., 165, 165 n., 166 n., 183
Söderblom, N.   62, 86 n., 91, 96
Sordi, M.   115 n.
Spencer, H.   37 n., 71, 193
Spiegel, Fr.   148
Spiro, M. E.   *202-206*, 207
Stalin, J. V.   167
Stella, L. A.   110
Stucken, E.   108
Suzuki, D. T.   183

Tagore, R.   165 n., 169
Tempels, B.   82
Tiele, C. P.   27, 68
Tillich, P.   203
Tokarev, S. A.   193, 193 n.
Toynbee, A.   26 n., 177 n.
Tylor, E. B.   16, 32, 33, 37 n., 61, 71, 72, 75, *84-86*, 87, 88, 195, 196, 203, 207

Vatke, W.   136
Vercoutter, J.   110 n.
Vermaseren, M.   120, 120 n.
Vernes, M.   27
Vico, G. B.   61, 64

Virolleaud, Ch. 111

Wach, J. 62, 178, 181, 215
Weber, M. 26, 137
Wellhausen, J. 62, 136
Widengren, G. 29, 113, 116, 116 n., 117 n., 118, 120, 120 n., 123, 154, 155

Wilson, J. A. 127
Wikander, St. 117 n., 123
Winckler, H. 108
Wundt, W. 62

Zolla, E. 25 n.

LIBRARY OF DAVIDSON COLLEGE